THE BLUE PRINT PART TWO

Sheroes & Heroes

BK FULTON
AND
NICHOLAS POWELL

DEDICATION

We dedicate this book to every person working to be the best version of themselves. The journey is rarely easy, but it's always worth it.

BK   Nick

FORWARD

We were pleasantly surprised when *The Blueprint* released at #1 on Amazon in both the film industry and media categories. It's the first time that has happened for our team and the honor was humbling. Our readers were eager to learn about our "secret sauce." *The Blueprint* delivered.

Soon thereafter, my publisher asked me if we could pull together a sequel. I did not hesitate. I asked Nicholas (Nick) Powell, my co-editor from SoulVision Magazine, if he wanted to take the sequel journey with me and he agreed. Excited, I began formulating my thoughts for how to follow up on a book project that covered over three decades of my life. Nick and I decided that since we both loved biographies, we could share select cover stories that we collaborated on over the course of publishing SoulVision.

The Blueprint: Part 2 - Sheroes & Heroes is the result of several years of faithfully interviewing diverse industry leaders, icons and artists. We believe that we have captured the essence of their journeys. Most of them said they are just getting started. All of them were encouraging and remained convinced that their best is yet to come. The 52 leaders profiled in this book will inspire you to do more. Proximity to power is in proportion to our willingness to let it go. These leaders have let go and they have allowed us to share their stories with the world.

Buckle up because you will vicariously experience what is possible as you turn up the rocket boosters of success in the pages of *The Blueprint: Part 2 - Sheroes & Heroes*. Enjoy.

BK   Nick

TABLE OF CONTENTS

Erica Ash: Spirit of the Hummingbird

Every day, two hummingbirds dance around Erica Ash's warm home. Her home office is bookended by two windows that respectively face both the front and back of her home. Erica looks out at her front window and sees one of the hummingbirds feeding off her banana tree. The other eagerly flutters at her back window—a glorious dance. Like these two hummingbirds, Erica isn't occupied with the superficial aspects of life. She keeps moving forward, enjoying the blessings and simplicity God has given her the privilege to enjoy.

As an army brat, Erica traveled around the world. It was enough to make her think so much travel was a normal experience for everyone. Her perspective changed when her father settled out of the military into civilian life. Erica met people who hadn't left their hometown nor the country since the day they were born. "I realized how special my childhood was, just being able to travel and take trips to different countries." Because of travel, friendships were always a challenge. "Having moved every three years, maintaining friendships always seemed difficult. When my family got out of the military and I was able to interact with children who had basically lived in the same town their whole lives, I began to observe bonds and friendships that began for others as early as kindergarten. Even so, the grass always appears a little bit greener to a child. I really wouldn't trade my traveling childhood-years for anything."

"Do your best, let God do the rest," is the motto Erica came up with on the spot during our interview. It perfectly explains Erica's approach to life and her career. As she explains, too many people try to "push, press, and stress" for moments and experiences they think should happen. No matter how much you push and pull, what ends up happening, happens. She makes sure to point out, you should always work hard and try. But there is a point where one has to let go and let faith do the rest.

Being too serious takes the fun out of the spontaneous nature of life. Therefore, Erica doesn't take herself too seriously. She thinks you should let your ego go because there is always someone who has done more or has more. "As soon as you think you've made it, you realize there is more to

"The grass always appears a little bit greener to a child. I really wouldn't trade my traveling childhood-years for anything."

reach, more to do like, 'oh I just got into this country club but there are tiers in this country club and I'm just on the bottom tier. Or, when you get your luxury car, you realize, 'oh my gosh, I'm just in the luxury car world. This isn't the best luxury car. I don't have a driver.' You shouldn't take yourself too seriously and you should learn to enjoy what you have at the moment."

Even with all of her success, Erica still doesn't believe she has made it. She doesn't feel like "making it" is even a real thing. "I don't think you ever really make it because it's never about 'making it.' It's about enjoying the lessons of the journey towards the goal. Realizing there is not an 'it,' could be seen as making it," she says. "Getting on TV was a huge deal for me but if you blinked, you missed me. So, I needed to get on TV for longer. I then became a series regular but I still wasn't number one. Then I become number one and I thought, 'oh yeah, I made it.' Only to realize the network isn't doing so great. So, then I had to get on a better network. And on it goes. You can always make it and realize there is more. I'm still "making it" but I'm enjoying the journey. I always want to be in this space because I think once you stop learning and growing, you die. I'm not ready to die."

BK FULTON AND NICHOLAS POWELL

"I don't want to fully step out of the mold of being a comedian because that will always be my default."

For many actors, the fear of being typecast is real. While Erica embraces her comedy stage-roots and the "comedian mold," she takes on dramatic roles too. "I don't want to fully step out of the mold of being a comedian because that will always be my default. Comedy is something I will always fall back into and something I quite enjoy." As Erica explains it, when you do great in a specific type of role, people will typecast you. They think it is how you will make the most money. However, Erica has embraced the power of diversity. She started to turn down roles she felt were too similar. "If serious actors want to avoid being typecast then they may have to sacrifice a few paychecks until a role that explores their range of talents comes into the picture," she says. This has paid off for Erica in the end. "I feel like allowing myself to turn roles down and wait for different roles has allowed me to be less typecast."

"I feel like my greatest achievements are the lessons I'm learning about myself and how I'm growing and changed spiritually."

When asked if there were any actors she would like to work with, Erica's voice heightens with excitement. "I would really love to work with Jeffrey Wright. I think Jeffrey Wright is not only one of the most brilliant actors out there, but one of the most underappreciated and unsung," she says. "He takes his craft very seriously. His focus and his commitment are just beautiful to watch. I could watch him rake leaves and be impressed," she laughs. "The first time I actually saw him was in the film, *Lackawanna Blues.* It was a small scene but was enough to make me wonder about this person because he was so focused and so committed to his character. I really appreciated that."

To the many young actors and actresses trying to make it in the industry, Erica suggests to "show up, but stop driving too hard." I think a lot of young actors and actresses have in their heads exactly how their career should unfold, how things should be, and what roles they should get.

'I'm gonna get this role and meet this person and then I'm going to be successful.' They have it all planned out in their heads and when one little thing doesn't work out, they get discouraged and quit. They just assume it's never going to work out," she explains. "You never know what the path is going to be, how you get in where you're supposed to be, or exactly when it's going to happen. Definitely show up to every opportunity that comes your way; that's obviously reasonable and doesn't compromise your integrity. However, don't try to be like other actors. Don't try to pattern your career after other actors. Don't try to control so much. Show up, be your best and simply do your best."

When Erica isn't out working on set, she's traveling the globe. "I love to travel. My favorite places usually have a beach where I can lay out and have a nap or some beautiful nature scene where I can take a nice walk. When I travel, I'm not tempted to be on my phone. When I leave the country, somehow it triggers in my mind, I'm leaving it all behind." I can fully commit to relaxing," she explains. Along with traveling, nature, and massages keep her grounded and calm. "I love being outside in nature, even if it's just being at my house and walking around my neighborhood or chilling in my robe in my living room or office, looking out at my trees," she says. "It's calming. Getting massages and getting my hair done and having someone touch my scalp calms and soothes me. I love a soothing touch."

Erica Ash has plenty of projects in the pipeline and a few she's currently starring in. She plays Veronica Greasley in *Legacies* on the CW and will star in *Family Reunion* on Netflix. She just finished the feature-length film, *Singleholic*. The film, which she executive produced (EP) and also stars in, was shot in Africa and screened at the 17th Annual Martha's Vineyard Film Festival. This is her first film as an EP.

Erica says her greatest achievement has little to do with her career. Instead, her greatest achievement is the total person she is becoming. "I feel like my greatest achievements are the lessons I'm learning about myself and how I'm growing and have changed spiritually. At this moment, I'm still in the process but I feel like a different person than when I started in the industry. My energy and outlook are different. My anxiety level has decreased," she says. "I learned the power and the privilege of meditating and how it stabilizes you," she says. "After I've done all of the things in my life God has for me to do, my greatest achievement will be the person I've become."

Note: Erica succumbed to breast cancer in Los Angeles on July 28, 2024 at the age of 46. She will not be forgotten.

"Talk about the story
of what we are"

Leroy Campbell

The Many Shades of Leroy Campbell

Self-taught artist Leroy Campbell was born in the Gadsden Green projects in Charleston, South Carolina, in 1956. He was raised in a culture that he describes as an "African village experience." "I came out of a Gullah Geechee culture. A culture rich with African food, dishes, words, beliefs, ways and traditions," he explains. "We were a close-knit community. Churches, schools, black-owned businesses, and grocery stores lined the perimeter of our village. A huge playground, swimming pool, and river were minutes nearby. Our food came from the farmers and fishermen. They drove throughout our village during the week selling their produce to us. The lawns were manicured and the entire community remained clean. We were a God-fearing people who loved spending time with each other. We kept our spirits up by dancing, playing games, telling jokes, and speaking positively to each other." He was surrounded by intergenerational storytellers who would become the inspiration for his art. Growing up in the backdrop of the civil rights movement, Leroy knew his worth and potential. "There were many teachers and members in the community who were determined that we would go into the world and share the best of who we were. Educationally sound, spiritually strong, respectful to our elders, and ready to work hard, and together," he says.

His father taught him hard work. He was a butcher with a passion for electronics. He would see his father bring home old thrown out radios and toasters to repair. While he wasn't much of a talker, he made sure his family had what they needed to survive. "I saw my father as a larger than life figure," he says. "He was dedicated to his church. On weekends, we would go and clean the shrubs outside of the church. That was when we spent most of our time together." In the neighborhood, Leroy looked to local athletes for inspiration as well. "I still embody their drive and winning spirit," he says.

In the early years of his career, Leroy learned that there were many people who were willing to help him with his art. "When people want to help you, you should let them," he advises. "They often see things in you that you don't see, not just in yourself, but see things in your career that you need and want." After high school, he moved to New York City and worked as a nurse's aide at a hospital. The workers there encouraged him to pursue

IT'S OUR TIME BY LEROY CAMPBELL

his art. As he became acquainted with the art scene in New York City, other artists saw his potential. He recalls Alvin Ailey dancer Donna Wood supporting him and his work early on. "Throughout your career, there is always someone there at the turning point of your career who is willing to move you to the next level," he says.

There have been many "I made it" moments throughout Leroy Campbell's career: Max Roach invited Leroy to dinner at his Central Park apartment to discuss designing his next album cover. Cicely Tyson visiting his studio to look at some artwork for a fundraiser comes to mind. Leroy also remembers the time he was interviewed by acclaimed sports journalist Bryant Gumbel with pop and psychedelic artist Peter Max at the Javits Center. "That was big, but that wasn't it," he admits. One of the most humbling moments in his career was when he went back home after his career was in "full bloom." He was talking to the pastor after church when an older woman grabbed the pastor's shirt and shouted out, "This is Leroy Campbell! He is our artist!" "After all of these years that still stays with me," he says. "I still feel that right now. When I was recognized by someone who knew from whence I came, that's when I knew I had made it."

> "I have a house. I'm living well, but there is nothing more important than having a young person connect to their own sense of worth and self."

Leroy's greatest achievement is making an impact on the youth. He loves to work with middle school children in Atlanta, Georgia and in the New York City education system. He believes at that age, it is easier to touch their spirits and minds. "People got to me when I was

BK FULTON AND NICHOLAS POWELL

in my middle school years, and that's why I am the person I am today," he explains. "When children remember who you are, they are going to make choices based on the things you pour into them." He wants them to move with confidence and purpose. "I cannot take for granted the life I am living," he says. "I have a house. I'm living well, but there is nothing more important than having a young person connect to their own sense of worth and self."

Leroy Campbell's creative process is thoughtful and substantive. His art interprets history and attempts to say something about our present. "I'm living in the present even though I'm drawing everything from the past," he explains. He starts with a story or a concept. Once he has a concept in his head, he will sketch out that concept. He then creates a character that brings context. He'll read news articles to find that character. "That silhouette with an elongated neck. Now that figure has an environment, a background, a thought process," he explains. "I focus on not only what the figure believes, but what he wants you to believe."

In his artwork, there are quotes around the characters, often inspirational. "You see this figure with no eyes and no nose, only a mouth. I want the viewer to think the figure itself is actually saying these things to them," he explains. Once you're done looking at his art, a conversation often begins.

> "When people look at a painting and it resonates and moves them, they are not only looking for what is conformational but also motivational."

He notes that his work is not random and that an extensive amount of research and thought goes into his work. He strives for each element to be cohesive—the backdrop, the figure, the choice of colors, etc. "I am always about uplifting—spirit uplifting, higher consciousness, education and empowerment," he says. "Because that is what I lived. That is what I got. That is what I know. I am documenting our story because without the documentation of our art, of our history and culture, there stands a chance it will be rewritten or reappropriated."

Leroy sees art as self-reflection and a means to heal. "When people look at a painting and it resonates and moves them, they are not only looking for what is conformational but also motivational," he explains. "Something that is already self-identified. Artwork is a direct connection to the energy that is our birthright in the universe."

He goes on to explain further. "We are using elements—paint. We are putting the elements in balance. We are putting in science. We are putting in math. All of those elements are embedded in art. The healing force in all of those elements is in us every day. So how we arrange them, and how we put them together matters. The organic forces, the spirit's underpinnings are of those elements and energy we all need to survive and thrive."

After viewing his paintings, Leroy wants viewers to understand that we do not become who we are by ourselves. "I don't care how old you are, what age you are, you are not a whole person without the input and connection, that multigenerational connection, of all of the people in your life," he says. "When you are connected and whole, you find your individual walk. Your individual walk is your contribution to that whole network."

Leroy believes young artists are in an excellent time to get their work seen. He suggests using social media and building out a website to showcase their work. He also suggests they find a mentor and they should ask for what they want. "As an artist, find your voice," he says. "Find out what you want to say. Tell your story and talk about your own journey." Reading is also important to Leroy. He suggests reading the stories and bios of other artists as well as the history of art. Apprenticeships and having an entrepreneurial spirit is also key. "Be open to working for an artist who is doing work in the areas you're interested in, and work at your craft," he suggests. "Try different mediums, paint, stay busy, treat your art like work. Get up. Just like you get up and work hard for someone else, do the same thing for yourself. Don't disrespect yourself: eat right, eat healthily, exercise regularly."

He admits it is not easy, and the people who really care about your well-being won't be easy on you. "Stay connected to those people who have your best interest at heart. People who fuss at you care about your future," he says. He believes in the midst of adversity, the ones that persevere can reach success. "After failure, get the lesson quickly, and keep going . . .," he emphasizes.

"When you are connected and whole, you find your individual walk. Your individual walk is your contribution to that whole network."

BK FULTON AND NICHOLAS POWELL

The idea of the artist having to starve to be successful doesn't sit well with Leroy. "Don't let yourself starve. It's not necessary to starve to be motivated, but it's necessary to find an environment that is conducive to your creativity," he says. "Try to find a lifestyle where you can be at peace and be comfortable so that the creativity can flourish." He believes the gifts of being an artist and the gift of creativity come from God. "These are gifts given to you by the ultimate gift-giver," he continues, "a gift that you can't keep to yourself if you choose to and a gift you cannot give back. You have to protect it and take care of it. You will find your place and enjoy the opportunity your gift creates, and you will enjoy the success and the benefits that it gives others."

Right now, Leroy is working on his first "autobiographical children's book" entitled, *Super Power*. "It is about a boy born with a birth defect on both his hands and left foot who is bullied and teased," he explains. "He tries to find a way to make the children accept him. They kept teasing him and made him feel isolated." The young boy starts to learn how to draw and trace. It makes him feel stronger. When he returns to school with his new talent, things become different. When the kids start to bully him, he pulls out his sketchbook and starts to draw. The teasing stops. "He realizes that what made him feel good, made others feel good too," Leroy explains. "So, the moral of the story is that if a child knows their worth, they don't have to try to be like anyone else or make anyone else like them."

He suggests that bullies wouldn't exist if they knew their worth.Leroy is working on more art as well. It will be a series that celebrates the many ways we enjoy each other and life, titled *Black Joy*.

GIVE AND TAKE BY LEROY CAMPBELL

To see more of Leroy Campbell's work,visit leroycampbelloriginals.com and follow him on Facebook, Instagram, and X.

Rob Chesnut: Bringing Ethics and Values to Silicon Valley

ROB CHESNUT,
CHIEF ETHICS
OFFICER OF
AIRBNB. PHOTO
BY ASA MATHAT.

"Lead by example."

Rob Chesnut's open-mindedness to the possibilities of the internet led him to be a part of some of the most influential companies of our times including eBay and Airbnb, among others. A graduate of Harvard Law School and the University of Virginia, he began his career as a federal prosecutor for the U.S. Justice Department. Unsatisfied with the negative nature of being a prosecutor, he left to go work for eBay in the late 90s. He cites AOL's dial-up internet as a precursor for his early use of eBay. He knew there was a place for him in tech when he found out AOL had hired a person who had previously had a background in federal government. Seeing there were no jobs posted on the e-commerce company's website, Rob sent his resume and cover letter to jobs@ebay.com. In his cover letter, he outlined their need for someone who could deal with fraud, the sale of illicit items on their platform, and regulations. The next day, he received a phone call (they had left a voicemail on his home phone) to come in for an interview. Almost immediately, he was on a flight to San Jose, California, to meet with the CEO at the time, Meg Whitman. He got the job. Two months later, he resigned from his role as a prosecutor and moved out West. His life was changed forever.

He would retire as the chief ethics officer of Airbnb (after serving a long run as Airbnb's General Counsel). Rob laid the groundwork for more companies to have dedicated departments that thought about what is ethical and just. Now, he has written a book titled, *Intentional Integrity: How Smart Companies Can Lead an Ethical Revolution*, which was released on July 28, 2020, to help companies become more ethical and fair to their employees, customers, and the world at large. In our interview with Rob Chesnut, he gave us a look into his upbringing, his time at eBay, Airbnb's culture of ethics, what intentional integrity means, and the issues that most concern him today.

"Intentional integrity is a recognition that leaders need to talk about integrity and they need to talk about what it means in a specific way so that everyone in the company can get aligned around it."

Where are you from and what was it like growing up there?

I grew up in Southeastern Virginia in the Tidewater area. My dad was in the Marines and retired in that area. It was, in a number of ways, a typical suburban neighborhood. I had a good childhood, although my father left when I was fairly young. I was an only child raised mostly by my mother.

Who or what was your biggest inspiration growing up?

I was always inspired to make the world a better place, but I had no idea how to do it. I figured perhaps being a lawyer would give me the greatest number of options. There's a picture of me in the high school yearbook with one of my classmates, each of us holding a briefcase. I guess people thought we both would end up being lawyers and we did. I was influenced by the legacy of John F. Kennedy. I was very moved by public service and sports, too.

Dr. J was my role model growing up. He played for the local professional team. Back then, Norfolk had a professional basketball team—the Virginia Squires. He was fantastic. I remember meeting him as a kid and shooting baskets with him. He had some relatives that lived in the area. I was so impressed with him as a human being. He has gone on to be such a well-regarded figure even well after his playing days, but he had a certain way about him back then that I had always admired.

Did your parents give you any valuable advice growing up?

Yes, I'd like to think so. There is one thing worth mentioning in particular. My parents held a belief that you may not be the smartest person in the room, but if you have a smile on your face and you work hard, good things will happen to you. From a young age, that was something that was always instilled in me and I kept that with me throughout my life.

What was it like working for eBay?

I was a senior hire for them and they didn't do much recruiting outside of Silicon Valley. I didn't know what I was doing. The CEO at the time, Meg Whitman, was going over these numbers with me and I saw these lines going up into the right. It struck me that they had the best business model I had ever seen. Even though I didn't understand much, I knew I wanted to be a part of it. I was so impressed by how the company could connect people from different parts of the world over a common interest and how trust was at the heart of it.

BK FULTON AND NICHOLAS POWELL

I remember the first time I was on eBay. Back then, you couldn't buy an item with a credit card. You could only send a check or money order. I was thinking: 'Wait, I'm going to put this money order in an envelope and send it to somebody I don't know, just to get this item? What are the odds that this is going to work out?' I trusted it would come and sure enough, it did. In a way, eBay restored my faith in mankind. To be able to make successful transactions over and over again on eBay and then to be a part of the company that was enabling it was pretty cool.

Do you feel like you have made it?

I don't think you ever feel like you've made it. I recently turned 60. I always think of it more as a journey that doesn't have a clear destination, but you kind of have an idea of the direction you want to go in. Every day is a new adventure. If your goal is to contribute in a positive way to the world, then the task is endless and in a sense, you never really get there. You evolve and learn to figure out new ways to do it.

> "If I come into the meeting and everyone in the meeting looks like me or has the same background as me, then we're heading towards the wrong path."

Greatest achievement?

I guess I don't reflect on that too much. I reflect on what my mom would be most proud of: me being open to the journey and not afraid to try new things.

You were the chief ethics officer of Airbnb. How would you describe your role and why do you think this role is so important for companies?

It was a relatively new role in the business world. I spent the first five years of my corporate career at eBay as a lawyer and then Meg Whitman said to me, "We need to start a fraud department. We need to start something that will proactively detect fraud before it occurs and protect people from getting ripped off." She knew I could figure it out and they gave me what I needed to get it done. We ended up creating the first trust and safety department in Silicon Valley. Now everyone has a trust and safety department—Facebook, Uber, Google, etc.

ROB CHESNUT SPEAKING TO UC BERKELEY MASTER OF ENGINEERING STUDENTS ABOUT THE IMPORTANCE OF INTENTIONAL INTEGRITY IN THE WORKPLACE. PHOTO COURTESY OF ROB CHESNUT.

I think similarly when I got to Airbnb and I started as their general counsel, I noticed that the world was changing. #MeToo became a movement. Leaders who were getting away with things for so long were getting called out for bad behavior publicly and it struck me that this is powerful stuff and a company needs to get ahead of this. In other words, how do you drive integrity into the culture of a company? This was new territory.

How did companies handle ethics in the past?

In the past, at least from what I've seen, companies worked on something called compliance. Compliance might be a code of ethics. You may put a poster on the wall in the break room that's got that tiny font that nobody reads or a sexual harassment video that people just click through. We asked: *How do you get people to pay attention? How do you get people to see that this is the way we want to operate as a company?*

That is when I became really invested in the issue. I knew then that I wanted to write a book about it and really focus on the issue. Airbnb is one of the first companies, not the very first, but one of the early companies to actually devote a senior level person full-time to thinking about integrity and ethics and drive it as the culture of the company.

You have a book coming out titled *Intentional Integrity: How Smart Companies Can Lead an Ethical Revolution.* Can you explain to us what *intentional integrity* means?

Intentional integrity is a recognition that leaders need to talk about integrity and they need to talk about what it means in a specific way so that everyone in the company can get aligned around it. In fact, it's a powerful force in business but only if you make it a part of your culture by having a real human conversation about it.

BK FULTON AND NICHOLAS POWELL

I talk to all of the new hires at Airbnb. It can be anywhere from a dozen to a hundred people. I think folks are quite surprised that we have an open conversation in the group about things like alcohol and relationships in the office. The reaction has been overwhelmingly positive. We do reviews with blind surveys at the end of these classes. It is the number one ranked class at orientation. People walk up to me and say, "You have no idea what it is like to work at a place that genuinely cares about this and actually talks about it and makes it a part of their culture."

In the old days, they thought, "Oh, it is a dog eat dog world out there. Ethics will get in the way." I think the way the world is evolving now is that ethics and integrity are superpowers for businesses these days. It's something that actually resonates with employees, with customers, and the community at large. Companies that intentionally act to do the right thing will be rewarded and outperform companies that don't.

That message is similar to Harvard professor Lynn Sharp Paine's. In her book, *Value Shift*, she makes the case for a more ethical perspective in business decision making. Being ethical benefits your company in the long term.

The problem today is that so many companies are forced to do what is in the interest of today's stock price or this quarter's numbers. We talk about the long-term perspective at Airbnb. Brian Chesky, the CEO of Airbnb, calls it an "infinite time horizon." I think that phrase comes from Simon Sinek and having that long-term perspective makes it easier to do the right thing.

I love what you said about the Harvard Business School professor. So often people don't ask the right questions. Is it legal? Is it ethical? Instead, companies ask: Can we figure out how to budget? Can we find a way to skirt around the law? Nobody asks if it is the right thing to do. I think these are distinct questions, and both are important. Even if it is legal, how would it look? My mom would always say, "How would it look if it was on the front page of the paper? Always think about what you do."

In today's world, you have to assume it will end up on the front page cover. Back when I was growing up, a whistleblower was an anomaly. It was maybe one Edward Snowden. Today, everyone walking in your building is a potential whistleblower because the internet has given everyone a platform. One person has the power with one blog post to change the course of a brand or company. Look at what Susan Fowler's blog post did for Uber. I think companies have to recognize, and this is a good thing, that anything they do is going to be written about online and therefore, be proud of it and if not, reconsider.

What advice would you give to young people who would like to make their mark in the tech industry, but are not necessarily software engineers or computer programmers?

[Laughs] Learn to code. No, there are so many ways to bring value to the table. At Airbnb, we talk about diversity as another superpower and we talk about it in so many different ways—the color of your skin, your background, your religion, your political affiliation, your gender. I think what's dangerous is when companies start to think that engineers are king or we're just going to hire the best person that's defined by "us." When more backgrounds and perspectives are represented in the room, the better decisions you will be making. A room full of 10 engineers is not going to come up with the best idea in the room. A room full of 10 lawyers is not going to come up with the best decision or 10 white people or 10 women or 10 men, etc. If I come into the meeting and everyone in the meeting looks like me or has the same background as me, then we're heading towards the wrong path. I love rooms that have people that think in different ways and when that happens, we are a lot less likely to miss something important.

How has Airbnb thought about diversity?

Airbnb was really torn up about three years ago when it came out that users were discriminated against based on the color of their skin. Black users were having trouble being accepted by hosts on Airbnb and the first reaction in the company—I had only been with the company for a few months—was surprise. There were genuine people in the Airbnb leadership who were shocked because that was not Airbnb as we saw it. Airbnb is headquartered in San Francisco and the environment in San Francisco is very open and accepting of people of all races, nationalities, and sexual preferences.

Why would we think Airbnb is immune to that when there is so much discrimination in the world? Maybe because Airbnb itself was not diverse. If we had more employees of color, it would have helped us to see it earlier. We learned we needed to be more diverse so that we could have a better understanding of what our customers have to go through every day. There has been more of a conscious focus in the last couple of years to understand this.

How do you relax when you are not working?

I love hanging out with my kids. My daughter is in college in New York studying to be an actress. Watching her perform gives me tremendous joy. Like me, my son loves basketball. He plays AAU basketball and he

BK FULTON AND NICHOLAS POWELL

and I will spend time watching basketball on TV and playing basketball out in the yard together. He is only 13 and his feet are already bigger than mine and he is growing like crazy. Just getting out in the yard and hanging and playing one-on-one with my son is something I get a great deal of joy from.

What's up next?

My mom used to love to read. There was always a book on the coffee table right where my mom would sit on the sofa. My mom instilled in me at an early age a love for reading. I'm saddened that my mom is not around anymore to be able to see that her son actually wrote a book.

> "I am deeply concerned about climate change. I am deeply concerned about the world I am handing off to my kids."

I'm still not over the fact that I've written even one book. I think when I see it at the bookstore, it will become a little bit more real. I haven't given one second of thought to another book. We will see where this one goes. As I said, I love the idea of changing things up in life and I like the idea of changing it up again. At age 60, there is still a lot to give and a lot to do.

I am deeply concerned about climate change. I am deeply concerned about the world I am handing off to my kids. My mom always told me to leave the room better than you found it. My generation hasn't done that when it comes to the Earth. I think we failed. I'm doing a lot more reading and thinking about climate change. I think that is an issue that needs a lot of people thinking and contributing in many different ways.

Order Rob Chesnut's book on Amazon.

"Inevitably, history is about how we are living in the present."

Christy Coleman

Christy Coleman:
Rethinking Our Relationship With the Past

Christy Coleman is one woman with the knowledge and expertise to help us build a more inclusive nation. Her passion is history. She lives and breathes it. It is a result of a knack for resourcefulness and a determination that many adults in her youth found inspiring enough to open the doors of opportunity for her to walk through. Like many African-Americans of her generation, Christy grew up in the church, a place that she credits for building the foundation for the values she carries with her today. "Of course, when you are a child growing up in the church, you not only learn to sing and learn the word, but you also learn how to comport yourself publicly and how to share ideas respectfully," she explains.

She grew up in Williamsburg, Virginia, a place rich in the history of the beginnings of our nation. "Colonial Williamsburg was literally in our background, five minutes away from where I grew up," she explains.

"So, I remember my church family and school friends who had parents that worked there in a variety of capacities. I got to see history behind the scenes on a daily basis and it helped cement my love for history and museums." She references a master printmaker named Willie Parker, who worked at the Book Bindery. He was an African-American man who was a "master of his trade." For Christy, her love for history never began with dates and facts, but it was what Coleman calls a "living experience from people like Parker and others." "The connection between what people do and what they are and how they interacted was brought to life for me pretty early," she explains.

Christy's parents also played a positive and critical role in her upbringing. "My parents taught me the power of using your mind. They taught me to stand up for myself," she says. "They were fearless and brave in how they stood up for my well-being, even in the face of systemic discrimination." When Christy scored exceptionally well on her standardized test but was not put in a gifted program, her parents advocated for her education and made sure their daughter was not pushed out of places where she would be able to blossom. She credits

their approach to them being young and having a lot of energy. "My parents led the way for our family in addition to working every day and making sure we were cared for. We were able to do what we needed to do to be contributing members of society," she says.

Dr. Rex M. Ellis, the former Associate Director for Curatorial Affairs at the National Museum of African American History and Culture (NMAAHC), was the man who gave Christy her first museum job at the Colonial Williamsburg Foundation. She applied for the job at the age of seventeen (a fact Dr. Ellis was not aware of). He hired her as a living history character. She would portray a young slave girl. After finding out she was still in high school, they worked around her schedule until her June graduation. After graduation, the museum gave her the opportunity to continue to work. "Dr. Rex M. Ellis has been a mentor, a friend, and a colleague for 35 years," she says. "Watching his grace, passion and power was inspiring. I will always be appreciative of the care that he gave to us in providing a safe space in a really emotionally unsafe environment." She credits him for helping her understand the work that they were doing was more than just a job. Even when they didn't agree, he was still supportive. "His example has led me to try to be the same kind of mentor to young museum professionals, particularly those who are black," she says.

As Christy went about her career, she learned the importance of using her voice. "I understood there was a special lens that I could look through and question the past to bring about new answers and a deep understanding of the past and that there were stories I wanted to share," she explains. "It allowed my creativity to really shine because I wasn't trying to do the work from someone else's lens." She learned to be prepared. In her work, people will always question what you know or what you are thinking. "You have to be twice as good. Always be prepared because inevitably—whether by my gender or by my ethnicity—there will be people that will question my place or try to define my place," she says.

BK FULTON AND NICHOLAS POWELL

"My parents taught me the power of using your mind. They taught me to stand up for myself."

When asked if she has made it, Christy Coleman looks at it a little differently. "I believe I've reached a point in my career where the impact that I had hoped to have in my field is, in fact, coming to fruition," she says. "Am I impactful? Am I making a difference?" She refers back to 25 years ago when she became the director of public history for the Colonial Williamsburg Foundation and as part of an estate sale, executed a reenactment of a slave auction. The response from other museums made it all worth it. "They would say, 'my god, if you guys could pull off such a powerful program that gave pain a face and helped us understand the intersection of our early republic and its connections and its paradoxes, the least we can do is get more research and just talk about enslavement and what it did in our location," Christy Coleman explains that in her role at the American Civil War Museum in Richmond, Virginia, she continues to think about the impact of her work and what role history plays in contemporary life.

"Inevitably, history is about how we are living in the present and the issues that we can confront and our desire to understand their genesis," she explains. We asked Christy about her view of Richmond and the conversation surrounding the Confederacy and monuments. "What is remarkable is that the conversation has expanded," she explains. Christy Coleman remembers the time she first came to Richmond to run, what was then called, the American Civil War Center. One of her first tasks was to go out and introduce the Center to the funding and grants community. While everyone was polite, there was one member of a foundation who was more direct and honest with his opinion. "He said to me, 'Listen, I'm going to tell you, we are sick to death of dealing with the Civil War in Richmond. We don't know what to do with it. It's a mess. It's divisive. We don't want it. We will not be funding anything related to it.' I greatly appreciated his words because it helped me understand what a heavy lift I had," she says. Christy's hard work did not go in vain. Today, people of all ages and ethnicities have walked through the doors of the American Civil War Museum. "I could not have asked for better," she says.

Christy emphasizes that to say it is "just a Confederate story" neglects the story of so many others. "There are people of every hue who lived through that crisis. People of every ethnicity and religious background and gender identifications which you can imagine have been impacted by our collective past. Yet, the story of our past has traditionally either been told as a military or a political one, when in fact, it is so much more," Christy explains. Christy acknowledges and is grateful for the changing dialogue surrounding the Confederacy and monuments in Richmond and around the country. "How are we going to reconsider what we have allowed to be venerated? Do these things or places reflect our values now? Those are really powerful conversations, and though I don't really have the answers myself, I think every community needs to decide those issues for itself," she says.

As the public marvels at Kehinde Wiley's *Rumors of War* statue as it stands proud in front of the Virginia Museum of Fine Arts (VMFA), Christy references the role of art in our lives and in history. "The unveiling of *Rumors of War* is a really interesting statement about the power of art," she says. Christy co-chaired The Monument Avenue Commission, which was formed to recommend what to do with Confederate monuments on Monument Avenue in Richmond, Virginia. She references one of the recommendations for the community to "align with the artistic community to look at ways to reframe what already exists." "That was one of the suggestions people often forget about, but it is absolutely one of the suggestions that we made and to see that come to fruition is a beautiful thing because it is sparking conversation and you couldn't have a better artist than Kehinde Wiley whose whole series of work has been about getting us to reframe our images, particularly of black men," she says. Christy believes the museum has done its job in providing resources to communities that will allow them to understand how nuanced and complex the Civil War period was.

"How are we going to reconsider what we have allowed to be venerated? Do these things or places reflect our values now? Those are really powerful conversations, and though I don't really have the answers myself, I think every community needs to decide those issues for itself."

Days after the unveiling of *Rumors of War*, it was announced that the "Honor the 14 Foundation" was planning to raise money to erect a statue to commemorate the 14 Medal of Honor recipients from the United States Colored Troops at the Battle of New Market Heights. "These fourteen men received the Congressional Medal of Honor for valor by pushing back Confederate forces outside of Richmond. Several of them were Virginians; several of them were formerly enslaved men who had run off to find their freedom and to display their own valor," she emphasizes. "It is an extraordinary thing."

Beyond her professional life, Christy calls herself a "big ole fan girl" of movies, music, graphic novels, and comic books. "I escape to fantasy and sci-fi," she says. She is also an avid reader of fiction and nonfiction books. "Losing myself in a wonderful book is always fun," she says. When asked what has been the biggest blessing in her life, Christy says it is the two people who call her mom. "Even though I know they are independent, free thinkers learning from their own mistakes, I'm still learning how to give them the freedom to be and discover even when they fall and mess up," she says. "So, I'm waiting to see what happens and what kind of people they become in adulthood. I just love and adore them."

When we spoke with Christy in December, 2018, she gave us the news that after almost 12 years, she will be leaving the American Civil War Museum to become Executive Director for the Jamestown-Yorktown Foundation in Williamsburg, VA. She began her new position in late January of 2019. As a professional in the history and museum space, Christy Coleman advises young people who want to work in museums to not be afraid to take a chance and to let what truly interests them lead them. "Don't feel like you need to be on a strict plan because some of the best things happen unexpectedly," she says. No matter what path Christy decides to take, she will always push the boundaries and make us rethink our relationship with our history as a country.

Jacqui Coles' Call to the Word

JACQUI COLES.
PHOTOS BY
JEFFERY MABRY.

"Know what you will and won't tolerate."

Jacqui Coles

Jacqui Coles is from Goochland County, Virginia, a small rural town in central Virginia, where "everyone knew each other." Her mom was one of thirteen and Jacqui would spend almost every Sunday at her grandmother's and Papa's house. "We grew up surrounded by love and laughter," she says. "We didn't have a lot of money but as kids, we didn't know how poor we were. I would often tell Mom to just write a check if I wanted something and she said we didn't have the money." Her mother was a voice of reason for Jacqui as a child and young adult. She taught her the golden rule and the value of one's character. "She would say, not to me in particular, 'You might be pretty on the outside, but if your inside is ugly, then you ugly." Growing up, Jacqui's dream was to be either a model, hair stylist, or airline stewardess. When she was in the 10th grade, she attended the Richmond Technical Center for Cosmetology. She accomplished two out of the three. She went on to model for the Ford Modeling Agency (now Ford Models) in New York City and later, opened her own salon. With the support and encouragement of her mentors, Dr. Myles Munroe and Dr. Kingsley Fletcher, Jacqui also became a minister.

Jacqui does not just see herself as a salon owner or a hair stylist, but as a counselor. Her clients don't just come in to look their best, but to learn and to share wisdom. While Jacqui is the one who is usually giving advice, her older clients have taught her valuable lessons. She recalls one client in particular who spoke about the loving nature of women. "She told me, 'If you are dating someone, you need to date someone who loves you more than you love them,'" Jacqui says. "So many times, as women, we love people who don't feel the same way and then try to change them. They never do." While Jacqui believes her talent as a hair stylist and owner of a salon are her gifts to the world, she does not believe those things are her purpose. "Once I wrote my book, *Do You Want His Will or Your Way?*, I began to feel I had a clear purpose on this Earth. I now feel like I'm on the right path and believe I can change many people's lives for the better through my ministry," she says.

"Once I wrote my book, *Do You Want His Will or Your Way?*, I began to feel I had a clear purpose on this Earth."

Jacqui recalls a client who was a beautiful, young pageant queen. Jacqui taught her the importance of presence and how to enter a room. "Pull your shoulders back, hold your head up and walk," she advised. "When you go into a room your mind has to say, 'OK, I own this room.' This doesn't mean you are a conceited person. Inner confidence is the only way you're going to grab that stage when you walk out." Her client went on to be the first runner up for Miss Virginia and a couple of other pageants.

Jacqui blames poor use of social media and reality shows for too often limiting the scope of young women's ambitions and creating a culture

BK FULTON AND NICHOLAS POWELL

that rewards outrageousness. "Media teaches women to not look at themselves as the queens that they are," she explains. "Some folk will do almost anything to get attention. I even tell my boys to draw the line with what you will and won't do or tolerate." When Jacqui was working as a model, she was offered a job for a smoking ad. "I don't smoke but I was offered the job for $50,000," she recalls. She didn't have to go to casting. All she had to do was show up. She ended up turning the job down. "I didn't want these young girls who looked up to me to think I did something that I didn't do. They may not know that it was my job," she says. Jacqui remembers when she was young, she wanted to be a smoker because she thought all of the pretty girls smoked and looked

cool doing it. "I've always agreed with the saying, 'If it cost you your peace of mind, it is too expensive.'" The temptation of money and fame can be tantalizing. Jacqui believes you have to have a sound moral compass. "If you wait until you are in a situation where the money is in front of you, a lot of times you will make the wrong decision," she says. "It is easier to walk away when you have a set of values and morals as your guides."

After readers finish her book, Jacqui Coles simply wants people to understand what God teaches. "Be holy for I am holy." She urges her readers to develop the *fruit of the spirit*. This means living with love, joy, peace, patience, kindness, goodness, faithfulness, gentleness, and self-control. "Just treat people the way you would like to be treated," Jacqui says simply. "When you are in a situation, run it through your mind and think about if you would like that comment being said to you or that act done to you. If the answer comes back no, then you shouldn't do it."

Jacqui believes we should all strive for God's definition of perfection. This means making a conscious effort to be the best person that we can be. "We can't always say that we're just going to make mistakes," she says. "Yeah, we're going to make mistakes, but we can't keep making the same mistakes because at some point, it is not a mistake as much as it is a conscious decision."

Jacqui hopes young people will contribute positively to the world and have their voices heard. She says that first they must develop integrity. "Develop your integrity and your character early," she advises. "The fruit of the spirit is not necessarily a religious thing; they are just principles. Life is based on principles. When we develop good principles, our lives will change for the better."

In 2020, a time where citizens were protesting against police brutality, Jacqui Coles had to reread her book and reflect on what she wrote. "I had to ask God to guard my heart because it is natural to be angry. However, we have to be careful that the anger doesn't turn into iniquity," she says. "I asked Him to guard my heart and reflect back on myself through this process." Jacqui believes without citizens risking their lives on the frontlines of the protests, we would not have any change. Jacqui believes her job is to research, understand, and give financially to those protestors and help rebuild some of the businesses that were lost in the unrest.

"Change for good and deliverance from evil is going to cost you something."

She compares Jesus confronting the money changers in the Temple of Jerusalem and destroying their property with the present-day protests that have caused some occasional destruction. "You get tired of evil, so you have to stand up to evil," she says. "I sent out a post, telling all of my friends that they cannot stay quiet."

Jacqui looks to future generations and hopes those who are older will have a change of heart, specifically those who are against having grandkids or great-grandkids who are mixed. "You might be part of the problem if you have an issue with that," she says. She hopes the religious community will give more than just prayers. "Prayer doesn't cost us anything. Prayer is free. If you are going to pray, you need to add fasting or help financially or be on the front lines. Change for good and deliverance from evil is going to cost you something."

Buy Jacqui Coles' book, Do You Want His Will or Your Way?: Holiness is Obtainable on Amazon.

"Make music that
unites us all."

Eric Darius

Eric Darius: The Sax Sage of SagiDarius

Saxophonist Eric Darius knew he had to work harder than everyone else to become a great musician. He grew up inspired by the saxophone greats before him: John Coltrane, David Sanborn, Grover Washington, Jr., and Cannonball Adderley, among others. His upbringing in Tampa, Florida, was essential in developing his musical growth. He studied at the Howard W. Blake High School of the Arts in Tampa, Florida, and went on to study music at the University of South Florida. Before he reached the age of 18, he was well on his way to stardom.

Eric considers his father to be a guiding force in his life. At the age of 11, his father became his manager and was by his side 24/7. Eric grew up in a family of musicians. His Haitian father plays bass, his Jamaican mother plays piano and sings, his younger sister plays clarinet and sings, and his older brother plays the trumpet and drums. Both of his parents inspired a young Eric to follow his dreams and stay true to himself. Some musicians wait for what feels like an eternity to find some success, but at 17, everything began to make sense for Darius after he heard one of his songs on the radio and was overjoyed. However, it wasn't until 2008 that he felt "validated." In that year, he got his first number 1 song on the Smooth Jazz Billboard chart with his single "Goin' All Out," released under the legendary jazz label Blue Note. "That was the point where all of my hard work had paid off, and I knew my work was being appreciated around the world," Eric says.

While he has achieved many milestones and wins throughout his career, Eric considers starting his own record label, SagiDarius Music, his greatest achievement so far. "I've been making music since I was 12 years old," he says. "Starting my own label was the ultimate achievement for me from a career standpoint and something I can now call my own."

Eric Darius has shared the stage with many music legends such as Prince, Babyface, and Mary J. Blige, to name a few. "One thing that was consistent, was they were always pushing themselves constantly," he recalls. "Their standard of excellence was on such a level that I had never experienced before." For Eric, being excellent wasn't from just a

**ERIC DARIUS HOSTING THE SAN DIEGO SMOOTH JAZZ FESTIVAL
IN SAN DIEGO, CALIFORNIA. PHOTO BY ERIC DARIUS.**

performative standpoint, but from a business perspective as well. He continues to aim higher. One day, Eric would like to work with Stevie Wonder. "He's one of the guys who truly influenced me and inspired me as a musician and as a songwriter," he says.

> "My ultimate goal is to make music that is relevant to all of the generations and bring people together."

When asked if his music inspiration comes organically or externally, Eric says it's a little bit of both. "As a musician, music has always been organic," he explains. "I grew up listening to R&B, hip-hop, jazz, rock, reggae, soul, and funk; so, my music is not just jazz." Eric has stayed true to his style even when record labels and management teams tried to pull him in different directions. His artistic vision has always stayed intact. It's important for him to continue to evolve and push what he can do musically. He works with no boundaries or genre labels. "At the

BK FULTON AND NICHOLAS POWELL

PHOTO BY ERIC CURTIS

end of the day, it is just music," he says. "My ultimate goal is to make music that is relevant to all of the generations and bring people together."

Eric pays it forward with his talents and gifts. His music education program, On a Mission in the Schools, exposes youth to the wonders of musical expression. He teaches his students the 5 Ps: practice, patience, persistence, perseverance, and prayer. "These 5 Ps have truly guided me throughout my life," he says. "Not just from a musical standpoint but from a life standpoint." Eric tells his students that there is nothing wrong with imitating the masters of their instruments. In fact, he encourages it. He recommends using the creativity of others as a blueprint to eventually innovate and take on their own style and embrace their individuality as musicians. "At one point everyone, even those outside of music like athletes and entertainers, has had someone they looked up to and studied to better themselves, incorporated their style and made it their own."

By choice, Eric Darius doesn't take much time to rest. He says he always had a strong work ethic. In high school, he played basketball, ran track, and was part of the marching band, the jazz band, and wind ensemble. "I was doing over 100 shows a year as a 14-year-old in addition to writing and creating my own music," he says. "So fast-forward to today and not much has changed." Eric is busy building a musical empire, as well as creating music on his own. He released his last album in 2022. His new single, "Summer Feelin' (featuring Paul Jackson, Jr.)," is a must-have, feel-good song to carry you through the summer. He got married a few years ago and while he is always working, he understands the importance of building a healthy relationship with his wife. Eric and his wife have made a pact to go on vacations periodically to decompress, recharge, and reflect.

ERIC DARIUS LIVE AT THE SEABREEZE JAZZ FESTIVAL IN PANAMA CITY BEACH, FLORIDA. PHOTO BY JIM CLARK.

Eric says cooking is therapeutic for him. This was even more apparent to him during a time when we were encouraged to stay in as much as possible. "It is something that I've been doing more of these days, so that's been fun," he says. Eric is usually in the gym about 4 or 5 times a week and maintains a healthy diet. He tries to stay active, whether that means golf or basketball, but he's okay with working out at home too. He jokes that since the pandemic, he has been at home the longest he's ever been. "I remember the first week, I was like, *this is cool*," he recalls. "I get a little bit of downtime. Fast-forward to the second week and I'm

BK FULTON AND NICHOLAS POWELL

like, *now what?* By the third week, I had completely immersed myself in my work, working on my business and music. So, I was back into that constant workflow."

During COVID, to keep up with his fans, Eric put together concerts every Saturday on his Facebook page @OfficialEricDarius. "It was one way that I liked to connect with my fans and keep uplifting spirits and performing every single week for free," he says. "I believe God has given me this gift to share with people and so I use it to inspire others."

As if he's not busy enough, Eric continues to work with his nonprofit that gives instruments to underserved kids. He is also looking to sign new talent to his label. He's not looking for any style in particular, so send him your best stuff if you think you have what it takes. "I'm simply looking for people with talent who need an outlet and are looking for that opportunity," he says. With a nation in the midst of radical change, it is easy to imagine there are plenty of musicians who have a lot to say. Eric Darius is giving them the platform to express themselves freely.

To learn more about Eric Darius and his music, visit ericdarius.com and follow his Facebook, Instagram, and X.

Chris Denson Has an Appetite for Exploration

Chris Denson watched a lot of stand-up when he was younger. He was a latchkey kid and when he returned home from school in the afternoon, he would turn the channel to *Caroline's Comedy Hour* and *Def Comedy Jam*. He didn't know it then, but he was enamored with the way the comedians used observation to explain universal experiences like romance, food, or the mundane details of everyday life. "I had a lot of guys and women that I liked in that space. Comedy was something I actually ended up doing for about seven years after I graduated high school," he says. "So it led me to Los Angeles. It led me to California and it set me off on the path I am on now."

In the early days of his career, after graduating from Michigan State University with a degree in packaging engineering, Chris worked as an engineer for Daimler-Chrysler. It wasn't too long before he realized it wasn't the right fit, so he left to pursue a career in the entertainment industry. His coworkers weren't so understanding about him leaving though. "It was this midwest, 'I can't believe you are going to change your life' type of thing,'" he jokes. But his boss' reaction was different. She had a best friend who lived in Los Angeles and had connections within the industry. While this connection didn't go as planned, Chris was now in the perfect location to express his creativity.

In Los Angeles, Chris made a name for himself as a producer, writer, marketer, and host in the media/entertainment space. He worked for companies like Paramount, BET, Playboy Television, Machinima, and Pluto TV and has partnered with platforms like Art Basel and Fast Company on content creation. But one particular moment stood out for Chris and changed his career trajectory. He got a job with the American Film Institute's Digital Content Lab. He describes it as a "think tank for the marriage between technology and entertainment." He admits that he took the job reluctantly, but it allowed him to find his spark. He was working with some of the top networks, content makers, and video game platforms. He found himself around some of the smartest and most creative thinkers he had ever met. This satisfied his attraction to business ingenuity. "The relationships that I have 'till this day have come out of trying to think outside of the box and being inspired by what other people are doing and finding some connective tissues," Chris says.

Putting these connective tissues together, Chris launched the podcast *Innovation Crush* in 2014. He describes the podcast as a mix between Fast Company and the Daily Show. It went on for nearly seven years and amassed 750,000 subscribers and inspired a #1 best-selling book on Amazon. "I got to be silly and goofy but also have really smart conversations with some of the best people in the world like Janice Bryant Howroyd, Steve Wozniak, Jean Case, Nolan Bushnell, and a lot of pioneers in their respective industries," he recalls.

> "The relationships that I have 'till this day have come out of trying to think outside of the box and being inspired by what other people are doing and finding some connective tissues."

Looking over his career, Chris feels like 33 is the age when you reconnect with your inner thirteen-year-old. He thinks about his mother who met his dad at 13, got married at 18, and was married for 16 years. At 33, his mother's curiosity resurfaced again. She took belly dancing lessons, eventually taught at colleges, went roller skating, and as an elder, participated in the Senior Olympics as a dancer. Chris calls this curiosity an "appetite for exploration" and this appetite developed in him as well.

BK FULTON AND NICHOLAS POWELL

However, his "appetite for exploration" came with a sense of otherness. "Along the way you sometimes feel like you don't belong, especially on paper in certain environments," Chris says. In 2020, his 48-hour think tank Gov City was honorably mentioned as a Fast Company World Changing Idea. Chris and Molly Cain, who was director of ventures and innovation for Homeland Security at the time, came together to create a "curated society" between government, business, and community.

At GovCity, Chris found himself working with government agencies, companies, and the Los Angeles and New York City mayor's offices. He had never worked in government, so he wondered how he would fit into all of this. But he used this to his advantage. "I don't know the rules that you live by, so I break them," Chris explains. "And to the right teams and individuals that is a very exciting value proposition, but it doesn't work for everyone. It can be a low percentage of conversion but the ones that do convert, become really amazing opportunities. My confidence came from an 'I don't know exactly what you do but I know what I do' mentality.'"

Being an outsider has led Chris to relate to those who move in spaces that are not necessarily thought of with them in mind. Chris' first celebrity interview for *Innovation Crush* was with rapper and entrepreneur, Chamillionaire. They discussed Chamillionaire's "graduation" from hip hop to business. He was the first entrepreneur-in-residence at Upfront Venture in Los Angeles. He was one of the earlier investors of Maker Studios and is an owner of a host of car lots and beauty salons. Chamillionaire explained to Chris how there was a public perception that he fell off career-wise. But Chamillionaire simply pivoted in a new direction. "This kind of response happens when you evolve and innovate," Chris says. "Which is something we all want to do. We all have some aspiration that doesn't necessarily align with what our past history may indicate."

In Chris' many interviews, there is always a lesson to be learned, a lesson he and his audience can take with them. He recalls his interview with author, mentor, and criminal justice advocate, Shaka Senghor, a fellow Detroiter. At the age of 19, Shaka Senghor was convicted of second-degree murder. Turning his life around, his story of spiritual redemption has led to him becoming a *New York Times* best-selling author, calling Oprah a best friend, and talks at universities to tell his story about ways to fix our criminal justice system.

"You are not going to be the same person you are tomorrow as you were ten years ago, five years ago, or sometimes even last week."

"We have sons that are around the same age. And come to find out he lives around the corner from me," Chris says. "He was saying as a parent, there is a generational difference between us and our kids. In today's culture, kids are exposed to so much all of the time. And so they have different entry points. I even picked up on a lesson on how to be a better dad by chatting with Shaka. In his case, he is applying the fatherly wisdom he didn't have with his older son to his younger one, age 9, because he was in prison for most of his older son's life. I have an older child and I have a younger child. I think about what I would do differently and how I can show up differently and still make an impact. How do I abandon my own beliefs? What have we unconsciously agreed to as an operating system for ourselves that may not fit or work in today's society and who you are as a person?"

Chris jokingly advises young people who want to work within media and entertainment to not do it. In all seriousness, he advises young people to be smart with their money because when starting out, they will hear a lot of no's that can set them back financially. "There is a lot of waiting and hurrying up and waiting," Chris explains, "No matter your craft or skill level or whether you are in development or in front of or behind the camera, creative projects come and go. I've worked on pilots of shows that didn't go anywhere. I've worked on seasons of programs that suddenly ended. You have to make sure that you are being smart about this kind of thing."

Chris admits that the entertainment industry is subjective when it comes to what content gets the green light and what doesn't. "I've gone through multiple bouts of imposter syndrome and the need to reconcile and be very deliberate in how I want to show up," he explains. "Because you can get lost in someone else's expectations or someone else's feedback. Feedback is great. You have to learn how to be able to adjust, but you also have to do what feels right for you, in the end, no matter what feedback or response you get from the industry."

But he also wants young people to be open to change. "You are not going to be the same person you are tomorrow as you were ten years ago, five years ago, or sometimes even last week," Chris says. "Your

BK FULTON AND NICHOLAS POWELL

appetite or approach might change. Emotional intelligence is not as often addressed as it should be."

> # "I really get inspired by people who don't have any business doing what they are doing and they do it anyway."

With a new season of the video series *The Work In Progress* with Fast Company now available to watch, Chris is proud of the work that he has done. "We had a bunch of really great guests from the CEO of PayPal and celebs like Taraji P. Henson to a bunch of really great folks at Nike and so on and so forth," he says. "We went into production in February and I am excited about it."

In 2022, Chris interviewed former professional baseball player Micah Johnson. After retiring from professional baseball in 2018, Micah pursued a career as an artist. After learning about how to sell his art as an NFT from a patron who bought one of his first art pieces, Micah created and sold the NFT Aku, a Black boy in an astronaut helmet, to inspire kids to dream big. In 2021, Aku was the first NFT to be optioned for TV and film. In a way, Micah Johnson is the epitome of why Chris does what he does.

"How do you keep learning and keep evolving and finding new passions?" he asks rhetorically. "Yes, there are pioneers of the industry. But I really get inspired by people who don't have any business doing what they are doing and they do it anyway."

To learn more about Chris Denson, visit www.chrisdenson. co and follow him on Instagram and X.

Raheem DeVaughn:
A Changed Man

"Believe in yourself.
Take every lesson and turn
it into a blessing."
— Raheem DeVaughn

Raheem DeVaughn just wants to be the best man that he can be. The prolific R&B singer released his intimate sixth album, Decade of a Love King, a testimony to monogamy. DeVaughn is now in his 40s and has rearranged his priorities. He's realizing his place in the world. He has new insights on life, romance and the importance of showing character in times where some men still refuse to be accountable for their actions, even in an age of #MeToo and #TimesUp." We spoke with Raheem about his career and what he's learned about himself at this point in his amazing.

Where are you from and what was it like growing up there?

I was born in Orange, New Jersey, in what was formerly known as Orange Hospital. I grew up in the Maryland, DC, and Virginia metropolitan area or the "DMV" as we refer to it around here. I would spend my summers in Newark, New Jersey with my dad. When I was with my dad, I saw the inner city and the effects of things like the crack epidemic. I saw a lot. My mom lived in a more suburban setting. It was total night and day. And even to this day, the difference from one setting to the other helped me tremendously in terms of balance. It's one thing to be analytical or book smart and another to be street smart. My upbringing gave me an edge. I think people who get to experience both the city and the suburbs have an advantage. It gives you a better understanding of the haves and have nots and how to relate to everyone.

Coming up, who was your biggest musical inspiration?

I love all the greats: Stevie Wonder, Donny Hathaway, Sade, Bob Marley, and Earth, Wind & Fire; you name it. Great music is great music. But if I had to describe Raheem DeVaughn in a combination of three different entities, I'd say it would be a sprinkle of Prince, a dab of Marvin Gaye and two teaspoons of 2Pac.

That's what's up. In your early career phases, before you took off, were there any important lessons that you learned?

I'll be honest with you, I'm still learning. I think life is a lesson. I think

the profound lessons are the ones that change your life forever. I used to wonder what it would be like to be in my 40s and how great it might be. I feel like as you mature in the business, you start to come into your own. I'm definitely in that state. I think making "food music" has taught me patience, humility and forgiveness. It's taught me the purpose of and the gift of time; the gift of one another; and the gift of decision making and how important those things are in shaping and growing the man I am becoming.

Well, tell me this. At what point in your career did you think that you made it?

I can't say that I've made it yet. As crazy as that sounds, I feel there's so much more in store for me and that once you tap into your greatness and understand the keys of life, that's when things begin to open up. So, I'm starting to see opportunities manifest and I understand how to move certain things my way. Everything isn't for me and every dollar isn't a good dollar.

I can tell you one aspect where I feel I have made it. I realized, I won't just be held accountable for what I did on stage but also for what I did off stage. That's where the humanitarian in me comes in. I started the LoveLife Foundation, a non-profit organization to help people. Who I am matters in the sense that when I pick up the phone or go on social media and make something happen, it is for somebody other than myself. You see, the homeless man that I gave $20.00 to, he doesn't care who I am. He just knows that the twenty might be his next meal or place to stay. There's an old saying: 'You don't know when you're entertaining an angel.'

What I hear you saying is that your voice has become a vessel?

Yes. It's way bigger than singing the panties off of women. I have the power to help other people without picking up a microphone,

BK FULTON AND NICHOLAS POWELL

without parting my mouth to sing a line. It's how people have come to respect me. Having integrity is a lane that I have created for myself. It's important.

Throughout the years, you've done a lot of collaborations. Have there been any favorite artists that you've collaborated with?

It would definitely be The Roots. That's probably my biggest accomplishment. I'm a huge Roots fan and I would love to do an entire album with them at some point. That is something I'm extremely proud of—the work that I've done with them. Of course, I am proud of all of the work that I've done. It's a very vast catalog, from the Roots to Boney James to UGK to Usher to Jamie Foxx, and some obscure collabs. Last night, I did some features for some boys down in Richmond, Virginia who just got talent, so we vibed. Again, it's about lifting people up and assisting one another.

Your last project, *Decade of a Love King*, was about being faithful, loving and giving and receiving. Why was this message so important to get out to the public?

At this point in my life, I believe in transparency. I've been very vocal in the last few months about celebrating the relationship that I'm in. Having that awakening and understanding of what monogamy is about is driving me. Life partners are gifts that come from the Universe and God. They are tailor made for you. I believe your blessings flow depending on whether or not you abuse them or appreciate them. It's so important for me to put that message out there.

I can help men who have been where I've been. I want to expose the detrimental effects of womanizing and lack of self love and abusing yourself and spreading yourself too thin. At the end of the day, nobody would rather be at their lowest low when they could choose their highest high.

I like that. Man, you are always working! When you're not working, what do you do to relax?

I'm still trying to learn that. I love to be with the fam, kick it with my lady and kick it with my kids. I try to get in there with my parents 'cause they're getting older—just valuing things differently. I used to think everything came after music. Now, it's a different list of priorities for me. It's God, faith, my family and then music. This order allows me to put everything into perspective. My work takes a lot of my time, but I appreciate those other things a lot more. I wouldn't be able to do any of this without God.

Consider for example, my day ended at 6 a.m. this morning. I was back up at 8:30 a.m, and then took a nice nap in the car service on my way to a reading in New York. I'm headed back to the crib tonight. I may get to the studio for a minute and then tomorrow, I fly to Houston for a show. It doesn't stop. You'd be surprised at what you can do when you put your mind to it. I try to find some time to recharge my battery 'cause I'm not a spring chicken anymore. My philosophy: When I leave here, I'm going to leave empty. Not to say we don't sleep, but we leave here empty because we put that work in and build that legacy.

What advice would you give to the next generation of singers/ artists who want to have a successful career in the music industry?

Believe in yourself. Understand early in the process that the gift of time is yours to claim. The gift of decision is yours to make and use wisely. And the gift of relationships and people will put you in rooms that you never thought you would be allowed to be in. You must be prepared when you get your shot. God and the Universe do not give you anything until you are deserving of it. If you want to make God laugh, make your own plans. Listen for the voice of discernment. Believe in yourself. Take every lesson and turn it into a blessing. Failure is imminent. It's going to happen. Failure breeds success. You can't be successful without taking some Ls (losses). And be prepared to hear a lot of no's. The most successful people are those who are determined

BK FULTON AND NICHOLAS POWELL

to change those no's into bonafide yes's. In the business that we're in—music, television, and film—and as public figures, few people want to be first. Nobody wants to be the first person who has someone come up to them and say, "You told me this was going to work and it didn't." Some of those people, may end up out of a job. So everyone wants to be second (or follow) 'cause it seems easier to be that cheerleader on the sideline, saying "Man, I told everyone that you would make it! Now, let's go spend all of your money!" Just be mindful of those things. There is no "I" in the word team. Everything has its point in time. You can't rush perfection. You can't rush the creative process. Take risks and be smart about it. Be the first to believe in you.

That's real talk and great advice. What's up next for Raheem DeVaughn?

I'm part of this great film called *Love Dot Com*. I just signed on for a couple of other projects that I cannot talk about just yet. I started a new company, DeVaughn Multimedia Group, which will allow me to do other work besides music. Additionally, moving forward, I'll own my masters so my art will be owned by me. I'm proud of that. It will allow me to jump into the world of television and film with more to offer. I've also been inspired to work on some self-help books. I think I'm a walking testimony for a lot of different reasons. This makes me want to share my story in the hopes that it helps people, particularly black men—young and middle-aged—in crisis who are trying to figure it out.

"A generous life is a
life worth living."

Brad Formsma

Brad Formsma Is Creating a Culture of Generosity

Brad Formsma has made it his life's mission to spread the message of living generously. Brad is the Founder & President of I Like Giving, and author of the best-selling books, *I Like Giving: The Transforming Power of a Generous Life* and *Everyday Generosity: Becoming a Generous Family in a Selfie World.* He inspires people to live a life of generosity through storytelling. I Like Giving has reached and inspired more than 120 million people in 170 countries. Brad has inspired major corporations to change their culture to one that cultivates kindness. Brad spoke to SoulVision Magazine about his humble beginnings in Grand Rapids, Michigan, the inspiration behind I Like Giving, and how he thinks people should practice the "seven ways of generosity" in their lives.

Where are you from and what was it like growing up there? Did you have any inspirations growing up?

I was brought up in Grand Rapids, Michigan, a conservative Midwest town. It was a nice place to grow up.I really looked up to my grandpa, Don. My grandpa was a large contract baker. He made croutons and stuffing, the food you would often have at Thanksgiving. He had a test kitchen where he would make 16 loaves of bread every Saturday morning. I would tag along with him and he would teach me a lot about life, including his modeling of the seven ways to live generously. At first, I thought it would just be Brad and Grandpa enjoying the fresh loaves of bread on a Saturday morning. But they cooled off and we put them in the trunk of the car and off we went to deliver the bread

to people around town. He would model the generosity of words by giving them a kind word. He would model the generosity of money by giving them money with the fresh loaves of bread. He would show me the generosity of thoughts, of words, of money, of influence, of time, of attention, and the way you should share your stuff. It just stuck with me. I looked up to him and followed in his footsteps. I started a business in high school. I ran that business for 20 years and used those seven ways of generosity in the formation of the business and the way I operated the business.

I still do this today by helping companies understand how to have a culture of generosity and how to bring the seven ways of living generously to work. The impact and the culture of the business not only affects the daily temperature of your venture, but it also affects the bottom line positively. I'm just an entrepreneur who loves God and people.

What was the most important lesson you learned in the early phases of your career?

In 2005, I was on a good run. My business was doing great, but I had a series of thoughts. How can we inspire people to live generously? How as a business person and a giver, do I like to be communicated with? What motivates me? I kept coming back to the fact that stories are great motivators and such phenomenal teachers. The average TED talk has 65 percent story content if they're good. So stories, in my opinion, are the best communication tools. I was moved by the vision to start I Like Giving to inspire people to live generously and show generosity in a multitude of ways. We started using short films as one delivery vehicle. Our short stories will make you laugh, make you cry, and most importantly, motivate you. We have great data that says when people watch these films, they get excited about finding new ways to be generous.

At what point in your career did you begin to feel you had made it?

I'm not a typical "I made it, so I'm going to do something good" guy. I sold a service business in Michigan. It wasn't a big liquidity event that compelled me to go do something good. I had put some practice into my business with these seven ways and thought I could take it further and positively influence the world.

Today, we have over 120 million people who have watched our short films and we continue to tell these short stories of just ordinary people doing extraordinary things. I feel like I'm still trying to make it. I believe a generous world is a better world for all of us.

What I need is help from people that agree with us. Together, we can multiply the giving message. Sharing stories broadly gets that thinking out there.

What would you consider to be your greatest achievement?

I think that for me—I don't want to be overly religious—by God's grace, I have been faithful to my wife and my family in terms of positioning them before the excitement of career, being a known author and having a best-selling book. I think my greatest accomplishment is that I just haven't screwed that up.

How has your faith influenced and/or guided your work?

Well, there is this idea that says, "It's better to give than to receive . . ." and I have found that to be true. However, I do have an interesting cut on it. I also like to receive. I like nice things. I like to go to a nice restaurant, play golf and yet, I have found it to be true that when I give

in the seven ways [of generosity], it is always better than me getting. When I find truths I pick up in the Bible, I apply them. It's kind of fun to validate things and way better to give than to get.

How would you describe a "lifestyle of generosity?"

I think about it in terms of what I do daily, weekly, monthly. It is so important for people to see that they can be generous multiple times, every single day because now they know they are not limited to just giving away money. When you know you have something to offer every day, you can develop a lifestyle of generosity. I don't think you ever simply arise; it's a process—and it's an exciting process. I always say I just want to do better, and not out of performance. I just want to try to be a little better every day.

How should the next generation of leaders apply generosity to their personal brand of leadership?

Be encouraged that you want to be known as generous. Think about this. We have better relationships when we are generous. The way to apply it is to just start. I find it to be contagious. You know, there is a

proverb that says, "the world of the generous gets larger and larger" and, drum roll please "... the world of the stingy gets smaller and smaller." And so I believe it is encouraging to know your world is going to get bigger, you're going to go places, and do things you didn't think were possible when you begin to live a lifestyle of generosity.

How do you relax when you are not working?

I really like to go on 3-5 mile walks. I like to listen to podcasts, golf, and clean my garage. I don't get a P&L every month saying, "Oh, more people are generous! Great! Let's keep going." We only get the anecdotal feedback that comes to our I Like Giving website. So sometimes, you just want to see progress, even if it means in your personal space.

What's up next?

We are doing more "Lunch and Learn" workshops in companies. Employers want to give good-hearted inspiration and hope to their employees. There is something powerful about giving employees the experience of an outside voice of inspiration. We're finding this is super powerful because parents are looking for ways to talk to their kids about their values. This comes through loud and clear at our "Lunch and Learn" events at many great companies across America and beyond.

If you want to learn more about Brad Formsma, visit his website bradformsma.com. To join the I Like Giving movement, visit ilikegiving.com.

"Never take.
Always give."

Vivica A. Fox

Vivica A. Fox: The Best of the Best

The all-around mega-talented, Vivica A. Fox, or "Angie" Fox to those who've known her since her days in Indianapolis, is kind, motivating and straightforward in her approach to life. She is an entrepreneur and in a more urban vernacular, she is a bona fide "hustler." All one has to do to appreciate her talent is take note of her bestselling memoir, *Every Day I'm Hustling*. With her own syndicated talk show, *Face the Truth*, and various media projects with Lifetime network, Ms. Fox has entertainment industry longevity that most people can only dream of.

We sat down with Ms. Fox to discuss her early years at home and in her career, her inspirations, and her hopes for 2019 and beyond. She provides an uncut look at what needs to be done to succeed in the entertainment industry and in life.

Vivica, thank you so much for agreeing to spend some time with us for our inaugural issue of SoulVision Magazine. It's going to highlight you, Debra Martin Chase, Quincy Jones and a few others. We have a few questions we would like to ask. Our aim is to help people appreciate your journey to become Vivica A. Fox. Let's start off with your life at home as a child.

Well first of all, I want to say congratulations to you guys on starting up this magazine and I think that it is a wonderful platform to celebrate African Americans that are doing so well and it's amazing that two of the people that you mentioned are people that I know and have had the wonderful opportunity of working with. Debra Martin Chase—We did the series *Missing* together. I've known her for many, many years and she's just an awesome lady. Quincy Jones—I've known him forever. I always see him at events and he's just always an amazing, energy force when you see him. So, I'm glad that I'm in good company for your inaugural issue.

Becoming Vivica A. Fox started years ago when I left home at seventeen. I remember in my senior year of high school, everyone was saying what they were going to do. Some were going to get married. Some were going to college. I had decided that I was going to go to California and I was going to become a movie star!

My nickname was "Angie"—that is what the A is for 'cause growing up no one could pronounce "Vivica." I used to be called Vivika, Vivicha—all kinds of stuff but not Vivica; so I always made people comfortable and was just like, "Call me Angie." It was all good. I had a wonderful childhood growing up in Indianapolis, Indiana.

I had a beautiful Christian momma that raised four kids, basically by herself. Our father was in our life, but my mother did most of the raising. We spent the summers with our dad. I lived across the street from Breeding Tabernacle Church, so we were always in church, which made my momma happy. I graduated from Arlington High School. I am the youngest child of four. I have an older sister, Alicia "Sugie" Williams, two brothers—Marvin Fox and William Fox, and I was the baby girl. I played sports: basketball, volleyball, track and I was a cheerleader. So, I've always been a Type A personality.

Can you still hoop a little bit?

Oh yes! Are you kidding me? Child, I can still do a cartwheel, the splits and jump up and shoot a jump shot on you!

BK FULTON AND NICHOLAS POWELL

When you were growing up, who or what was your biggest inspiration?

I was in love with Michael Jackson. I thought Michael Jackson was just the cat's meow. Michael and Diana Ross; I always said what a huge influence they were on me. I remember going to see them in my teenage years and had never seen such dynamic and amazing African-American talent. Diana Ross—I've never seen a black woman with hair and nails and one that changed clothes six times. Michael Jackson—just a dynamic performer so I was just like, "Where do they live?" I would also say that my late Aunt, Madame King, is a major inspiration. She was one of the first and few African-American females that owned her own beauty salon on the South Side of Chicago. She was the first one to cut my hair and put me in a fashion show. So those three people were an inspiration, but I would say Madame King was my biggest inspiration. I was bit by the entertainment bug early.

Thinking back to that young actress as you were coming along, what was the most important lesson you think you learned on the road to becoming Vivica Fox?

For me it would be learning to get out of my own way. It was the biggest lesson that I had to learn. You have to realize where you are in your life and your chapter, not to force things. This generation nowadays is so used to this "insta-fame" that they have no idea that building a career that has longevity takes time. You have to realize that what is for you will be for you. You have to work towards it and know that when it's your turn, that it's your turn. So for me, I used to be so impatient and I wanted everything to happen so fast. Trust me, it can't happen too fast because life goes by even quicker. My biggest life lesson was learning to get out of my own way and I always pass that on to young talent who ask me, "How did you make it?" I say, "I had to learn how to get out of my own way. Just learn to know my place, play my position and stay in my lane."

Very well said. As you think about your television roles your movie roles, do you have a favorite character that you've played?

Gosh, I've been blessed to be in a lot of films. One of my favorite roles was Frankie—everyone loves Frankie from *Set it Off*. *Set it Off* has become such a classic film that everyone is like, "Why did they kill y'all! Y'all could have done a sequel!" But some things need to just be a classic and there doesn't need to be a sequel. I also have to say Shanté from *Two Can Play That Game* because I'll never forget that night getting out of the limousine at the Premiere and looking up at the marquee and seeing *Two Can Play That Game* Starring Vivica A. Fox. I was like, (astonished) "Wow!" So if I could pick my top two, it would be Frankie from *Set It Off* and Shanté from *Two Can Play That Game*.

Is there a particular formula or some kind of criteria that you use to make your decision about what roles to choose versus what roles not to choose?

Let's talk about my passion. How much I come through and how much I'm dedicated. There are two people who are really responsible for that. The first person would be my very first acting coach, Sheila Wills. Sheila and I met during the soap opera, *Generations*, and that was my very first acting role.

She was on the show and I remember she came to me and said, "You know, you're very talented but you got to learn to sharpen your chops" and I was just kinda like, "Wow!" This can be a business where people will just let you fall on your face so they can look good and make you look like an amateur. She did not let that happen. When the show ended she became my acting coach. She was really instrumental in me getting a lot of roles. She would say things like, "You have got to understand that when you go into a room, you think you're cute. There are going to be ten other cute girls just as cute as you and they think they are cute too. So you got to show up prepared, look the part, act the part and leave no room for doubt that no one else should get this part." And so, I would get to a point when I was going for a lot of roles and I would get really close and it would be given to a bigger name and she was like, "Vivica just stay ready because when that role is right for you and if you're not ready, you can't blame anyone but yourself." She would always tell me to work out, take care of myself, have a good attitude, be prepared, be professional. I commend her for that.

Then my passion, once I really started acting regularly, was amplified when I worked with F. Gary Gray; who was the director of *Set It Off*. Gary was one of the most serious, professional directors I've ever worked with. In rehearsals, he wanted you to be on time. He wanted you to be dedicated. I remember one time we came back from lunch— Me, Jada, and Queen Latifah. We would be 3 to 4 minutes late and he would look at us like, "Y'all think I'm playing with y'all. Y'all better respect this now."

Really?

Oh yeah! He was like, "People think they are going to come to the movie and laugh at y'all because it's four girls supposedly robbing banks. So they think, 'Oh wow, let me go see this, it's going to be wack.' "

People walked out of that movie theater in tears and it's because he was so dedicated from rehearsals to when we wrapped the film. I could really say my work ethic came from my first acting coach, Sheila Wills and one of my amazing directors, F. Gary Gray.

Wow. You know what, I often tell the team, you gotta do the work and then the magic happens. God shows up and I think that even your career really exemplifies that. In addition to the modeling, the acting, you've also been an entrepreneur. You've got beauty products. You have a TV show. Is being an entrepreneur as fun as acting?

What drives me crazy is that when you meet people and they say, "Oh, I want to be an actor." and you say to them, "What are you doing to become an actor? Are you taking drama classes? Are you studying? What are you doing?" We make it look so effortless that people just think, "Oh, I can do that!" Not realizing that you gotta hit marks, gotta have a good memory, you gotta cry on cue; there's a whole lot of different

BK FULTON AND NICHOLAS POWELL

dynamics: love scenes; all kinds of stuff that's really uncomfortable but it's an art form. I always tell people as you said, do the work. Learn to be a triple threat—learn to sing, act and dance—because you never know what the role may require. You have to do the work. And just know that it doesn't happen overnight. A lot of people say, "Oh such and such was an overnight sensation. Well, most of the time that's many a long night that it took to become that overnight sensation."

You have a recurring role on *Empire*, a hit TV show with an all time high rating called *Face the Truth*, you have a wonderful book— *Every Day I'm Hustling.* How do you balance all of that?

In my book, I share the secrets of my success and also with *Face the Truth*, I'm helping people live their best lives. I am so blessed to have this amazing chapter that's happening in my life right now and that's because I have built my "dream squad." You have got to have people that look out for you. I have an excellent publicist, BJ Coleman, who looks and finds opportunities for me. He's the reason I got my book deal for *Every Day I'm Hustling*. He would say, "Hey, time for you to do a book" and I would say, "Wait, I got some more living to do." He would then say, "Nope, we're going to do a motivational memoir. You are a woman in your 50s that's having an amazing resurgence in your career. Share those secrets of your success. Let folk know that you understand how hard it is to achieve success, but more importantly, how hard it is to maintain success for as long as you have a shot."

My business partner, Lita Richardson, who is my entertainment lawyer and best friend, always saw opportunities for me. When I started green lighting movies back to back to back, she would say, "Nope, now we're going to get a producer credit" and I would ask, "Well, how can we do that?" and she would say, "Because your name is green lighting movies so that means you now get a producer credit and another check" which was magic to my ears.

My wonderful agent, Sheila Legette, is always out there hustling: looking for roles for me, looking for opportunities for me. My executive assistant, Darren Bond, who is also a savvy business partner is on the team. He is someone that I've known for over twenty years and is always out there looking for gigs. You want people on your team that are not takers. You want people that are contributing to your career and not just sitting there waiting to get paid and just like, "Well, what we doing today?" Like, "Na, well what are you doing to help us do something today? Help me and we all win!"

Well, I'm going to combine these next two questions because I think you're touching on something really inspiring and I love the idea of building a "dream squad." There are times when we all need to take a break and relax. But what I also hear coming out is some faith in action. How do you relax when you're not "working" and where does your faith come in?

Wow, I definitely had to learn that because I recently had been working just so much that I got a little sick and that was the Lord telling me, "Slow it down now. Go on and rest now. I know you're working." But I've always been a Type A personality and you gotta strike while the iron is hot but you've also have to find that balance of when to take time off or rejuvenate and take care of yourself. I always tell people, when you start working a lot, there is nothing wrong with saying "no." Everything is not for you and you got to learn when it's like, "Nope. I need time off . . ." because people will run you into the ground and then when they've received what they wanted from you and you're over there tired and worn out then what do you do? So, you've gotta learn sometimes to say "no."

My time off for me is going to the spa, sleeping, taking some vacations with the family—going to Jamaica. I've celebrated my birthday at Montego Bay, Jamaica, about four or five years in a row. Next, I want to go to Europe and take other trips. So, you've got to learn to balance that out and have some fun time and some work time. If not, you're just going to run out of gas.

Faith—My mom raised us in church. I'm always so grateful. I know I'm a blessed child of God. The reason why all of these blessings are coming upon me right now is because I'm not just a taker. I give back. I support my community. I always put God first and I help others. So you've got to find the balance in that as well. Don't just be a taker from your community. Contribute back into your community and support others.

Wow, Vivica those words are powerful! This interview is going to be a blessing to a lot of people. I totally agree with what you are saying. When we give back and work together, there is nothing we can't do. Anyone from the outside looking in, would say "she's got it all." Is there anything missing right now for Vivica Fox?

Honestly, right now, I'm so fulfilled in this wonderful place that I'm at. I've got six beautiful godchildren. I've kind of created my own extended family that I enjoy. The next chapter—something that I may look for in life again—is probably to direct in the future and then to possibly fall in love again. But I don't feel less of a woman because I don't have them right now. I've directed a video before and I've been married before and I've done love before, but I'm taking the time to do me and I'm really happy right now. I've got a wonderful extended family with friends and life and my career is great. So right now all the seeds that I've planted are all blossoming and have created this wonderful floral bouquet of success—I'm taking the time to smell and enjoy all these fragrances.

There you go and they smell good. You got a bouquet going! I have one last official question for the interview: Is there any advice you want to give to the next generation of actors and actresses or would—be authors and entrepreneurs? Anything you want to tell them about becoming who God has blessed them to be?

Yes. I love to tell people that are wanting to become the next Vivica A. Fox or the next Barack Obama or Michelle Obama that to become successful—we've been saying it the whole interview—you have to do the work. You have to make good choices. Please know that the choices that you make today affect your tomorrow and your future. Make good choices. Do the work. Get your education. Be good to people. Try to be kind to others and know that if you really want to build a career, it takes time. There are no shortcuts to success. Do the work so that when all of it happens, you can claim it all; that you did it. Do you.

CREDITS

Makeup Artist:
Nordia Cameron-Cunningham
@nordia_ffaceit

Hairstylist:
Micah Cook
@micahmiami

Stylist:
Toni Lowe
@toniposh

Photographer:
Zavier Deangelo
@Zavierdeangelo

BK Fulton Has a Vision for the Future

BK Fulton believes we should all adopt excellence as a guiding principle. In everything he does, he strives to do it at the highest standard. BK was born in Hampton, Virginia. He attended Virginia Tech for college and accepted a full scholarship as a "Sloan Fellow" to attend Harvard's Kennedy School of Government and the New School's Milano School of Management for his Master of Science degree. While living in New York, he worked at the National Urban League during the day and attended law school at night.

BK went on to serve in executive positions at some of the most well-known American businesses—American Online (AOL), Time Warner and Verizon. Today, he is Chairman & CEO of the media and film production company, Soulidifly Productions, as well as the founder of SoulVision Magazine. BK says that he spent the first fifty years of his life doing what he was trained to do. Now he gets to spend the rest of his life doing what he was born to do—showcasing the important stories in the human narrative his art are inspired.

Soulidifly Productions is the first independent film company in the history of cinema to produce four feature-length films in its first year of business. SoulVision Magazine has kept a steady readership in its first few months and has acquired article placements from big names like Vivica Fox and Quincy Jones. Soulidifly is on the move with movies, magazines, books and music for their growing fan base. For this interview, BK Fulton sat down with his co-founding editor, Nicholas Powell, to talk about his early childhood and career, his vision for Soulidifly Productions, and the need for the next generation to carry on the torch of excellence.

Where are you from and what was it like growing up there?

I was born in Hampton Virginia. I had a great childhood with loving parents, lots of friends, plenty of cousins and two sisters that were a constant presence. We moved a few times between Hampton and Newport News but I have always lived in a neighborhood that felt like a community. We knew our neighbors, there was a lot of playing outside and lots of sports. We did everything from swimming and karate to basketball and football. Riding bicycles was huge fun along with riding go-karts and minibikes! My childhood was rambunctious to say the least. I also started my first entrepreneurial venture, cutting grass for pay, at 10 years old.

Who or what was your biggest inspiration growing up?

My parents were school teachers, so education has always been something that informed how I operated. Outside of that—when I was growing up—I really wanted to play basketball. I was inspired by the likes of Julius "Dr. J" Irving, George "The Iceman" Gervin, Larry Bird and Erving "Magic" Johnson.

I played basketball on the junior varsity (JV) team at Denbigh High School. After the junior varsity season ended, I went on to play ball for the varsity team. When I went to Virginia Tech, I played JV for a little bit. I didn't get a scholarship or anything, so I decided to focus on my studies. My intramural team did win the championship at Tech, so I'm proud of that as well.

What was the most important lesson you learned in the early phases of your career?

I would say, figuring out how to do school. I learned reading was a critical part of success, not only in school but in life. I remember my first couple of years in engineering school at Virginia Tech. I was struggling a bit and hadn't quite developed the study habits of reading the material, going to class and reaching out to my professors. It's amazing to see what can happen when you actually do the work that has been asked of you. Going to class and reading the books made things a whole lot easier!

For me, reading African-American history, which was something that was missing in my earlier training through high school, inspired me and still inspires me today. Reading about folks you relate to allows you to figure out what you want to do in your life and how you fit in the human story. Once I realized that people like me have

always been central to the progress of the world, I approached my education differently. I was proud of who I was connected to and felt a responsibility to do my best, as my ancestors had done.

Do you feel like you've reached your goal of doing the good work for the people and communities you care about?

For the most part yes. I was a part of some very large teams at some important companies that were doing great community work, and I enjoyed those roles. At the National Urban League, I founded the Technology Programs and Policy Department and built their very first website. The National Urban League was the first non-profit of any kind to broadcast over the internet. We partnered with a company called Broadcast.com, which would later have a successful IPO on Wall Street. Mark Cuban was the founder. At AOL, we created "Power Up!" which was a project to bring technology centers to low-income children all over the world. We brought technology centers to Appalachia, big cities, and Native-American reservations. At Time Warner, I had the opportunity to work with some of the most legendary and iconic brands of the day, including HBO, Warner Bros, Marvel, and *Time Magazine*. It was a real eye opener for me and gave me the chance to

THE BLUEPRINT PART TWO

see first-hand how major media worked. At Verizon, I helped to clear the way for FiOS TV and learned about the importance of distribution and getting to your market.

I even spent some time in government—at the Department of Commerce. There, I learned how expansive government's reach was. I appreciated how it takes all of these sectors—private, non-profit, and government—to make the country and the economy work. These entities shape the world as we know it. Each role allowed me to walk away with lessons that inform what I do at Soulidifly Productions. Today, I make films, write books, and invest in companies. I have become somewhat of a serial entrepreneur and a very serious artist. With my art, I try to deliver a more inclusive and complete narrative of people of color. It turns out that we are a part of so much more than most folks realize and that more often than not, people of all ethnicities work together in different ways to achieve the best examples of human expression.

A lot of the media, then and now, is filled with what happens to women and minorities, instead of what we do for ourselves. The latter is the more inspiring to me. Accordingly, I created a career that would allow me to be a part of the doing in life—doing good work for the communities and people I cared about.

BK FULTON AND NICHOLAS POWELL

At what point in your career did you begin to feel like you had made it? Any great achievements?

I think I'm still making it? I'm not done yet, so I think the book is still open on whether or not I have "made it." I feel successful and happy. I have a great wife, my children are alive and free, and my parents are still on this side of heaven. I have a great family (blood family and in-laws) and lots of friends. So by all those measures, I feel like I've made it.

As a person who creates content, I feel like I'm in the early stages of my outpouring. I'm starting to get some success with my writing. Most of our early films came out in 2019. I enjoy being able to work with a collective of really wonderful people who are doing some fantastic work. I feel like our efforts are inspired. This year, we will release four movies, a soundtrack, seven to ten books, twelve issues of our magazine, and launch a few companies; so, I'm excited. I feel privileged to have the life and the opportunities I have.

Soulidifly Productions and SoulVision Magazine are fairly new ventures for you. Respectively, what have been the biggest challenges?

For Soulidifly, the biggest challenge has been getting people to take us seriously. Even though we are the first independent film company in cinema history to produce four feature-length films in our first year of business, we're still considered newbies. But we are serious and we've brought in people who have been making movies for over 40 years to help make our venture a success. Building a solid reputation takes some time.

SoulVision Magazine is a few months in and it's been fun. I think figuring out all of the content each month and delivering what our subscribers and readers want to see is always a bit of a challenge, mostly because of how time-consuming it can be to put all the content together. We want the magazine to reflect a certain quality and character each month. We want it to be respectful of the intellects of our readers, while also being accessible to anyone who wants to know, for example, how Vivica Fox became Vivica Fox or what a pioneer like Quincy Jones is thinking today. Putting all of that together in a way that is digestible and accessible was an initial challenge. I think we're doing pretty good with it. I have faith that our readers will tell us when we need to do better.

There is more content being created than ever before. How do you decide what is worth putting out into the world?

Too many stories on film and TV today speak from a deprivation narrative. They portray mostly what people are doing to us. This leads to a lot of "boys in the hood" narratives, slavery films, and domestic violence films. There were some civil rights narratives but even these are mostly framed around the difficulties women or people of color have had in this country. While I think it is important to tell those stories, I rarely find the way they are portrayed inspiring. However, noting how our ancestors overcame those negative and horrific circumstances is inspiring. I believe that our fans want to be continuously inspired the way that *Hidden Figures* or *Black Panther* moved us. Even if *Black Panther* was fictitious, it was still uplifting and made me want to be a better person. I decided we could create an entity that produced more of the *Hidden Figures* and *Black Panther* kinds of stories.

We don't have to go back and create mythical characters however. Our history is so ripe with real heroes and sheroes—John Kenney, Joseph Bologne Chevalier de Saint-Georges, Dr. Charles Drew, Booker T. Washington, Harriet Tubman, Frederick Douglass and so many more— that we could make hundreds of films about our excellence and what it takes to build in spite of the obstacles. If you think about what some of these people did during their times and under their circumstances, they were real-life superheroes!

They were challenged for being excellent. What I realized is there is an opportunity today, in 2019, and beyond to tell the stories that complete the tapestry of the human experience. These stories won't be told from one group's point of view or the sadness of another group. They will tell the good, the bad, and the ugly but focus primarily on the good because I think that's the kind of stuff that motivates and inspires people to be better—the achievement narrative. I hope that with our publication, movies and other art, we will empower, encourage, and motivate. Unfortunately, too few of these amazing stories have been told on the big screen using the full splendor of media and today's digital formats. This leaves open an opportunity for brands like Soulidifly. We can choose from a cornucopia of exceptional content that inspires. The possibilities are endless.

What projects are you currently working on?

Hell on the Border is about the legendary Bass Reeves and will be released this winter. Soulidifly plans to release *Love Dot Com* this summer and *1 Angry Black Man* in the fall, so we have a great slate of films coming out this year. Atone released in late February and has received some acclaim. *Sweethearts* is an upcoming project about, for the lack of a better word, the strip-club world. It will probably be the most edgy concept we've done so far.

We have a set of children's books we plan to release this year. *The Taste Buddies* series has a five book arrangement with Owl Publishing. Books two and three in the series will be releasing soon. *Mr. Business: The Adventures of Little BK* has a seven book deal. The entire series will release this summer. For Mr. Business, we're working with a very talented artist, Salaam Muhammad who is a photorealistic illustrator. My first book, *Shauna*, has been re-released in paperback on Amazon. Also, the soundtrack for *Love Dot Com* will be released in the coming months.

We're viewing other scripts and talking to creators about a series based on *Love Dot Com*. We've got an opportunity for a stage play about Nina Simone. We have a person writing a screenplay on Saint-George. We hope to have that polished by Misan Sagay, the writer of the film *Belle*. Right now, we're busy building a fanbase so we can share our work more broadly.

What advice would you give to the next generation of business leaders who would like to become the next big executive/ entrepreneur?

As I recently told over 300 students at SXSW, don't give up and learn from what people have done before them. Every billionaire I know has created their own business. Every person I know whose net worth is in the 100s of millions has created their own business or worked their way up through excellence in a big company and acquired stock options and other perks that lead to wealth. The point isn't really about the money, but about being excellent. When you pursue something with excellence, the best results tend to come out. My advice to young people is to be excellent by design—that's number one. And number two, you don't have to reinvent the wheel while you are figuring out how to get from where you are to where you want to be. You can read the biographies of three or four people you respect and follow their plan—which is what I did.

When you read those biographies—and you can read the short version—see what they did, lay out the common denominators of their success and mirror that. It will often go like this—go to college, get an internship, get a job, find mentors, work at this place and that place. You can use someone else's plan and eventually, add your own nuances and interests as you discover them. But please remember, it is important for you to develop your own plan and write it down.

When I was in engineering and architecture school at Virginia Tech over 30 years ago, I wrote a 50-year plan. What I've been doing ever since then is executing that plan and checking off boxes. If something came up that didn't contribute to my plan, I didn't do it; and if it contributed to my plan, I would consider it and might do it. The point here is that I had written it down. I had a standard of excellence. I used the blueprints of others until I could add my own scaffolding to my plan. This has worked for me, and now I find myself in a position to use the power of art to help other people find things that inspire them.

How do you relax when you are not working?

I like to sleep, watch good movies, listen to great music, chat with good friends and eat. Sometimes, I will sit on the couch and put on a good movie and get me a Little Debbie oatmeal pie or a slice of cake, kick my shoes off and enjoy the blessings. It is important in life to be able to pause and take it all in.

As I've gotten older, I like to sit out on our balcony and watch nature, letting the stress drip away. I try not to do things that cause me too much stress, but we all live in an imperfect world and we have to prepare for whatever is to come. Likewise, whatever I choose to do, I like to give it my best. Once I've done all I know how to do, my faith says God will do the rest.

PHOTOS BY JESSICA KNOX AND STYLING BY NIKKI TUCKER

BK Fulton: Faith In Action, Deeds Not Words

Faith is how BK Fulton describes the force that motivates him to keep going and to keep helping others as he climbs. "At the end of the day, it is my faith and prayer that helps me get it all done at a very high level," he says. He wants to make sure that we know he doesn't do it alone. "The secret sauce," as he describes it, is a team of passionate individuals who are willing to put in the work to make his vision a success. They are counting on him and he is counting on them. He believes we are all connected in a giant and friendly universe, and it is up to us to bring our best selves as individuals to collectively create a better world. Even in times of uncertainty, BK is hopeful, passionate, and excited about the future of his Soulidifly Productions. More importantly, he is confident that he and his team will have an impact on this country and the world.

His media empire's mantra is "to create media with a message." Since its inception in 2017, Soulidifly Productions has released five feature length films. By the end of the year, Soulidifly will have released a total of eight. Its latest release, *1 Angry Black Man*, came at a pivotal time when citizens took to the streets in mass to protest the murder of George Floyd. *1 Angry Black Man* has been used as a resource to understand America's uncomfortable past and the trauma we are still dealing with today. The film, released by Byron Allen's Freestyle Digital Media, is thought-provoking and essential viewing. Films like *1 Angry Black Man* capture BK's cinematic vision. He believes diverse art can heal. While Hollywood has been scrambling to produce more diverse films for a more diverse world, creating inclusive content has been the driving priority for BK's Soulidifly Productions from day one. Soulidifly films have been on Netflix, Amazon Prime, Hulu, HBO, Apple TV and Starz, among others. Company distribution partners include Lionsgate, Cinedigm, Gravitas Ventures, Freestyle Digital Media, and Urban Home Entertainment.

BK's vision extends beyond creating more inclusive narratives in films and books. He also aims to teach the next generation of media makers how it's done. The Soulidifly chief is working with former

Disney **executive** Adam Leipzig to launch MediaU — the first online film school with transcripts and transferable credits from the University of California (UC) System. It's a big deal. MediaU will launch in 2021 and will allow students from all over the world to access working professionals as they pursue careers in media and film production. "Diversity and inclusion are sorely needed in the film industry. MediaU will reduce the time it takes to earn the requisite training and certifications needed to land a career in the industry," BK explains. "It will reduce the cost of quality film education and increase the number of people that can access the best media training available."

Those who complete the MediaU programs will receive credits from the UC System. "It's exciting to be a part of the MediaU journey."

BK is also one of the lead investors in PreShow.co, which anticipates a launch during the fourth quarter of this year. BK says PreShow will allow people to go to the theaters and pay for their tickets with a virtual credit card after watching a few ads on the PreShow app. Basically, consumers get to watch movies for free, forever. "It is going to be a game changer," he says enthusiastically.

> "My prayer for everyone is that they do their work and go forward guided by their hopes for humanity rather than their fears."

While audiences have appreciated the range of Soulidifly's current films, the company has not yet created a film or cartoon specifically geared towards children. That is about to change. Soulidifly Productions is working with the Oscar-winning animation studio Lion Forge Animation (creators of *Hair Love*) on a *Mr. Business*-inspired animation series. "We

BK FULTON AND NICHOLAS POWELL

are working with Lion Forge Animation on a series we have been asked to pitch to several networks," he says. "We will have at least one cartoon or children's movie in production soon. "Children's programming is important because when you reach children with positive programming early enough, you don't have to work so hard later in their lives to get them to unlearn things that could hurt their future." Before *Mr. Business* makes his animated debut, fans can purchase the current seven book series online and soon will be able to purchase his eighth adventure – *Video Games.* "In the eighth book, I share lessons from a time in my life when I was thinking about running away. I decided against it," he says laughingly. "Who wants to leave all that fun and love and food at home to go into the unknown? Not me! I stayed with my parents and my dog."

Within the next year, BK hopes to have a film fund established for Soulidifly. It will include funding for new work and funds for additional marketing of their films. "That will be the next level for us," he says. "We have been able to successfully make quality programming with bankable talent over our first few years, culminating in a $10 million first-look deal with GoMedia Productions out of Atlanta, GA. The foundation for growing Soulidifly is in place. Beyond the day-to-day work to produce films, write books and manage the company's other brands (a TV network – SoulVision.TV – and a magazine – SoulVision Magazine), taking on investors and going public is within the realm of possibility for us."

Soulidifly recently produced BK's new book, *The Tale of the Tee*, with co-author Jonathan Blank. The book details a strong friendship that grew out of a series of e-mail communications between the two authors as they discussed the local and global protests that occurred after the murder of George Floyd. The two men try to make sense of where we go from here. The book demonstrates the power of truth and honest conversations to heal.

BK believes change is overdue. He believes we can build the "civil society that our children deserve" but it will require collaboration. One group alone cannot do it. He was pleased to see the NFL apologize and admit that they should have listened to Colin Kaepernick from the beginning of his civil protest. Similarly, he is encouraged by the NBA, Lebron James, and others who are leading and showing solidarity with Black Lives Matter. He shares that he did not expect either of these moments to happen in 2020. He is most proud of the professional athletes for using their standing and their stage for justice. "It means a lot when our leaders and heroes take a stand for people on the margins," he says. "I think it elevates the meaning of humanity when those with a voice use their standing to advance decency and to help others find their own voice. Their example gives me hope and nourishes my faith."

BK says the next steps beyond protests that must happen are policy changes. "Tearing down statues is one thing, but you have to be ready to build up statutes (laws and policies) that change society," he explains. "Our society is one that is governed by rules and laws. In today's world you don't have to terrorize with white sheets. If you know how to use spreadsheets, you can disenfranchise people through voter suppression tactics like gerrymandering, voter ID laws, and purging. This is why voting is so important. If people don't vote, they effectively abdicate their rights. Very little good comes from civil abdication. Citizenship has always been about the right to vote and then actually doing it. A lot of good people risked everything so we could have and exercise the right to vote."

BK continues to reflect on making America and the world better. "I believe you have to act on what you believe to be true," he explains. "My prayer for everyone is that they do their work and go forward guided by their hopes for humanity rather than their fears." He explains that when we see systematic injustice like violence against particular communities or inequitable investments in education for low-income areas, they are the consequences of people acting out of fears and prejudice. "They say . . . 'don't you come to my country,' 'I have to build this wall . . . ,' 'these people are good people and those people are bad.' This is not leading from a place of hope,'" BK explains. "We need more hope. We need to vote from a place of our dreams not our fears."

"We have to put less time and money into the instruments of hate and war and go all-in on love and peace."

BK sometimes gets exhausted by issues surrounding race and what he says are "old problems" that generations have been fighting to resolve since the founding of this nation. "When we can get past these issues, we will be able to do more for the collective good." He envisions a world that can collectively work to cure cancer, ALS, and rid the world

BK FULTON AND NICHOLAS POWELL

of ailments like Alzheimer's and dementia. He wants to see a world that prioritizes a higher quality of life for everyone. "It means we have to invest in all of our children. We have to put less time and money into the instruments of hate and war and go all-in on love and peace."

He's optimistic that it can happen. "I think we can do it once we realize the value in every person," he says. "It starts with yourself. It starts at

THE BLUEPRINT PART TWO

home. We have to learn to feed the good in ourselves and work on our awesomeness. If you are amazed at life, you know that we owe our very best for future generations. Mediocrity has no place. When you embrace that philosophy, it is a lot easier to put your faith into action and do the work required to win."

BK is an advocate for integration of more diverse history in our schools. "Learning about inventors who looked like me changed my life for the better," he says. "This is why I know that art can heal." He names a few African-American men whose contributions are not widely known: Lewis Howard Latimer and Dr. George Franklin Grant. "Lewis Latimer improved on Thomas Edison's light bulb by creating the carbon filament that provides the luminescence in the electric lights we use in our homes today." George Grant is the man on the cover of *The Tale of the Tee*. He invented the golf tee in 1899. "When golfers all over the world drop that tee, most have no idea that an African-American man invented it," BK says. "There are so many stories like these that get left out of history. They are inspiring and should become a standard part of what is taught to all children year-round, not just one month."

When we don't see people as contributors, BK explains, it is easier to rationalize their dehumanization. "It is ok to put those people off in a ghetto if you don't value them," he says. "It is ok to put those people off in the slums. It is ok to put those people in an underfunded barrio. It is ok to push those people onto a reservation if you think they don't matter. They say, 'These people don't love our country.' That is a lie. The more you expose yourself to the truth, the harder it is for discrimination to be tolerated." BK hopes when people see his films or watch documentaries like *After Selma, The Uncomfortable Truth and read books like The Tale of the Tee, Begin Again, White Rage, Caste,* and *One Person, No Vote* they will internalize the lessons and find the courage to fight systemic racism.

BK finds pleasure in reading biographies, especially those of business leaders. "I'm a person who doesn't believe in reinventing the wheel, so I find inspiration and learn quite a bit from what others have done," he says. "I read bios and then develop blueprints and plans for myself." Even with these blueprints for living he isn't afraid to try new ideas, and he encourages young people to do the same. "Don't be afraid of failing," he advises. "The win is in the work and you have to take small steps in the beginning and then bigger steps later." He says "the path to your best life isn't often easy but it's worth it. Looking at the biographies is just the start." BK advises young entrepreneurs to "get busy and be inspired by what others have done while adding their personal touch; then just keep going."

Soulidifly Productions has many initiatives that will help in the fight for social justice and equality. Soulidifly is working with three nonprofits to deliver national programs for youth: Media Mentors, the Joan Trumpauer Mulholland Foundation, and Riverside Community Development Corporation. Media Mentors has created a new initiative called "TikTalks" that will invite celebrities like Pharrell Williams and Missy Elliot to meet with school children nationwide to inspire their creativity and expose them to the creative

process. Riverside Community is the sponsor of an innovative news service that hopes to update people on what is happening in the social justice space real time. Finally, in projects with the Joan Trumpauer Mulholland Foundation, Soulidifly is working to produce and promote civil rights training and documentaries as well as a podcast with civil rights legends. "We want to highlight interracial cooperation and show how working together leads to a better society," BK says.

> "At the end of the day, deeds not words will shape the world we deliver to our children and their children. We have to put our words into action."

Follow BK Fulton on Instagram and X. To learn more about Soulidifly Productions, visit their website www.soulidifly.com and follow them on Facebook, Instagram, and X.

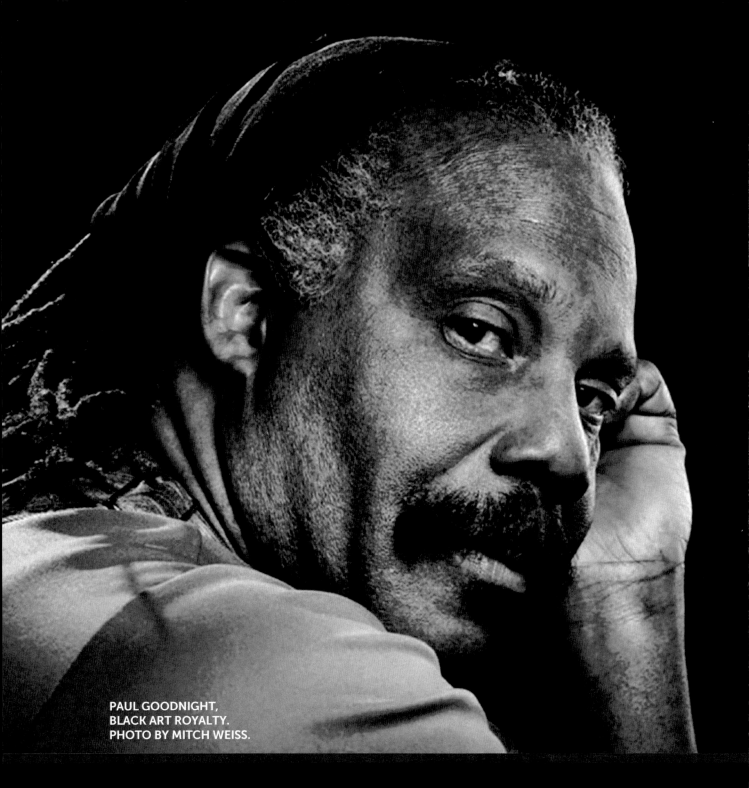

PAUL GOODNIGHT,
BLACK ART ROYALTY.
PHOTO BY MITCH WEISS.

"Great art
moves you."

Paul Goodnight

The Genius of
Paul Goodnight

Paul Goodnight has dedicated his life to creating art that uplifts and empowers his community. He has seen the destruction of war firsthand and is doing the work to make a peaceful world a tangible reality. Goodnight's art is beautiful and can be emotionally overwhelming. His subjects sometimes provoke images of the famous (Jack Johnson) and others are common folk who could be a close family member or a neighbor. His paintings can express happiness and freedom, but his shading and color choices can make one sympathize with the struggle and pain of being marginalized in this world.

For many, Goodnight's paintings are cathartic. Sometimes in order to find happiness, you have to overcome tragedy. For a man who has seen tragedy, Goodnight continues to be a positive light for young artists and is forever evolving his craft. He sat down with us to talk about what being a community artist means to him, his creative process, and the projects he's currently working on to make our neighborhoods a much more loving and welcoming place.

> "Through art, I can hopefully express myself, along with other artists to talk about what needs fixing in our communities."

Where are you from and what was it like growing up there?

I'm actually from three different places. I was born in Chicago and we were moved to Connecticut and then to Boston and then back to

MUSIC THUNDER BY PAUL GOODNIGHT

Connecticut. I ended up back in Boston and I have been here for the last 40 plus years, so I suppose I'm a Bostonian. I grew up a foster child. There were eight of us kids in the family. We were always active and always getting in trouble. We enjoyed each other's company and we maintained a close relationship because we were all foster children – the same. That is one of the things that I admire the most of our foster parents. We had someone who cared enough to take in eight misfits and blend them together as a family. We came to understand the gift that we had been given. It gave me purpose.

Were there any blood relations?

There was a blood sister and brother, Gloria and George. Gloria died recently, but we were all like brothers and sisters; all eight of us.

Who or what was your biggest inspiration growing up?

My grandfather was my biggest inspiration. Everyone knew that he didn't lie. To this day, I don't know anyone who never told at least one lie. He was the only person who said what he meant and meant what he said. And he taught me the truth of *clarity.* As a child, I didn't understand it at the time, but I fully accepted it. I realized how important he was as a role model. He was that person that was willing to take on eight children and made sure there was a constant sense of peace and a place in his house for all of us. Now that's God.

What was the most important lesson you learned in the early phases of your career?

I think the most important lessons were the lessons that muralist John Biggers gave me. We met in Africa and he was a pure, true mentor. Although he lived in Texas and he came to Boston for a visit or show, we always kept in close contact. During one particular show of his, I badgered him to see my work. I said, "John, I want you to come over to my place to see my work." And he said, "yes, yes, sure Paul, I will." Clearly unsatisfied with that answer, I took to repeating my request and asked again, "John, I want you to come by and check out my new work." Again, not the reply I was looking for,."Soon, Paul, soon." Now I'm trying to get a specific day from this man, "Well, Wednesday, Thursday or Friday?

Exasperated at me riding this man, he turned to me and said, "Paul, let me ask you this question: Are you committed or are you involved?" I told him that I was committed because of all of the things that I learned from him. *Who do we do it for? Why do we do it? What's our inspiration? Why is this our expression?* He said, "OK, son. That is all I needed to know. You see, it's like a ham and egg sandwich. I acted like I understood what he was saying for a couple of minutes, although I had no idea what he was talking about. I admitted that I didn't know what the heck he was talking about. He then gave me a lesson I will never forget. He explained, "You see son, in the ham and egg sandwich, the chicken who laid the egg is involved, but the pig who gave his life (the ham) for the sandwich, now he was committed. Always be the pig, son and I will see your work and so will everyone else." True to his word, he came over to my studio soon thereafter and I remember telling him, "Damn, John, that was the first time I was ever called a pig and enjoyed it!"

That's the kind of mentorship that I had. I had a great mentor. I had great teachers, great advocates, and a loving family. And now I have great art colleagues. I think that is the best part of my journey.

At what point in your career did you begin to feel you had made it?

Although I've shown internationally, been the Olympic artist for both Atlanta and Beijing, I'll never feel like I've made it and that's a great

SALSIFIED BY PAUL GOODNIGHT

place to be. I think anytime you think you've made it, you deprive yourself the room to go even farther. If that stops you, it means you aren't curious enough about the gifts that you've been given; that you have honed. There is always more to learn. I'm in school right now, learning and honing my skills around sculpture. No, I never thought about making or not making it. I think about growing and evolving. I let the business people do the business—Karl McLaurin does a great job for me—and I let that "do what it does ...." This way, I stay grounded.

Would you consider any of your work so far to be your greatest achievement?

No, I like what people like and I'm blessed that a lot of folks really dig my work. You see, your best teacher is your last painting or drawing. So I keep learning. My best is still within me because I feel there is still more to come. But you know, the business of art is a whole different animal. And I think that is why I have Karl and a bunch of other people who understand that the business of art is completely different than creating and teaching art.

Can you give us an overview of your creative process?

There are three things I want to see in a piece. Since I work in a medium that is devoid of true movement, it has to first move me. If it does, then I proceed and hopefully, it will move you as an audience. Second, it has to challenge you. It can challenge you from a lot of different vantage points. It can be political. It can be racial. It can be in the technique itself. It can be very religious and that sometimes can be very, very challenging. Third, it should entertain you in some ways.

I think if you have those three ingredients, along with the skill set that you've learned, applying what you know, and having the patience to

BK FULTON AND NICHOLAS POWELL

stop and start, to draw over and over again, then you're pretty much in business because the rest is all creativity.

You have been labeled a "community artist." What does that label mean to you?

It means that I cannot afford to paint pretty pictures all of the time. My reality and my people's reality is that we live in a community that has a lot of problems. Through art, I can hopefully express myself, along with other artists to talk about what needs fixing in our communities. And that just isn't in my neighborhood, but neighborhoods around the world.

In the 1990s, you started Color Circle Art to help young artists develop their artistic and business skills. Can you tell us why this initiative was so important for you to start?

When I got started, I didn't know much about the business of art. Most artists don't know much about the business of art and the business is something that we should be familiar with but not always do. But once you know what another person is doing, you basically have some say in where you want to go. I was lucky enough to find some people who were really in the business, Elba Vargas, was a hard-working, beautiful woman who was really intelligent and a great marketer. She told me not to do the business but to know the business. She wanted me to know the business so when we sat down and talked about the business (contracts, commissions, etc.) that I had an idea of what was going on. Always remember that you are still working to get better as an artist. The art is and has to be your focus. At the same time, knowing the business and working with business professionals is important. Just remember to not impede your growth as an artist from getting caught up in making deals. It is the art that inspires.

What advice would you give to young artists who want to get their art noticed?

Make sure you have a strong enough skill set that you can build on because the art craft is about evolution. You just can't be a one-hit-wonder and then be angry at the world for the rest of your life. If you are always curious, you will always grow.

Also, it is important to start to brand yourself in a way that people are interested in seeing the work you do.

If it's consistent and you work hard at your craft, you will taste success. Then you will start to recognize the separation between the business

**ROAD TO RHYTHM BY PAUL
GOODNIGHT**

of art, the education of art, and the artists themselves. And then, hopefully, the world will take note.

I've been saying this a lot lately: Your JOB is what you're PAID for, but your CALLING is what you're MADE for.

How do you relax when you are not working?

I swim. I'm curious, so I also like to read books. I tell you what people don't feel comfortable talking about but I do, is *intimacy*. Intimacy has a real calming effect and you can take that any way you want to. It can be physical intimacy. It can be mental. It can be a spiritual intimacy.

Bishop Barbara L. King out of Georgia gave me a prayer book (*Daily Thoughts from the Hill*) that I read every day and it sort of sets the tone of where I'm supposed to be and how I shouldn't let what bothers me just linger. I pray with that prayer book every morning and it makes all the sense in the world.

What's up next? What projects are you currently working on?

I am working on a Frederick Douglass sculpture. That's why I am back in school and learning how to sculpt. This is just another evolutionary period in my life. We are doing the Frederick Douglass sculpture right here on Frederick Douglass Square in Boston. It is time to salute him here. I wish he were here to see it.

As I mentioned earlier, I hope a new series that I'm working on will have a ripple effect. We are doing a collection of pieces called *The K.K.K. Series* and I make no apologies for that name because I think what we are doing is right. K.K.K. stands for "Kids Killing Kids." There is an epidemic in all of our cities and small towns. Young men and women are destroying their future and our own communities. We have to stop the epidemic of violence because if we don't, then what good are the gifts we are given? We have to deal with the problems in our neighborhoods.

BK FULTON AND NICHOLAS POWELL

We have seven different artists working on this project and we just need funding to keep it going. We are going to auction the paintings off and the money we make from the auction will be given to the organizations that are keeping kids off the streets. That is our goal and we want to do it in every city with different artists.

Each participating artist has to paint two pieces: one that addresses the problem and one that chronicles the solution. Every one of these artists working with me has to search within their soul. Whether depicting how our culture is being taken away or how we've been bamboozled or learned to hate each other. Art can help us to remedy these issues with a visual medium. *What have we learned? Who are we learning from? Who are our role models? What have our contributions been before we got here and why has that not been publicized?* We come from people who are strong and productive and helped build this community and this world.

"If you are always curious, you will always grow."

There is one artist named L-Merchie Frazier who is creating a curriculum for the schools. We are finding people who want to contribute because they know that youth violence is a problem in their neighborhoods as well.

I've seen too much destruction. I've been to Vietnam and Nicaragua and Mozambique. Imagine seeing those wars; going to Sierra Leone and helping the amputees there . . . my God. You realize no matter how many weapons you have, you are not going to solve the problem. Weapons and wars are not the solution for humanity. They are part of the problem. Loving yourself first, then others around you seems like the right path to me!

BACK STAIR STEPS DUET BY PAUL GOODNIGHT

BROTHERS MIKE AND JOSH GRIER ARE THE CO-FOUNDERS OF EMBER LAB, AN INDEPENDENT ANIMATION, DIGITAL, AND GAMING STUDIO. PHOTO BY LUKE FONTANA.

"Find what speaks to you."

Mike Grier

The Game Theory Wizardry of **Mike and Josh Grier**

It was June 11, 2020, and Sony would be showcasing their lineup for the PlayStation 5. At the 27 minute mark, two new faces appear on the screen. They were the faces of brothers Mike and Josh Grier, co-founders of Ember Lab, an independent animation, digital, and gaming studio. They were there to introduce the world to *Kena: Bridge of Spirits,* a new game platform for the console. It was surreal seeing themselves in the showcase. It surprised their family and friends too. "My phone blew up with messages from people I hadn't talked to in a while like, 'I saw you on the PlayStation 5 showcase,'" Josh explains. "Most people didn't know we were working on *Kena*, but no one was expecting our faces to be up there."

Back in the 90s, Orlando, Florida, wasn't quite as densely populated as it is today. Mike recalls when they would play around in the woods around their neighborhood and shoot hoops in their yard. They lived around dirt roads and meadows. They were surrounded by magic and wonder. Their dad was an executive for Disney's theme-park operations. "Our dad worked for Disney for a long time and worked his way up into management over the years," Mike says. "We got a sneak peek of how the parks were operated and what was possible when you had the right team."

When Josh was six and Mike was four, their family moved to Paris, France, for 18 months. Their dad was tasked with opening Euro Disney. It was during this time that the two brothers bonded over shared experiences. "Oftentimes, we didn't speak the language, so a lot of that bonding involved watching animated films and playing video games, like the old classic *Zelda* game from Nintendo," Josh says. These games and the experience of living abroad influenced the kind of naturalistic and environmental elements found in their work. "Everything we do has a lot of texture," Josh says. "We create fantastical characters, but we try to give them a realistic spin, whether that is in lighting or the art style."

CHILDHOOD PHOTO OF JOSH AND MIKE GRIER WITH THEIR LITTLE BROTHER DANIEL IN PARIS. FROM LEFT: MIKE, DANIEL, AND JOSH GRIER. PHOTO COURTESY OF EMBER LAB.

"I hope people connect with the story and the themes of the game as much as the gameplay," Mike says

In the 2000s, their father would become vice president of Tokyo Disney. During this time, Josh was studying business and economics at Northwestern and Mike was still in high school. This was years before he would go on to study film at Chapman University. The family lived in Tokyo, Japan, for three years. Living in Tokyo sparked Mike's creativity and influenced the creative choices behind *Kena: Bridge of Spirits*. Kena was in development long before it was revealed at Sony's PlayStation 5 showcase. Josh and Mike founded Ember Lab in 2009. Josh is the chief operating officer and Mike is the chief creative officer. The team at Ember Lab cut their teeth creating ad campaigns for the MLB, Coca-Cola, and KFC. These ads illustrated Ember Lab's ability to create beautifully rendered animated ads for a global audience. But their greatest success story came in the form of a short animated film, *Majora's Mask − Terrible Fate*, that paid homage to the classic *Zelda* games. It went viral. As of this writing, it has over 10 million views on YouTube. So when it came to pitching to companies, Ember Lab was at an advantage. Sony was among a list of companies that fell in love with what the team was doing. They partnered with Sony in October of 2017. "We started development on the PlayStation 4 platform and they gave us the opportunity to jump to PlayStation 5," Josh says. "They are pretty committed and passionate about fostering creative teams like ours who are doing this kind of work."

The main character in their game is Kena, a young spirit guide, who travels to an abandoned village to find a sacred mountain shrine. She is aided in her quest by spirits and adorable black creatures known as the Rot.

KENA TAKES A MOMENT TO MEDITATE IN THE FOREST TO INCREASE HER FOCUS AND POWER. PHOTO COURTESY OF EMBER LAB.

The Rot assists Kena in battle, platforming, and other actions that are required for players to progress through the game. The Rot are with Kena until the end. The game's Asian female protagonist was an easy choice for Ember Lab. "Diversity is natural for us," Josh explains. "We have always planned for a unique lead character that gamers haven't seen before. We try to be authentic no matter what we do." Mike adds that the storytelling is relatable. "The storytelling themes and the human connection and narrative are universal," Mike says. "It deals with people struggling with loss or struggling with a mistake they made and the desire to reconcile it. I hope people connect with the story and the themes of the game as much as the gameplay." Mike hopes that the game will create the same strong bond that he and his brother had when playing games. "It was a way for us to connect as siblings and I think part of the goal of making this game is to supply that sort of connection," Mike says.

> "I think a lot of people in our community have the potential but don't have the access or the exposure of knowing someone who is the industry," Josh says.

With the buzz surrounding Ember Lab's new game, Mike and Josh are dealing with the growing pains of operating a bigger company. Despite this, they operate Ember Lab like a family. "As you become bigger, collaboration and effective communication become even more important," Josh says. "Building a team unit and an atmosphere where

KENA FACES OFF AGAINST A TOUGH ENEMY BEFORE SHE CAN CLEANSE A CORRUPTED SPROUT. PHOTO COURTESY OF EMBER LAB.

everyone feels they can communicate effectively and have their voice heard was important to us."

In a moment of vulnerability, Mike says he struggles with what many creatives struggle with: he second-guesses himself more than he should. "I find that it is best to follow my gut and do what I think is good and true," he says. As the Ember Lab team grew, Mike says it was a challenge to articulate those creative ideas and get everyone on the same page. "As a creative director, it is just a matter of listening to your team and then making the best decision," he says.

Because they grew up with a father who was in the creative industry, the two brothers went into the industry with their heads held high. "We talked about it before, but for us, a lot of what we have gotten is based on opportunity, and seeing people like us in positions that we aspire to is critical," Josh says. However, it was a little surprising to see that there were only a handful of people who looked like them in gaming design. They want this to change. "I think a lot of people in our community have the potential but don't have the access or the exposure of knowing someone who is in the industry," Josh says. Mike adds that they have inspired those closest to them to the possibility of working within the gaming industry. "When we talk to our cousins, it is like wow. They didn't think it was a possibility before," he explains. "They didn't think this was a career path that they could take."

BK FULTON AND NICHOLAS POWELL

For those who would like to tap into the industry, Josh suggests keeping yourself busy with projects of your own. "Even if there is no budget, getting our hands dirty and getting in there and learning the tools through a project is something that we have found has helped us," Josh says. "That struggle of learning the tools on your own makes you strong when those doors are opened to you." He also advises those interested in game building and design to make connections within the industry.

"Talking to someone about their experience is just really valuable," he says. "We get people reaching out to us all the time and while we may not always be able to give everybody what they want, we always try to respond and give as much feedback as possible. Don't feel afraid to reach out and ask people for help." Mike adds that talking to community managers on social media is a path to build that connection. "It is a bit of a tough nut to crack," Mike admits. "But I would say there are so many avenues and different skill sets involved in making games. Find what speaks to you."

While their primary focus is Kena, Josh says they will hold off on a sequel. "I don't know if we will do a direct sequel next," Josh says. "It may be another IP, in the same style—in terms of gameplay and the story-driven experience." However, the duo is interested in exploring the world they created in Kena in different creative mediums. "Kena and the universe we built has a lot of storytelling potential," he says. "So exploring and taking it into a more linear experience like a TV show or film is a possibility."

To learn more about Josh and Mike Grier's Ember Lab, visit Emberlab.com and follow them on Facebook, Instagram, and X.

PHOTO BY LUKE FONTANA

"Time is the most
valuable thing you
have."

Hill Harper

Hill Harper:
Investing in Us

Hill Harper comes from a rich history of black entrepreneurship. "The family lore is that we were slaves in Kentucky and made our way to the Mississippi River," Hill says. "They made their way up North and like a lot of other folks, they wanted to get as far away from the South as possible." Hill got his name from his two grandfathers—Harold Hill and Harold Harper. His maternal grandfather Harold Hill, also known as 'Doc Hill,' started serving the black community in the Jim Crow era. He owned Piedmont Pharmacy in Seneca, South Carolina. As young Hill Harper read comic books and bit on popsicles, he saw his grandfather trade medical prescriptions for potatoes and chickens with those who couldn't otherwise afford their medicines.

His paternal grandfather Harold Harper was an OB/ GYN physician in the small town of Fort Madison, Iowa. He and his brothers were graduates of Howard University Medical School and operated their own hospital in Fort Madison. Black women from surrounding states would come to him and have their babies delivered. Hill recalls his grandfather's good fortune. They would visit during summers. He owned an 88-acre farm outside of Fort Madison. There was an indoor and an outdoor pool. "Not even white families had all of that," Hill says. He was inspired by his grandfather's pride. "My father inherited his pride, and I think I got some of it too," he says. "To see those two very successful men serve the community with so much class and dignity was such an inspiration."

Hill doesn't play into others' expectations of him. His intuition is his best guide in life. "It is so easy to let other people project their fears onto you and influence you to change your behavior and decision-making," he says. "Always follow your heart." When Hill goes through work and life, he thinks in terms of impact and legacy. "I have a deep desire to have a positive impact in the world and for that impact to last, which is legacy," he says. He quotes part of the Bodhisattva Vows: "Sentient beings are numberless; I vow to save them all." For Hill, this means no matter the impossibility of a situation, he has "the will to change the world and do all the work." Because he believes he has yet to achieve his highest purpose, he must continue to do the work.

Acting works as a springboard for Hill's greater purpose—becoming a guiding force in the world. His acting and fame have afforded him the ability to reach a wider audience with his words. He references his first book *Letters To a Young Brother: Manifest Your Destiny.*

"There were a lot of young men who needed guidance, role modeling and help to navigate the journey from adolescence to manhood and a lot of them didn't have positive male role models in their lives," he says. "For me, having a role model on paper changed my life, and I wanted to do the same for others." Hill says people of all ages have reached out to him to tell him how much the book has changed their lives and how they see and navigate the world. "These are people who I wouldn't otherwise have known or met," he says. "It won the Best Book for Young Adults award by the American Library Association. It is in every library across the country. So people have access to the book even if they do not buy it. I'm very proud of *Letters* and what it has done."

> "It is so easy to let other people project their fears onto you and influence you to change your behavior and decision-making. Always follow your heart."

As an actor, Hill understands that actors have a greater purpose and are perfectly suited to be activists. It is in his lineage. His late aunt, Virginia Harper, was an activist. "Harry Belafonte, Sidney Poitier, Paul Robeson: all of these people were activists in their own ways. I wanted to be that type of actor, performer, and activist." One of Hill's first major roles was in Spike Lee's *Get on the Bus*. He spends most of the movie sitting next to Ossie Davis. "He would tell me stories about Malcolm X visiting him

BK FULTON AND NICHOLAS POWELL

at his house, tell me stories about Godfrey Cambridge acting in theatre with him, basically telling me that my only purpose as an artist is to be an activist in some way or you are not being an artist," he recalls.

We see this mentality play out in the roles Hill chooses to play. He is Dr. Marcus Andrews on the hit TV show *The Good Doctor.* He loves playing the role of a doctor who is considered the best surgeon in the hospital. "It is certainly a stereotype buster, but it is also about making him and his life cool, making him something people want to emulate," he explains. He recently was involved in the documentary, *Black Men in White Coats.* The documentary advocates the need for more black male doctors. "So few black men are becoming doctors even though we must face the fact that we have disparities in the way that black men and black people, in particular, are treated by the medical profession," Hill explains. "The data certainly shows that we get higher and better and more complete care when we are treated by black folk, so black men becoming doctors is a matter of life or death." Hill hopes that his role as Dr. Marcus Andrews inspires "young brothers" to become doctors.

"They ask me what Dr. Andrews drives and I say he drives a fly 911 Turbo S," he says. "And I know doctors like that. He's confident. He's had an evolution as well on the show, so I love playing Marcus Andrews."

One of Hill's primary pursuits is working to close the wealth gap. "All of these big issues we want to see solved—criminal justice reform, health disparities, education gaps, housing, and poverty—can be dealt with through a prism of financial agility," Hill says. "We can solve these many problems or at least create a foundation for solving these problems." Years ago, Hill wrote the *Wealth Cure* about this exact issue. Some of the solutions he proposed in the book are now able to come to fruition due to technological advances. He has created Black Wall Street, an app and digital wallet that allows people to directly invest in the black community. The name is inspired by Black Wall Street, the Greenwood District in Tulsa, Oklahoma, that was an epicenter of black wealth in the early 20th century. In 1921, a white mob stormed the town killing hundreds, destroying their livelihoods and assets. This atrocity set their descendants back generations. "Today's dollar leaves the black community after six hours. In contrast, in the brick and mortar version of Tulsa's Black Wall Street, the dollar changed hands 36 to 100 times within the ecosystem," Hill Harper explains. "With digital currency, we are seeing the dollar move out of the black community even quicker." His Black Wall Street is the solution to this issue.

"I have a deep desire to have a positive impact in the world and for that impact to last, which is legacy."

In Hill's eyes, most artists will have a hard time making money solely off of their art in the near future. "Why? Because technology is allowing anybody and everybody to create content," Hill explains. Hill believes content creation will be even more decentralized in the future. "There will be micro-communities where you can create content, but it is not going to be easy doing it for a living,' he predicts. Hill sees the creative

BK FULTON AND NICHOLAS POWELL

world going back to the days when people would create for the love of it instead of for money, so having a nest egg is important. "Get into an asset class that is growing," he says. "If you have a strong financial foundation, then you can make the choice of how you want to use your time, which is the most valuable thing you have. Don't let anyone lie to you and say that money is more valuable. No. Time is the most valuable thing you have. If you have the resources to have more time, then you have invested well."

To learn more about Hill Harper, follow him on Facebook, Instagram, and X.

"You are in the driver's
seat of your life"

Brandi Harvey's
Mission for You to Be Healthy

Growing up in the Midwest town of Cleveland, Ohio, Brandi Harvey was taught that excellence was the standard she should live her life by. Brandi's elementary school principal, Mrs. Stella Loeb-Munson, was one of her earliest exposures to excellence. She had an entrepreneurial spirit in the way she made her own clothes and relied on her own intuition and smarts to navigate the world. Brandi wanted to emulate her style and swagger. Outside of school, Brandi was inspired by the writings and grace of Susan Taylor, the former editor-in-chief of Essence Magazine. As a little girl, Brandi sat at the hair salon and would eagerly grab a copy of the latest issue of Essence Magazine to read her column "In the Spirit." At eighteen years old, Brandi had the opportunity to meet Ms. Taylor. For the first time in her life, she was star struck. "She embodied grace, style, poise, and beauty," she says. "She was this tall black woman with these braids and very striking features. She, to me, was the epitome of womanhood. I wanted to be that. She was one of the reasons why I fell in love with words and spirituality."

> "I needed to find the thing that was going to make me get up early in the morning and make me want to stay up late at night."

After graduating from Ohio State University in 2005, Brandi became a high school history teacher. She recalls that while teaching high school history was rewarding, it wasn't her purpose. "I was young and fresh out of college," she says. "I had just moved to Los Angeles and had these big dreams of being this young engaging teacher.

I remember being in college and thinking, 'I'm going to change the world!' I realized all of those big ideas that I had didn't quite fit into the space of school bureaucracy. It just wasn't for me." So she had to change course. She needed to find her passion. "I needed to find the

thing that was going to make me get up early in the morning and make me want to stay up late at night," she says.

Her parents instilled in her the importance of service to others. "When you are here, you are here to serve the needs of God's people," they would say to Brandi. She realized teaching was not necessarily confined to the classroom. After she left teaching and moved to Atlanta, her mother said to her, "That wasn't your classroom to teach in. The world will become your classroom." After leaving her teaching position, her mother's wise words rang true. In 2018, she started Beyond Her, a wellness brand for women, specifically for those of color. Brandi has traveled the world as an advocate for women's health and wellness.

Brandi recalls the time she was executive director of the Steve & Marjorie Harvey Foundation, her family's non-profit that focuses on educating and mentoring underserved youth. After being executive director for seven years, her dad fired her. "People couldn't believe it," she says. "They would say, 'How could your dad have fired you?!?' but I'm so thankful he did." Brandi says her dad had to navigate his way to success and in seeing similarities in her that he saw in himself, he wanted to allow her to grow and create her own lane. "He said to me, 'You got to go do the thing that's going to make you happy. The thing that's going to make you smile. The thing that's going to make you soar.' And when he released me, I was released into my destiny," she says. "So many people wait around because we are so afraid to get out of the boat of mediocrity. There is no outside source that's coming to save you. You put the "S" on your chest and save yourself."

> "You are 100 percent responsible for the life that you have. You can heal your life, but it's going to have to start from the inside-out."

When Brandi started to be intentional in her life, she saw a significant change in her happiness and well-being. "We must put intention and action behind our daily lives. I became intentional about how I get up in the morning," she says. "I became intentional about how I practiced my life during the day— e.g., my rituals for meditation, going to therapy, journaling, and praying. When you match intention and action, you are on the road to success."

In her book, *Breakthrough Sold Separately: Get Out of the Boat of Mediocrity and Walk On Water*, she advocates for living the life you want to live. "I want readers to get that you are in the driver's seat of your life," she says. "You are 100 percent responsible for the life that you have. You can heal your life, but it's going to have to start from the inside-out." She understands everyone has self-doubts, but she says you have to remind yourself that you are valuable and loved. "I'm a spiritual person and that connection plays out in my life in many ways," she explains. "When I get a little anxious or don't know what's going to happen next, I just focus on my breathing and I start to feel centered and in control again."

Brandi started to consider therapy around the time her sister and brother-in-law were getting married. When they were dating, her brother-in-law told her sister that he wanted to marry her, but first, she had to work on some things. He encouraged her to go to therapy and so she did. Brandi could see a change in her sister. While she considered therapy, she did not take the action to go at that moment. This was also the time she was still executive director for her family's foundation. As she would talk to the kids in the program and discuss the issues they were facing with counselors and their families, Brandi started to question what was going on psychologically with these young people of color. This turned into a bigger question for Brandi: "Why do people of color engage in certain behavior?"

She began her research and came across Dr. Joy De-Gruy's book, *Post-Traumatic Slave Syndrome*. Post Traumatic Slave Syndrome is the theory that centuries of chattel slavery and institutionalized racism have caused multigenerational trauma in people of color. The theory goes on to explain how this trauma causes harmful behavior like internalized racism, anger, violence, and low self-esteem. The wounds were never really healed. "After reading *Post-Traumatic Slave Syndrome,* it kind of gave me the green light to say I wanted to heal myself," she says. "I never looked at my life as being traumatic because most of us view trauma as something big." She goes on to explain how we look at "big traumas" like death, assaults, and so on, but ignore traumas like abandonment or verbal assaults. "I started examining my life and I saw myself exhibiting so many of the signs that Dr. DeGruy talks about in the book as a black woman and I was like, 'I want to fix that,'" she says. In 2016, she began going to therapy. Therapy became, what she calls, her "non-negotiable." She went every week and has continued to since then.

She advises people to find their non-negotiable, specifically something that can be part of their self-care ritual. "I tell people to find something that becomes your non-negotiable," she says. She used the example of 5 am runs as an example of a non-negotiable. "That's you in the morning in the darkness on the pavement," she says. "Whatever it is, find that non-negotiable that you are not willing to compromise for anything or anyone and that is when you will see real change in your life."

"Wellness is a lifestyle. It doesn't work if you don't work it."

Brandi is proud of herself for taking the steps to stay healthy. Today, she has a great sense of self-awareness and love for herself. "If I can continue to keep walking in that way, then God will continue to bless me," she says. With more clarity and purpose comes self-mastery. For Brandi, this means understanding who she is as a person emotionally, physically, and mentally. "I think it's an old adage that says, 'your health is your wealth,' and as cliche as it is, it is true for me," she explains. "I have expanded my life in ways that I didn't know were possible 10 years ago, let alone five years ago."

Brandi feels like she's still moving and pushing along. "Being the daughter of a megastar, you have a real blueprint of hard work and work ethic," she says. She referenced watching her dad tape a show. She was looking at a 60 plus-year-old man who was still working. "He's still teachable and he's still coaching. I don't think you ever make it. I don't think you ever arrive. You just keep growing," she explains. In a journal, she has written down all of what she wants to accomplish. She feels she is on her way to accomplishing big things. "I feel like I'm in a place where I just keep being available," she continues, "And keep being open and keep allowing myself to surrender and trust the process."

Brandi says young people who would like to become wellness entrepreneurs must learn to "walk it like they talk it." It is important to be authentic. "I think so many people can easily fall into this idea of wellness careers being a gimmick," she says. "I'm not going to tell you to eat plant-based and I don't eat plant-based. No, I eat plant-based and vegan because that is the life that sustains me and allows me to do the work that I do. That's how I live." She says, "I'm not going to tell you to go to therapy and heal yourself and I don't do that. I'm not going to tell you to journal and I don't do that. It is about practicing what you preach. Wellness is a lifestyle. It doesn't work if you don't work it."

In 2020, Brandi has rolled out new video content on social media and has started a Beyond Her branded podcast. She will also create an audiobook version of her book later this year. Readers will have the opportunity to document their self-care journey in a journal that will coincide with her book. She says she will also be on a nationally syndicated radio show that she has to be on the hush about. Before we ended our talk, Brandi outlined the universal attention she would like *Breakthrough Sold Separately* to have. "I want to take this book around the world so that we have conversations, healing conversations with women, particularly women of color," she says. "I think this book is not just for women, I think this book has a lot that it can offer men as well." No matter your gender or race, self-awareness and care are important steps to living a long and fruitful life.

To learn more about Brandi Harvey and Beyond Her, you can subscribe to her newsletter on her website beyondher.co and follow @iambrandiharvey and @beyondherco on Instagram.

CHRIS HOWARD, FORMER
PRESIDENT OF ROBERT
MORRIS UNIVERSITY (RMU).
PHOTO BY MICHAEL WILL.

Chris Howard's
Principal of Integrity

Chris Howard's story began in Plano, Texas, where he experienced the difficulties of being one of a few black people in a predominantly white neighborhood. Chris recalls moving from Little Rock, Arkansas to Plano, Texas, and walking into his fourth-grade classroom. The school was modern for its time. There were no walls, so you could see into the next classroom. He was the only black student in his entire fourth-grade class. It was easy for young Chris Howard to feel alone in a sea of faces that did not look like him. At some point, he realized he was not as academically prepared as his classmates. The reality of inequality settled in. He became the stereotypical young angry black boy. "1979 Plano, Texas, was not a place where white people were politically correct and understood sensitivities around black people," Chris explains. "So hearing the n-word, not necessarily thrown at me, but just hearing it on the playground affected me negatively. I got into lots of fights."

When he reached middle school, he began to understand how he could amend his past transgressions. "In Texas, all sins can be forgiven if you can play football," he says jokingly. He was a great football player. He caught up academically and continued to work hard. By the time he had graduated Plano Senior High School, he was student body president, the cadet colonel commander of his ROTC battalion, and captain of his football team. "It was a journey from fourth to twelfth grade," he recalls. "There was a lot of blood, sweat, and tears from all parties involved, but by the end of it, they are people who I absolutely learned to love like they were my own kinfolk." Chris went on to graduate from the United States Air Force Academy, earning a BS degree in political science. He received the Campbell Trophy for his stellar academic and football performance. He then was named a Rhodes Scholar and earned his doctorate in politics at the University of Oxford and an MBA with distinction from the Harvard Business School.

Chris Howard believes that his family history holds the clues to how he landed where he is today. His parents' humble beginnings started in Texas. They both grew up picking cotton; black people were not permitted to work in stores. His mom, Caroline, who was his biggest inspiration, grew up with no indoor plumbing and, for a portion of her

CHRIS HOWARD BECAME THE EIGHTH PRESIDENT OF RMU IN FEBRUARY 2016. PHOTO BY JOE APPEL.

freshman year in high school, no electricity. Notwithstanding all of this, his mom was valedictorian of her high school and his dad was salutatorian at his. His parents met at Prairie View A&M University. While his dad graduated, his mom left school after they were married and went back to school off and on.

She ultimately graduated from college the same year his older brother graduated high school. Throughout his years as a youth, while he was going to school, she was too. He saw his mom sacrifice and work hard and diligently to make a great life for him and his brother. Caroline graduated cum laude from the University of Texas at Dallas.

He also saw how active she was in the community and the barriers she broke down. She was treasurer and head of the PTA at his high school and helped elect the first African-American City Council member of Plano, Texas. Yet, she was still at every band performance, football game, and track meet. He remembers the time his mom had gotten a C+ in one of her classes as a student at the University of Texas at Dallas. "She said to me, 'I got a C+ in this class. I am so happy. I worked so hard to get this C+,' Chris says. "It was the only C+ she had ever made. She had made all As and Bs throughout her collegiate career. But I thought to myself, what a great example for me to see this strong black woman who emphasized that if you worked hard and tried your best, you should be proud of that."

"I think people enjoy the most success when they do the things they do best."

Chris Howard loves the quote attributed to Mark Twain: "The two most important days of your life are the day you are born and the day you find out why." For Chris, that moment arrived when he became president of Hampden-Sydney College in Virginia around 2009. Sure, at that point in his life he had work experience in the military, corporate

BK FULTON AND NICHOLAS POWELL

America, intelligence, and the non-profit space, but he didn't feel those opportunities were his purpose. "When I got into this college presidency thing, it was challenging," he explains. "Then I started to think that this is challenging but rewarding. I'm giving back. I think people enjoy the most success when they do the things they do best."

Chris is an outlier in the pool of university presidents. "The average school president is a 61-year-old white male. I'm 51 and I've been president for over a decade," he explains. But he declares that the title or accolades are not what's most important. What is most important is that he feels he is doing something meaningful. Chris considers

RMU PRESIDENT CHRIS HOWARD AND FIRST LADY BARBARA HOWARD. PHOTO BY MICHAEL WILL.

his greatest achievement to be raising his two sons Cohen and Joshua Howard with his wife, Barbara, a native of Johannesburg, South Africa, who grew up under the Apartheid system. "These are the kind of young men who you would want to have sitting at your table," he says of his two sons. He tells his sons that regardless of who you are or what you've achieved, you should always be respectful. "You don't have to be a Rhodes Scholar to be respectful," Chris says. "You don't have to be a graduate of Harvard Business School to appreciate other people and what they do in their struggle. I'm very proud of who they are and who they have grown to be."

When asked how he manages to do so much, he says he is inspired by his ancestors who were born into slavery. He cites being just three generations removed from chattel slavery. "My great-great-grandfather Amos Howard was a slave," he explains. "I've been given a lot, so I must give. That motivates me. This history is not lost on the opportunities that I've been able to seize."

Chris is also motivated by his parents' characteristic of standing by their word. "My mom and dad were not wishy-washy people," he explains. "They did what they said they were going to do." In his job, he holds everyone accountable. He goes through the mental process of understanding what they need and if they can accomplish what is in front of them. If they can both agree that it can be done, then he will hold them accountable. This is the same standard he holds himself to. "I understand the world is gray," Chris says. "I understand that there are circumstances and issues, and I'm not inhumane, but I think as a leader if I can try my best to be transparent and fair and consistent, the organization will be successful."

COVID-19 has put a strain on higher education. He believes he has a capable team that will get the university through a tough and uncertain time. There is his nine-member cabinet that reports directly to him. Then there is the leadership council and a board of trustees. "We are like a battle-hardened combat team that is going on into the next fight with the hindsight of being successful in the previous battle," he explains. He references Jim Collins and his book, *Good to Great*. In the book, Collins explains that in hardships, you have to be pragmatic and realistic at the same time. Chris Howard and his team have made the decision to reopen their campus for the fall semester with the option for students to have the comfort of taking their classes online or in-person.

"You don't have to be a graduate of Harvard Business School to appreciate other people and what they do in their struggle."

We asked Chris what advice he would give to someone who would like to follow a similar path. He humorously responds, "Are you crazy? Are you sure you want to do this?" He then reframes his answer. "In all seriousness, it is a magnificent honor and—as they call it in the military—the covenant of a command," he says. "To be the chief empowerment officer, to be able to help people, students, staff, alumni, friends of the university achieve their hopes and dreams and aspirations is a real honor." Chris makes it clear that being a school president can be a "thankless" job, so if one is okay with that, then they are perfect for the job. While Chris took a non-traditional route to his position, the traditional route consists of moving through the academic ranks. "There is plenty of need here. We touch every aspect of the human condition in civil society. If you really want to make a difference in the world, take a look at it," he encourages.

Chris Howard makes it a priority to take care of his mental and physical health. "I try to keep my weight within 5 pounds of what my fighting weight was," he says. "That's how I calibrate how I'm taking care of

BK FULTON AND NICHOLAS POWELL

myself because quite often the stress is greatest when you think you don't eat right, don't exercise, or hydrate." Chris is aware of the immense responsibility leaders have on the success of the organization. "When you move up in leadership roles you actually lose grip of what you can control, but you're responsible for so much more," Chris says. "You recognize as a leader, you cannot do everything by yourself. It requires working through others to get things done and that can be really scary."

He recalls a meeting with his cabinet earlier in 2020. It was when the coronavirus was fairly new. He recommended focusing on what they could control. He explained that they could control staying fit, keeping up with dental hygiene, putting on sunblock, and staying hydrated. As he explains, all of these things were "good for them" and in their control. "It's a metaphor," he explains. "There are other things you can control in terms of your work schedule, discipline, attentiveness, how you run meetings. You have to distill it down to what you can control and do your best to be understanding that there are going to be things beyond your control and be at peace with that." As a leader, Chris recognizes it is his ultimate responsibility to revolve his work around empowering his team and the people he serves.

After a long discussion, Chris notes that he is proud to be the president of Robert Morris University. "We turn 100 in 2021 and I'm excited to see what we are going to be in the next 100 years," he says. "I'm excited about the arc and journey of the institution that I'm leading in a region like Pittsburgh which is very much a microcosm of society—medicine, technology, education, and very blue and red politically. Being a part of that and that vibrancy is going to dictate where our country is going to go in the future. I'm very excited to be on this ride."

CHRIS AND BARBARA HOWARD MEET WITH STUDENTS AT RMU'S ROMO'S CAFE AT ITS MOON TOWNSHIP CAMPUS. PHOTO BY MICHAEL WILL.

Richy Jackson Dares to Go Higher

Richy Jackson may not be the star you know, but he is the person the stars go to when they want that extra pizzazz. He has worked and continues to work with some of the greatest and most iconic pop acts of the millennium—Lady Gaga, Katy Perry, and Nicki Minaj, just to name a few. He works nonstop and lends his creative genius to those with the talent and work ethic to become icons. Richy is also an icon.

He grew up in the culturally and racially mixed city of Fairfield, California, 20 minutes north of San Francisco. Richy lived as most kids do from that area: carefree and endlessly curious. "I was a band geek, so it was all about the band and sports and having a good time with friends," he says. "It wasn't a lot of crime in the city. It was a town where everyone could just thrive and grow." His mother, Debra, and his uncle, Ricky, inspired him to pursue music and dance. "My mother was a cheerleading coach and it was through her coaching that I really started to get into dance," he says. "I choreographed her cheerleading team when I was 13." He had a love for dance, but before that point he never choreographed anything. Uncle Ricky was a percussionist. "He used to play the drums in bars and clubs for groups around town. He was the drummer everyone had to have," he says. After hearing his uncle play the drums, Richy started to play them too in the fourth grade. "The inspiration for what I do today comes from these two fantastic people that I love."

Early on in his career, Richy realized he didn't know everything. "I had to watch and learn and live by experience," he says. "I was just a dancer who wanted to become a choreographer." He learned how to work on a video set and what it took to work on tours and at rehearsals. "As a dancer, I had to see what was working for other people and what wasn't," he says. "I would watch the choreographers and see what they were taking on and how their relationships were with a client, the director, or the artist." He watched how choreographers would treat their colleagues, good or bad. "I would say, 'Yeah, that's cool or that wasn't really nice, the way she was talking to that person.' I studied and because of that, I knew how to stay successful as a dancer and as a choreographer," he says.

Even at this stage of his career, he doesn't feel like he's made it big yet. "There are so many levels of creativity and new challenges that are unforeseen at this point," he says. "To me, I've done great and I want to continue to do great, but I don't know if I'll ever be able to say I made it. I feel like as soon you say that, a notch turns in your brain and you might not create or approach opportunities the same way. So, for me, I'm climbing a never-ending ladder. There is always a new rung to climb up."

"I feel like we were able to entertain and still be able to capture the audience at a time where people were easily bored."

There is one special moment that wowed Richy and the world—Super Bowl LI with Lady Gaga. It was his first time working on an event like the Super Bowl. "There was a lot going on in my life and in the world, politically," he says. "I feel like we were able to entertain and still be able to capture the audience at a time where people were easily bored. The Super Bowl is a great venue and platform to be a part of, but at the same time, you have so many different kinds of people watching you." Richy is privy to the fact they had the opportunity to reach a diverse group of people: The audience included sports fans that could care less about "shows," people who just want to see the halftime performance, people who love Lady Gaga, people who hate Lady Gaga, and the people who don't know who she is. "It was amazing for us to be a part of one of the greatest, most viewed, most well-respected, and I think at this point, still unmatched Super Bowl halftime shows. It was the pinnacle of my career so far."

His creative relationship with Lady Gaga began in 2007. "I met her at a dance studio in Hollywood. She was fresh out of New York and after seeing her perform a few of her songs, I was amazed." She is the kind of artist that I always wanted to work with. She just had this conviction about her, that I hadn't seen from other artists." He liked how she was different and unique. "It was just this force that I understood," he says. "I always wanted to be a part of that world and take the road less traveled. When I met her, that was kind of what sparked my creativity." Their relationship centers around mutual respect for their individual creativity and ideas. "We create these shows, and we bounce ideas off each other, we challenge each other," he says. "It's not really

BK FULTON AND NICHOLAS POWELL

about what the industry is doing. Instead, for us it's about what we can do to create the best art. What kind of show can we do ourselves and how can we top ourselves. It's not about what everyone else is doing. That's what I always loved about us and our relationship."

No matter the background of the artist Richy is working with, the language of choreography is universal. "Whether I'm counting in English and they are from another country, they still understand what 5, 7, 8 means," he says. However, Richy does notice a difference in the degree of how involved international and American artists expect him to be in the creative process. "I think when it comes to international artists, they really do look to me to lead the way, like 'What do you want me to do?,' which is great. I think when you're working with traditional American artists, the project is more of a collaboration than me just leading the way."

Over the years, Richy has experienced first hand the changing of the music industry and how pop music's vitality has fallen by the wayside. "We need a change, a new system. I think pop music, in particular, lends itself to those groundbreaking artists and game-changing routines with elaborate sets, and fantastic tours," he continues, "but pop music has lost its magic over the last five or six years. It's time for pop music to get back up. I see that happening within the next 10 years as pop music evolves. Currently, the music industry is about how little we can spend. Should we look like this or sound like that? There is a monotonous approach towards music today and someone needs to break the pattern, create a new system, and bring back the magic of pop music."

"Figure out who actually has done a professional job. Look at their resume because if you want to learn how to dance, you have to learn it from the professionals."

BK FULTON AND NICHOLAS POWELL

Richy advises up and comers that want to be in the industry to watch and study music videos, tours, and live performances. "They really need to do their research. There's so much content out there that as much as they think they are learning, they're not learning enough," he says. "Many of the creators on the internet are false prophets. Having a lot of followers does not necessarily mean there is a lot of talent, so newcomers must investigate. Figure out who actually has done a professional job. Look at their resume because if you want to learn how to dance, you have to learn it from the professionals. When you get on stage, on set, or start to perform live, a professional is the one that is going to help you to become a better dancer and a better performer." When he's not working, Richy loves to watch movies. Mostly because it helps him escape from his busy work schedule. "For me, this business is 24/7. It's nonstop. There isn't one artist, one project, one video going," he says. "Multiple creative projects are happening all the time. So, when it's time to chill out, I love going to the AMC theater to watch movies. I can shut my phone off and dive into the movie for an hour and a half or two. But as soon as the movie goes off and the credits roll, the phone is back on. People are like, 'Well, don't you want to take a vacation.' and I say, 'Well I'm always flying and in some hotel.' So, for me, either watching a movie or doing absolutely nothing is enough. I love the work I do, and I don't run from it. Relaxing is just something I add to the mix."

Richy believes YouTube superstar JoJo Siwa will be the next big phenomenon in pop music. "She's a 21-year-old from Omaha, Nebraska," he says. "I met her when she was nine and for the past year, I've done five of her music videos. I creative directed and choreographed her "D.R.E.A.M. The Tour." The response has been incredible. She went from theater dates to arenas and she's getting more and more dates as we speak. She's selling out everywhere. I just love working with her. She inspires me. She knows her brand and I know how to turn her brand into something that's live for the kids to not only love, but for the adults that bring their kids to enjoy as well."

To learn more about Richy Jackson, you can follow him on Instagram @richysquirrel and X @RICHYSQUIRREL or Facebook @Richy Jackson Choreography.

Dr. Michael Jones'
Work Is Beyond Himself

Dr. Michael Jones grew up in the suburb of Ashton, Maryland, where his family was the only Black family in a neighborhood of seventeen homes. As a teenager, Michael found diversity at Saint John's College High School, a private Catholic school in Washington, DC. He remembers this time in his life as bittersweet. On the one hand, he was experiencing the wonders of adolescence in a big city. But on the other hand, there was rural farmland and simmering racial tensions. However, Dr. Michael Jones appreciates having both world experiences.

His father was a manager and executive for IBM. In the summers, Michael accompanied his father to work and learned the ins and outs of the business. "Those summers with my dad made me want to be an entrepreneurial and business-minded person," Michael says. However, his true passion lay in medicine. He set his eyes on becoming a veterinarian, but he didn't know anyone in his immediate family who was a doctor. "My only experience seeing doctors was when I went to the pediatrician or the dentist, but they were all white," he recalls. "They didn't take much interest in me or what I was doing in life." But things changed when Michael had an appointment with a Black dermatologist. After learning Michael was interested in the medical field, the dermatologist invited Michael back to his office to show him around. "That was it for me," Michael says. "I knew right then and there I wanted to care for people and as a Black man, I knew I could do that."

After Michael graduated from Columbia University Vagelos College of Physicians and Surgeons and finished his residency, he worked as a surgical oncologist. Michael found the work difficult as he grew attached to his patients. He would spend hours with them, taking out tumors and putting them back together just to lose them later to a stubborn or recurring cancer. "I knew I had to pivot," he says. "I had to do something more in line with my personality. I wanted to grow old with my patients. I wanted to know that I could give myself to them and make them happy to come back and see me again." Hence, his pivot

to plastic surgery. Michael believes he has found success doing what is best for his patients.

Michael is the owner of Lexington Plastic Surgeons, a plastic surgery practice with locations in New York City, New Jersey, Atlanta, Miami, Houston, Los Angeles, and Washington, DC. Expanding his business has come with its challenges. Specifically, the disparity between Black and white businesses' access to capital often creates a problem for

BK FULTON AND NICHOLAS POWELL

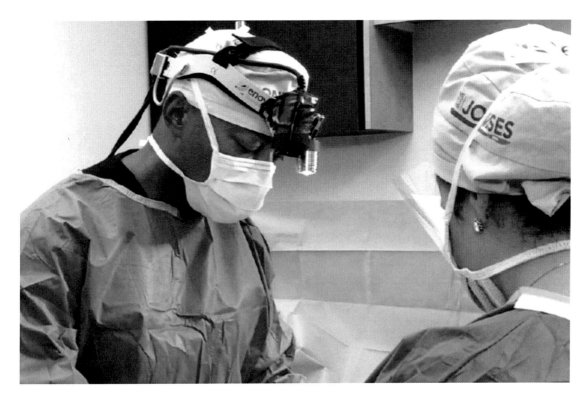

minority-owned enterprises. This issue has stifled Black businesses for decades. "The expansions didn't result from going to the bank," Michael explains. "Every office opened because we saved enough money to open it. That is not the typical way white businesses grow. They will go to a bank or a private equity firm and boom! You will all of a sudden see their footprint expand. Unfortunately, that was not going to work for this business."

"My only experience seeing doctors was when I went to the pediatrician or the dentist, but they were all white."

Michael's first business was a laundromat in Washington, DC. He was still a student at Columbia and no one believed he could get a loan. He went to what may have been thirty different banks before one gave him a chance after he promised he would get his parents to cosign.

"From then on, I learned how valuable it was to have good credit and how hard it was going to be to get access to capital," Michael says. As Michael moves through life, he is careful to appreciate what he has. "I feel at any moment all of this could be taken away from me," he explains. "It doesn't seem real that I can do what I do for so many people."

Outside of Lexington Plastic Surgeons, Michael's new project centers around digitizing plastic and non-surgical treatments. "It came to light during COVID when home delivery became popular," he says. Michael believes customers should have the choice and freedom to access these services at their convenience. He is quick to shut down any rumor that says all doctors have a successful life full of riches and luxury. "Doctors don't make a whole lot of money these days," he admits. He says this because of the amount of money spent on medical school, the number of hours doctors have to put in caring for their patients, and the unequal revenue share between private practitioners, hospitals, and insurance companies. He instead advises those who would like to go through medical school to do so for the sake of altruism. "Do it because you enjoy caring for patients and making people happy," Michael says.

BK FULTON AND NICHOLAS POWELL

"Every office opened because we saved enough money to open it."

Michael remembers his time as a pre-med student at Columbia University and the difficulty he had in his first biology class. He was forced to drop the class in the middle of the semester. "It was like learning a new language," he explains. "If you hadn't taken Latin, which I did take in high school, you wouldn't have known the letters or the words." Once Michael tapped into what he already knew, he ended up taking the class again and he did well. "You are going to have failures and you have to learn from your mistakes. Don't give up," he says. "Keep your eyes on the prize, but do it for the right reasons." He emphasizes again: "Don't do it for the money."

Dr. Jones was relaxing in the backyard of his vacation home in Puerto Rico staring at the ocean during our interview. It's his place to recalibrate and chill. "When I think of energy, I think I am a fire sign," he reflects. "I have a lot of heat. I have a lot of passion. So I spend a lot of time trying to calm that chi down." Michael enjoys his yoga and takes time to play his trumpet. He loves to create jingles for his practice and his wife's business.

"Two of the most important things in my life are my marriage and fatherhood.

While in college, Michael opened a restaurant and jazz club where he once got on stage and played the trumpet with his idol, Wynton Marsalis. Michael also played jazz clubs in D.C. and New York City to pay for college and medical school. As he has achieved his dream of expanding his practice, he still calls back to those days as a trumpeter. "Who knows, maybe that is the next chapter of my life: picking up my horn again and playing for a live audience," he says.

Michael is truly happy with his life. He has a purpose that is beyond him. "Two of the most important things in my life are my marriage and fatherhood," Michael says. "They give me the most sense of humility and stability. I believe I am grooming a legacy. After we are done, what we leave behind as a legacy is all that will exist."

To learn more about Dr. Michael Jones, visit Lexington Plastic Surgeons' website, www.lexingtonplasticsurgeons.com.

Adam Leipzig:
The Movie Yoda

Adam Leipzig is a "solopreneur" who believes there is always room for improvement. This is an interesting self-assessment when you think about all he has achieved in his career. He is a former Disney executive who was instrumental in the production of one of Disney's highest grossing live-action films, *Honey, I Shrunk the Kids*. As president of National Geographic Films, Adam was responsible for acquiring the international rights to *March of the Penguins*, releasing the U.S. version which garnered much deserved critical and commercial acclaim. Adam, with his degree in Literature from Yale University, has made a career out of what he loves—movies. In our interview with Adam, he discusses the people who inspire him, his wildly successful career and the keys to producing one's very best work.

Where are you from and what was it like growing up there?

I am from Los Angeles and I grew up in Reseda, which is in the San Fernando Valley. When I grew up, the street we lived on ended in a dead end, about a block away. All of the blocks surrounding us were orange groves and about a half-mile away was an actual dairy with cows and we used to go there to get milk and bottles. I know it sounds like we grew up in the 1860s but it was really the 1960s. Now, all of those orange groves are tract houses and shopping malls. The street is no longer a dead end. It cuts through into four lanes where the speed limit is 45 miles per hour. Things have changed a whole lot.

Very true. They always say "showing up is half the battle." At what point in your career did you begin to feel like you had made it?

I feel like I'm still "making it" or at least in the process of making it. I feel that having amazing kids is making it. Being with an amazing woman and partner is making it. I feel like I have those things in my life. But in my career, I feel like I'm always a work in progress.

What would you consider to be your greatest achievement? Anything from your body of work?

The projects from my body of work that feel like great achievements are always the underdog projects that nobody thought were going to work but ended up working. Launching and opening the Los Angeles Theatre Center in the 1980s which is a four-theatre, 1200-seat performing arts complex was pretty cool. It was a gigantic and amazing achievement career-wise.

I am proud of a little movie I did called *Honey, I Shrunk the Kids* that was supposed to be passed over but instead relaunched the Disney family brand in live-action movies. *March of the Penguins,* which everybody laughed at me for spending a million dollars to buy a movie about penguins, went on to great success and acclaim.

It always feels great when you have something that not only works creatively and financially but becomes a part of the popular culture.

Throughout your career, you were able to release films like *March of the Penguins*, *Arctic Tale,* and *A Plastic Ocean* that subtly and not so subtly dealt with climate change. Did you create these films because of your position at National Geographic or did you just feel the stories needed to be told?

Both. I did not start making documentaries until I came to National Geographic. Previously, everything I made was scripted, live-action feature films. But when I came to National Geographic, I became really interested in documentaries. It rather coincided with the renaissance documentary phase that we are currently still in. Documentaries are so much a part of National Geographic's DNA that it was only logical that we moved there. So we pivoted in that direction with terrific success.

　　　　　　　　BK FULTON AND NICHOLAS POWELL

I think I have a certain skill with documentaries. I have a way of approaching them, of putting them together. *A Plastic Ocean* is also a signature achievement for me and the team behind it because it was a movie that no one should have watched. Think about it, if you have a choice between watching a Marvel superhero blow something up which is a "good time" and a documentary called *A Plastic Ocean* which you kind of intuitively know is not going to be a "good time," what do think most people would choose?

Why would you go see *A Plastic Ocean*? We opened it on the right day which was the weekend Donald Trump was inaugurated as President. It opened as the number one documentary in the U.S., Canada and the U.K.!

It also got picked up by Netflix. We had a theatrical release as well. It is now in 35 countries and in 25 languages. It has changed more than 100 laws, nationally and locally. The film is still having an impact. Most

recently it was on a world tour at U.S. Embassies around the world, courtesy of our State Department. It's really extraordinary to have something that is that impactful. I really did not expect it to have the impact it has had. It's really gratifying.

Are you still making documentaries?

Yes, I have one that we are selling now and another that is almost wrapped through post-production. After these, I need to slow myself down a bit because I'm launching MediaU, a new film school, and I'm focusing myself entirely on that.

You're the Founder and CEO of two media companies (MediaU, Entertainment Media Partners), Publisher and Editor of Culture Weekly, and an educator at UC Berkeley's Haas School of Business. How do you manage all of your passions without feeling burned out?

I never really get burned out. But I do get overwhelmed. I'll completely admit to getting overwhelmed on certain days when I look at the long list of things to do. Largely, I'm a "solopreneur." I don't have the big staff, the big team, or a giant office. Largely, each one of these projects runs off of my energy and then the energy of a select few people doing very specific tasks very well. All of them are really solopreneurs too and usually doing their own things in addition to collaborations with me.

So I do get overwhelmed, sometimes at the scale of tasks in these different areas. But I think I am pretty good at critical path and triage and knowing what has to be done before other things can happen. I'm also pretty good at prioritizing what needs to be done today and knowing what can wait until tomorrow. I think that helps me a lot.

How do you relax when you're not working?

Believe it or not, I watch TV and my very favorite channel is the Movie Trailer Channel! I just watch movie trailer after movie trailer. I can sit and watch 30 movie trailers in one go. I love that.

What advice would you give to the next generation of filmmakers/ producers who would like to get their start in the movie industry?

That whole question is really at the core of what we're doing at our new film school, MediaU. It is in collaboration with the University of California so when people enroll, they'll get University of California

BK FULTON AND NICHOLAS POWELL

credits. It is also in collaboration with Slamdance Film Festival. We're building an ecosystem where learners of all ages, all backgrounds and all levels of resources and experience can learn from each other, and from those who have come before and who might be a few steps ahead on the road ahead and can point out the pitfalls and the cul-de-sacs and the good things you should look out for.

The advice I'm going to give is the whole philosophy of MediaU, which is "do it by doing it." Don't make meetings, make movies. Don't make plans just go do it. Right now, you have in your hand the capacity to make a movie, edit it and upload it to the world. Whether it's a long movie or a short video, you can do it. You will learn so much by just doing it and you'll learn so much by just getting the mentoring advice of people who have come before you and also of your peers and other learners.

Sometimes people ask me what they should make, what's going to be commercial, what's going to really work. That question is a blind alley because if you're making something for other people just because you think it's going to work, you're probably wrong. If I have had success in my career, it is because I have opted to work with good people on projects I care about. Sometimes they've been commercial and sometimes they haven't been commercial, but I feel good about every one of them. I feel as though every one of them was a good use of my time.

Time is the only resource that is truly limited in our existence on this planet. There is always more money, there is always another something to do, but we only have the time that we have. So, make good use of your time by being only with good people and only working on things that are the best use of your energies.

PHOTO BY TOMMY
OCEANAK

Harry Lennix: Move Forward With Faith

PHOTOS BY
THEO & JULIET
PHOTOGRAPHY

"Those things that don't kill us make us stronger"

Harry Lennix

Harry Lennix has spent decades carving out a path for himself as an actor and filmmaker. It was on the South Side of Chicago where he learned the value of hard work and thrift. A student of Northwestern University, he majored in Art and Direction. After moving around a bit from coast to coast, his breakout role came in the early 90s when he starred in Robert Townsend's film *The Five Heartbeats* as Terrence "Dresser" Williams. Throughout his career, he has played supporting roles in major franchises like *The Matrix* (Commander Lock) and the DC Extended Universe (General Calvin Swanwick). His performances have drawn acclaim from critics and fans alike including a role in 2002, when Harry performed as the lead in a biopic film about the late great Adam Clayton Powell, Jr. entitled *Keep the Faith Baby.* Harry has also garnered acclaim on the smaller screen as Harold Cooper in NBC's *The Blacklist.*

As a director and visionary, Lennix has adapted some of the most celebrated works of literature and turned these classic works into something fresh and new. In 2012, he created an urban version of Shakespeare's *Henry IV* titled *H4* and in 2020, *Revival!* about the Gospel of John. His project, *Troubled Waters*, is a character study on a comedian who is offered a second chance at a career. Lennix's legacy will be cemented when the Lillian Marcie Center of the Performing Arts is built for those on the South Side of Chicago. Those on the South Side will be able to experience and enjoy the greatest art and entertainment without needing to travel across the country.

We had a chance to talk to Harry about his upbringing on the South Side of Chicago, his calling to support great black art, and his advice for young people who want to know what they need to do to become exceptional actors as well as respected for their talents.

Where did you grow up and what was it like growing up there?

I'm from the South Side of Chicago. It's a tough neighborhood but a great confluence of people—blue-collar workers, doctors of science, gangsters and hustlers, Muslims, and recent migrants from the South. It was a heady time when I was growing up. I was born in '64. I came up in the political social stew of the civil rights and black power movements, but also the syndicate of the Chicago gang system was in full effect. It was a pretty trippy time. I am very much a fabric of that community.

Who or what was your biggest inspiration growing up?

We had not far from us the great Muhammad Ali who was living maybe a couple of miles away. I would say Muhammad Ali was my biggest influence and then Jesse Jackson with Operation Push.

What was the most important lesson you learned in the early phases of your career?

Well, certainly with working, I knew thrift, working hard, and discipline. Growing up, the biggest lesson I took away is that people in my neighborhood were not lazy. They worked hard and the harder they worked, the better they did. In Chicago, our motto is "The City That Works."

That has always been my ethic. I studied to be a priest as a young man. I studied at Quigley Preparatory Seminary South and our motto there was ora et labora or "prayer and work." I don't feel like I can relax when I am not working. It is a very strange thing. In some ways, it is a curse. I think hard work is really the biggest lesson that I learned. Obviously, I can say trite things like honesty and trustworthiness and those things like pride and political involvement. But even if those things are absent, the diligent application of the lessons I observed was really that you just have to keep at it and it will eventually come to be.

> "I don't feel like I can relax when I am not working. It is a very strange thing. In some ways, it is a curse. I think hard work is really the biggest lesson that I learned."

At what point in your career did you begin to feel you had made it?

Well, I'll keep you posted. I never felt that I've made it. I've never been the flavor of the month in the industry, per se. People have said kind things but in no way do I feel like I'm a star. I'm still working on that.

My great mentor as an actor and my big brother so to speak—we just lost him this past year—is the great Anthony Chisholm. Whenever someone gave him a compliment he would just say, "I'm trying to get better, man." He was well into his 70s at that time and he meant it. And I do too. I am nowhere near where I want to be.

What would you consider to be your greatest achievement?

Not to be overly cute about it but I'm working on it now. That is to say, I am working on what I know will be my greatest achievement. My single, greatest achievement will be the Lillian Marcie Center of the Performing Arts and the founding of the African-American Museum of the Performing Arts which will populate it.

I am currently in the process of developing the center on the South Side of Chicago. I hope it will be the black version of the Lincoln Center for the Performing Arts. We will attract entertainers and artists from all over the country who will be able to bring to people in their own backyards, the greatest entertainment that the United States ever created. We are the inventors of the only original art forms, culturally and to some extent beyond, but there is no home for it on the South Side of Chicago where much of it was created. That will be my crowning achievement when we pull it off.

In recent years, you've mentioned that there is a lack of substance in black entertainment. Do you still feel that way? What needs to change?

There is still room for improvement, growth and development. I think that is only natural. Undeniably, we were not given the same resources, the same access, the same opportunities. We were not encouraged to create dimensioned, nuanced and subtlety within various art forms. The most popular entertainment—and that is not exclusive to black people—for us is broad and low brow humor. We are still digging around the dirt of our past, like slavery and so forth. Not that that's been exhausted but that's not where the beauty of our story lies.

Is that where you come in?

I like to think that's where I come in rather than complain about it. I've been pretty diligent these past 10 years creating content of my own. I have a movie on BET+ which is doing very well. I think it is their number two movie?

It is called *Troubled Waters*. I play a comedian by the name of Ron Waters, who has gotten his second chance at a career. Think of a Richard Pryor, Lenny Bruce kind of guy with demons and that sort of thing. It is set in the present day.

> "My single, greatest achievement will be the Lillian Marcie Center of the Performing Arts and the founding of the African-American Museum of the Performing Arts which will populate it."

Do you have any other projects you are working on that promote your mission?

I have a great calling, a vocation really, to create a form of entertainment for the faith community. I refer to it as "greater faith entertainment," which is giving the church audience something good to look at. There is a lot of content that has a church focus but doesn't have faith or any of the life lessons. I don't want to be the only one doing it, but I want to speak to the souls of our people through entertainment. I believe that is the greatest platform, and the greatest form of lessons is through spiritual literature. Dramatizing that is what I hope will be my bailiwick.

I have a movie called *Revival!* which is the Gospel of John put to gospel music. Mali Music plays Jesus Christ and we use well-known gospel songs that tell the story of what happened, but we have never seen the stories in gospel music applied to our own people. It's really the most

146   **BK FULTON AND NICHOLAS POWELL**

effective way to get to the hearts and minds of people rather than being faith-adjacent or "faithy."

Right. These stories should be authentic.

I really want to take these stories and bring them to life like many, many other people have done and very, very successfully. There is no reason that Moses should be played by Charlton Heston and not be played by someone who looks like us. I mean, Charlton Heston was great in the film. He was a Northwestern man like me of course, but why not someone who looked like Moses? I think that other people, other races have done what we should have been doing. That is to make our God look like us and there is nothing wrong with it and in fact

there is everything right about it. I am not trying to deny anybody else the ability to do it. Whitewashing the history of it has been the popular choice for a while. Go right ahead, but we need to be able to see ourselves up there too.

And honestly, if you could reengineer and go back to 1619—really go back to the enslaved people who were brought over here in 1501—the thing that you would take out would be giving people a God that does not reflect or respect their faith traditions. Giving black people a God that is the opposite of who they are can be a death blow. If you could take that and just correct that, we would be a lot further along. We often become what we think of ourselves, right?

"Giving black people a God that is the opposite of who they are can be a death blow. If you could take that and just correct that, we would be a lot further along. We often become what we think of ourselves, right?"

Zack Snyder released his director's cut of the *Justice League* on March 18th, 2021 on HBO Max. On social media, he revealed your character, General Calvin Swanwick, was a Martian Manhunter. How was it working with Snyder and were you surprised as much as fans were about the reveal?

Zack is an innovative, visionary director. You know he's taken a very popular form. He did this before with zombies, too, but today he has taken these superheroes who are really like Gods. Some of them are Gods—like Thor and what not—but he gives what would be catchy, popcorn drama, a very serious artistic treatment. It is almost like Andy Warhol when he took a soup can and turned it into art. I think Zack has a unique gift. I am very proud that I am going to be in his version of the *Justice League*. I was originally supposed to be in it, but due to script changes, I was left out. I have been restored, so I am very fond of Zack for that. He didn't have to do it for me. I consider him a friend and a colleague and I am very enthusiastic about his vision.

There can be a lot of distractions on your way to greatness.

People see the trappings of it. They see the fame, fortune, and accolades that go along with it and think that it is exciting. They think it is what it looks like, but it requires very hard work and breaking down your psychology and comfort zones and doing an exploration of yourself and other people. That's where the great actors really distinguish themselves. You can be a star and not have to worry about those things. However, if you actually want to be a great actor, you have to be honest and say that it is not only just the outer version of what people see, but this is something that I have to master. That is where the years of studying, application, copying, rewinding tape, and seeing something 50 times comes into play. Doing the ugly work, the fundamentals, that's where you separate the wheat from the shaft.

What advice do you have for young people who want to get into acting?

The Bible puts it in 2 Timothy (paraphrase): Study to show yourself approved by God. The workmen need not be ashamed, rightly dividing the word of truth. That's the right side I lead with.

Of course, the great alto sax player Cannonball Adderley said to imitate, integrate, and innovate. Imitate someone that you find compelling. Someone whose career you admire. Whose work you are fond of. If you master it, it will become integrated. It will get into your bones. It will get into your DNA so to speak, more or less naturally. At some point you will have gone from copying a style to it being a part of your being. If you master that, you can innovate; take that base and create a style and a method of your own.

How do you relax when you aren't working?

I play piano, but not terribly well. It is probably my greatest meditation along with swimming. A nice long swim in the ocean or pool is my best exercise. It sort of helps me meditate, breathe, and stretch. On Friday the 13th of December in 2001 or 2002, I had a near-death experience. I was swimming in the ocean in Mexico and I got caught up in an undertow and almost "bought the farm." I don't go swimming alone anymore. I almost didn't make it. God be praised that I did. Even now when I have the opportunity to swim in the ocean, I make myself do it to confront that fear and I realize whatever mistake I made that day was a human error. It was completely innocent on my part, but I learned a lesson: Those things that don't kill us, do make us stronger.

To learn more about Harry Lennix, follow him on Facebook, Instagram, and X.

Leon: An Actor's Actor

Leon's path changed before he realized it. In a way, film and theater served as a way for Leon to live out his ambitions and dreams. He grew up in Mount Vernon, New York, a suburb outside of The Bronx. His all-boys Catholic school, Mount Saint Michael Academy, was mostly Italian and Irish. When his sister's high school put on a rock and roll revival, Leon convinced his school to put on their own version. He played Chubby Checker and one of his friends played Elvis Presley. Leon choreographed the entire production. It was a hit. Upon further reflection, Leon recalls the times he snuck into the Wakefield Theater, where they showed Elvis Presley films. Elvis became the catalyst for Leon's acting ambitions. "He sings. He acts. He kisses pretty women," Leon jokes. "I thought, 'I could do that."

Growing up, Leon's dad placed no limits on his son's dreams. "My dad pushed me to be the best I could be," Leon says. "I remember him telling me, 'Son, don't worry about it. Just do your best. The cream will always rise to the top.'" His father didn't know his son would become an actor, but his advice has helped Leon deal with the uphill battle that comes with being a working actor. "In this business, 'no' is something you hear 9 out of 10 times and that's only if you are very successful," he explains. "So you have to have a lot of faith in yourself. You have to believe in yourself for other people to believe in you."

In the early years of Leon's career, his first agent, Miriam Baum, from Artists First and the agency's attorney sat him down to give him a serious chat about the industry. "He said there are thousands of actors across thousands of sound stages," Leon recalls. "When you are on screen it doesn't say $40,000 or $100,000 or $4 million on your forehead. All they will remember is your role and the story you told. If you do memorable work you will be remembered beyond your time."

"You have to believe in yourself for other people to believe in you."

His agent's advice turned out to be true. Role after role, people noticed Leon's charisma and artistry on screen, even some of Hollywood's

PHOTO BY OGATA

greats. Leon recalls the time he met Sidney Poitier at the California African American Museum (CAAM). Before Leon could introduce himself, Poitier referred to him by name. ''I said, 'Wow, I didn't know you knew who I was,''' Leon recalls. "Mr. Poitier said, 'You are a very good actor. You played my friend Little Richard and I loved it.''' This was coming from a man who Leon looked up to as an actor. Poitier's appreciation for Leon's acting reminded Leon of the importance and value of his work.

Leon's roles in *Cool Runnings, Above the Rim, The Five Heartbeats*, and *The Temptations* have made him an icon. However, Leon is hesitant to use "icon" to describe himself. "When words like that are used around me, I am very flattered because I don't see myself to be one," he says. He references the sleeper hit *The Five Heartbeats*. It was a commercial failure due to a lack of marketing but became a success on home

BK FULTON AND NICHOLAS POWELL

video over the years, especially in African-American households. "You have to realize as much as *The Five Heartbeats* has become instilled and ingrained in our people as our movie that we like to watch at family reunions and holidays, it was still not a broad success in white America. If a white girl saw *The Five Heartbeats*, it was because she went out with a brother; not like she saw it on her own," he laughs.

"If you can tell the story without my character, then I am usually not interested."

In the film – *A Day to Die* – Leon plays the villain Tyrone Pettis. It is in this role that Leon shines as a multi-layered character with a

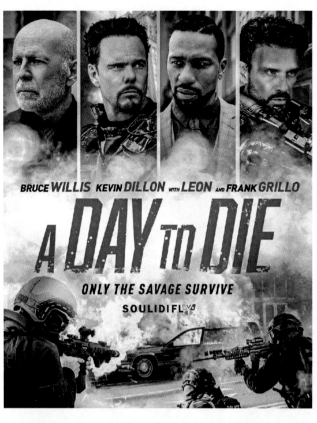

IN HIS LATEST FILM – A DAY TO DIE – LEON PLAYS THE VILLAIN TYRONE PETTIS.

redemption arc. Leon was initially drawn to the role because of its relationship to the plot of the film. "At some point in this movie, it is everyone against me," Leon explains. "And realistically, if I am not on screen in this movie, they are talking about me. The actor in you always wants to play these kinds of roles. You want to be the character that flips the plot on its head." Leon picks roles based on their importance to the film's plot and not necessarily for its size. "If you can tell the story without my character, then I am usually not interested," he says affirmably.

A Day to Die is Leon's first time working with director and writer Wes Miller. He appreciated Wes' openness to listening to his actors. "When you have a director who listens to you, then you feel free to be in your character and know that he is going to allow you to do things scripted or unscripted," Leon says. "Wes knows what he wants to do on screen, but he isn't close-minded."

Leon is an extremely versatile and talented entertainer even beyond the big screen. He is the lead singer of his band Leon & The Peoples. Just before COVID, they released their sophomore album, *Love Is A Beautiful Thing*, with two top 20 singles on Billboard's Hot Singles chart. His band couldn't tour due to COVID restrictions. Accordingly, he is planning some dates for a tour, which he hopes will bring more

BK FULTON AND NICHOLAS POWELL

positivity to the world. He also has several undisclosed producing and acting projects on his plate. "My belly is full, but I'm hungry," Leon says smiling.

As an actor's actor, Leon cautions young people who want to be serious actors to refrain from getting involved in the fickleness of social media. "You can have five minutes of fame on social media," he comments. "But five minutes is not a long career." He gives two pieces of advice: apply yourself to stand out from the competition and figure out what you have to offer the industry. "What you have to offer this business is your unique self," Leon says. "If you do not understand what you bring to the table, then you do not have anything to offer." This is essentially Leon's blueprint to success.

"You may know a better actor, a better singer, or even a better person than me," he says. "But there is no better Leon because I give you uniquely me."

To learn more about Leon, visit justleon.com and follow him on Facebook, Instagram, and X.

Ashish Manchanda:
Ambassador of Mumbai's Creative Arts

UJJLA AND
ASHISH
MANCHANDA

Ashish Manchanda believes that India's music scene has the power and merit to go global. As an esteemed mixing/recording engineer, producer and entrepreneur, Ashish has worked on over 150 Bollywood films and has been involved in the Indian music scene where he works with fresh, young talent. His work is coming full circle, having started from the U.S. where he worked on live and studio projects with American music veterans like Garth Brooks and James Taylor. Ashish graduated from Full Sail University, FL, in 1997 with flying colors. He was hand-picked by Michael Jackson's multi-Grammy-winning engineer/producer, Bruce Swedien, while still on campus and there began his "real world journey." While in the U.S., he established Flying Carpet Productions, a 360-degree production company that serves as a one-stop shop for artists to create and distribute their work. The production house extended into a training academy for young people in sound engineering and music production and Ashish's ambitions kept growing bigger. This gave birth to Boon Castle Media & Entertainment which not only encompasses Flying Carpet but includes allied services such as designing live music experiences, video productions, and music education. Extending roots back in the U.S. with Boon Castle offering these services there while the India story continues to grow, Ashish spoke with SoulVision Magazine to talk about Boon Castle, his career, and the future of India's music scene.

Where are you from and what was it like growing up there?

I was born in New Delhi, India, where I spent the early years of my life. I was about 8 when my family moved to the City of Pune which is known as the "Oxford of the East." My parents wanted to get away from the big, busy Delhi and start anew in Pune which was developing into an educational and industrial town. I have always considered them to be progressive and very supportive. My wonder years were in Pune and it's a lovely city. It is a city that offers a good work-life balance. It was very nice growing up in Pune.

Who or what was your biggest inspiration growing up?

I think my biggest inspiration has always been *Star Trek*. I think somewhere deep inside me, it resonated. I am an explorer. Through the show, I could go on a journey and discover strange and unexplored worlds. Imagine Christopher Columbus on steroids: get on a spaceship and explore the universe. What I learned from it, and it still stands today, is that you have to always be prepared to go through the unexpected hurdles or obstacles to get to your journey's purpose.

What was the most important lesson you learned in the early phases of your career?

I don't think it was very clear to me then, but I could feel what was coming. People at that time were seeking out a master of their craft or a role model/"mentor". I think even the word mentor was a fancy word back then and it was more about seeking a person who was an expert in a discipline that you're a fan of. It could be tennis or music or filmmaking. I think I was slowly gravitating towards that and that has become a very important factor in my life and also something I extend to others.

At what point in your career did you begin to feel you had made it?

I think "making it" is very relative. As a high school student, I was very interested in physics and math, so I was always exploring things like chaos theory and quantum mechanics and how you apply it to everyday life. I have had several milestones in my life. One of my "aha" moments was when I was a teenager. There was this young band at Loyola High School in Pune. This was the first time there was a band at the school. The youngest member was in the third grade and he was playing drums. He was making a hell of a noise, but he was the person who seemed to be having the most fun. I thought it looked like fun and I thought that I should give it a shot. So, in the 11th grade, I started to learn music and began to play the drums. I had never picked up an instrument before. I was a late bloomer. I thought I had made it.

To cut a long story short, when I got my first gig, I thought I had made it yet again. I had met my mentor, a very fine gentleman and a superb musician by the name of Ranjit Barot who was someone I respected immensely. He believed in me when I didn't even know what "believe" meant and where it could take you. So, I got a gig with him and was getting paid for it. We stayed in touch over the years and subsequently

BK FULTON AND NICHOLAS POWELL

have done a whole lot of super projects together. I am still closely associated with him and I am eternally indebted to him.

When I first met my future mentor Bruce Swedien, I thought I had made it. It was another major turning point in my life. So, I'm sitting here like, "How many times have I made it in my life? I'm still making it." So, I think it's relative. What would you consider to be your greatest achievement? When the people I have believed in have achieved their respective successes, that has been most gratifying! And it never ceases to amaze me what the power of belief in one another can do!

Do you feel Indian artists can have similar global success like those in the K-pop scene?

The Indian movie industry is super popular in India, and in its own way is all-encompassing. It is a self-sustained and successful ecosystem. The independent music industry in India has always acquired lesser priority simply by virtue of the tremendous success of the movie industry and lack of sustained effort for and by the independent music ecosystem— management, mentorship in all aspects, and creators. Having said that, the talent in India is world class whether it belongs to the movie industry or independent sector. It has the potential to crossover. You

will see both elements like what has happened with K-pop—a foreign language genre in an English territory that has a "Beatlemania" like reaction.

There are super talented youngsters and creators in India who are innovative, care about the arts, and are ready to showcase their talent to the world. It is only a matter of time when that crossover happens. Additionally, in India's music scene, there are English singing artists. And India is one of the largest English-speaking democracies. On YouTube, India is the largest consumer of English content, globally.
I predict that very soon we will see Indian artists picking up Grammys amongst other international accolades alongside global stars like Beyoncé, Adele, and Bruno Mars.

You created the Totem Pole music festival in 2016 to create a safe festival environment for youth in Mumbai. Why was this so important and how have the youth responded to the festival since its inception?

I think once you become a parent, you start to look at life a little differently. We have two teenage daughters now. The idea came from my lovely wife, Ujjla, who is also my business partner and a very talented and accomplished woman. We started brainstorming and thought about having a festival for youngsters, particularly those between the ages of 12-20 years old. Most music festivals are usually

BK FULTON AND NICHOLAS POWELL

alcohol and tobacco driven and hence outside the purview of young people below 21. Besides, such an environment is not the most favorable place to take young and impressionable kids. And then there are other festivals which are more "kid friendly" with activities for under 12 years of age. We understand that this demographic, 12-20-year-olds, are amongst the highest consumers of music. So, we created the Totem Pole music festival to promote a festival for young people and offer a safe environment for them to groove to music. Kids can also come in by themselves without their parents worrying about their safety. There are a lot of opportunities for youngsters of all disciplines to present themselves – through their music, art, etc. These new and unseasoned artists are what we call "state talent."

How do you relax when you are not working?

If I'm writing a song, working on a story, or strategizing the company's next move, I actually find that relaxing. When I would come home from "work," at a time when I used to mix a lot myself, I had a day full of satisfaction. At the end of the day, I would read some good stories or sit with loved ones and enjoy movies or TV series. I enjoy swimming, going for a walk, and most importantly spending quality time with my daughters.

I love to research and read about how I can be a better creator, innovator, and leader. Specifically, I have gotten into the various aspects of how to improve the business of our company. I'm very good at being a "vegetable" too. I can be in one place for hours, like a rock, and do nothing. At such times, I don't feel the "need" to run around and go up to the mountains or to the ocean. I can feel satisfied when I'm just sitting still.

What advice would you give to young music producers and/or entertainment business entrepreneurs trying to make it in the music/entertainment industry?

Just do it. I think we overthink and overcorrect way more than we should. We spend valuable time getting lost in unimportant things. Artists and creators have to just get out there and do it. They must put their art into the universe. It is very important to associate oneself with a team and people who believe in what you do. One has to have the ability to take in criticism and stick to your craft without fear of being rejected or criticized. I think making decisions and acting on them with timelines is a critical part of becoming an entrepreneur. Whether you're a CEO or a small business owner, you have to be prepared, have purpose, and be present. You have to have good people working with you. It's not something one can or I would recommend doing by themselves. The magic is in working together.

There are very few companies across the world today who have the courage and will invest in "state talent." We consider ourselves perhaps the only "state talent" investors in the creative arts.Totem Pole extends itself to a music conference too, where we have hosted Grammy-winning professionals amongst other stalwarts who share their valuable experience with young people. It is indeed fortunate for the youth to get this level of exposure at such a young age.

Tell us about Boon Castle and its purpose?

Boon Castle at its core is a platform for the creative arts, globally. The idea is to identify talent across the world; singers, songwriters, actors, writers, directors, etc. To offer the institutional support that young talent requires to carve out its true path is a gateway and backing that Boon Castle offers. We have been very fortunate to gain talent from Norway, Croatia, the U.S., and of course, India. We look at talent like it is sunshine. There is sunshine all over the planet. There is not a place on Earth that does not get sunshine. Everybody gets their share of sunshine. But what do you do with the sunshine? There are some people that have invented and designed solar panels. They harness the energy of the sun and make something useful for people, like electricity. So that is what talent is for us. Talent can be appreciated everywhere. But not everyone knows what to do with talent — for example, develop writers, dancers, and performers — and present the same to audiences. There are some countries and cities that have pioneered the creative arts better than others.

BK FULTON AND NICHOLAS POWELL

Our efforts are to create and present cutting-edge talent and content of tomorrow, today! Boon Castle provides all the services that help creative artists reach audiences globally. It was critically important for us to create a platform where we were responsible for end-to-end integration; from curation to distribution. It is a platform to break in fresh talent and tell new and old stories, from various cultures. The music and the visual medium are a great vessel to spread positivity and meaningful content. We cover the entire gamut from live entertainment to musicals, pop festivals, concerts, developing movies for movie theaters and new age media and of course music, where we started our journey. Boon Castle's main purpose is to truly make a difference by enriching people's lives. We have an opportunity to serve people. We really love this, so it doesn't feel like we're going to work. We are inspired and have decided to create something special.

THE BLUEPRINT PART TWO 163

Steve McKeever:
Still Grinding

"Tap into the power of the unknown."

Steve McKeever

Steve McKeever always knew he wanted to be a part of the music industry. It was arguably a wild idea, especially from a child who grew up in a family where his mom was an educator and his dad was a CPA. But the music spoke to him. It made the world clearer and just a little bit more balanced. He now owns the successful independent label, Hidden Beach, but the journey to success was no easy accomplishment.

Even when Steve did not know where he was headed, he had a dream and made the right connections in an industry that is constantly changing. The South Side of Chicago, Illinois, was a peculiar place for a young Steve McKeever. He grew up in Hyde Park, one of the few neighborhoods in Chicago that wasn't segregated. His family knew John Johnson. Muhammad Ali would walk the streets of his community. McKeever remembers riding his bike and passing Muhammad Ali's house. "It had an elevator in it way back then! The neighborhood was an unbelievably fertile ground for entrepreneurs, especially minorities. I got to see a lot of that," notes McKeever.

As a kid, he had very eclectic taste in music. His taste ranged from Earth, Wind & Fire to Stevie Wonder, Elton John, and Led Zeppelin. When he was down, music would lift him up. He never felt the need to get high off of substances in part because he enjoyed the feeling music gave him. He realized the power of music through his own spiritual experience with it. At a young age, he "assumed that the music business was one of the best businesses in the world and he wanted to be a part of it." McKeever repeatedly asked a local studio owner for an opportunity to work in his studio. The studio owner eventually gave him a job sweeping floors, but it brought him into the kind of environment he always wanted to be a part of. His interest was peaked even further.

His biggest inspiration came from an article he read in *Ebony Magazine* featuring entertainment attorney David Franklin, most known for representing Richard Pryor. "This guy's lifestyle and everything that he was doing in Atlanta was fascinating to me and I thought, wow, this is a way to appease my parents [by pursuing a law degree] and at the same time getting a toe into the business I wanted to be in." His plan was simple. He would become an entertainment attorney, learn the business, and then move out to California to work in music.

After receiving his law degree from Harvard University, he headed west to work for the elite full-service law firm, Irell & Manella, in their entertainment department. From there, he worked for the boutique law firm Mason Sloane & Gilbert. He was then recruited by his late mentor, Jeff Sydney, to work for PolyGram Records as the head of the business affairs department. Things changed for McKeever when Mr. Sydney set up a meeting with him to meet Dick Asher, the "head honcho" of PolyGram Records. Young McKeever was anxious to learn everything about the business. "Asher told me there was no limit to my aspirations if I genuinely wanted to help people." McKeever finished his time at PolyGram working in creative affairs. He brought in the late comedian, the iconic Robin Harris, and produced his first and only album, *Be-Be's Kids*.

McKeever was recruited next by Motown to work as the general manager and head of A&R. Two years later, his title had changed to executive vice president of talent and creative affairs. Here, he was able to work with the artists he would listen to as a young man from the South Side. "I was able to work with legends like Stevie [Wonder], Diana Ross and Lionel Richie—people I grew up admiring." McKeever was pivotal in guiding a new generation of artists who blended the new school with the old school, like Boyz II Men, Johnny Gill, and Shanice Wilson. Additionally, he signed artists like Queen Latifah and Norman Brown. During his stay at Motown, he also started Motown's most successful jazz imprint, MoJazz.

"I was able to work with legends like Stevie [Wonder], Diana Ross and Lionel Richie—people I grew up admiring."

Steve reflected on his age when all of this was happening. "When I got tapped for the Motown job I think I was 29 years old. When you think about it, that kind of opportunity is often wasted on a 29 year old. I look back now and I'm even more appreciative of how special it was to travel the world, meet people all over the globe, and work with unbelievable artists while developing creative projects. I'm sure I appreciated it then, but I was just working too much to take it all in."

He was on his way to start a record label with Sandy Gallin, who was Michael Jackson's manager; but after coming home from his honeymoon, spent touring the continent of Africa on safari, things started to fall apart. Doug Morris ended up getting fired from Warner

BK FULTON AND NICHOLAS POWELL

Bros. Music Group. This limited Steve's ability to start a new label as planned with Doug and Sandy. His very "plum contract" was no more. "It was a non-existent opportunity. I had just committed to buying a new house. I ignored all the voices in my head that were telling me to get out of the house and go find a job. I had a bunch of unsolicited offers to continue doing what I had been doing at other labels but I had decided that what I really wanted to do was run my own shop and do things a bit differently...." He felt that if he explored these offers, he would be enticed by the incentives offered and lose sight of his "entrepreneurial dream." He admits that he didn't know how to start a company from the ground up, so there was a moment when he was "... walking up the trails of the woods." But he knew what he wanted.

McKeever saw an opportunity that was not being taken advantage of in the music industry. He recalls seeing artists like Madonna recording music with Boyz II Men's producer Dallas Austin that was pretty left field of what the world was used to hearing from them. He knew songs like those would never be released at that time. One day he thought, "Wow, I have this vantage point that lets me hear this great stuff, but the public doesn't get a chance to hear it." Hidden Beach would be where artists could be free to experiment and make the records they really wanted to make without pushback from a major label. Success didn't take long when Hidden Beach's first release, Jill Scott's *Who Is Jill Scott? Words and Sounds Vol. 1*, was nominated for Best R&B Album at the 2001 Grammy Awards. It went on to be certified 2x platinum and is now considered to be one of the greatest albums of the 21st century. McKeever looked at everything Hidden Beach put out into the world as an experience. He would put a thank you note in every CD released to the public. In 2014, Hidden Beach Recordings became Hidden Beach Experiences. This transition made a lot of sense to Steve. Hidden Beach was already using tours and launch parties to drive music sales and to give their artists exposure. They just weren't capitalizing off of these experiences as a key part of the business. But things had to be put on hold for a moment when the unthinkable happened. Shortly after announcing the new brand, Steve and his family were involved in a major car accident. "It was one of those reset moments where I needed to reconsider my priorities. For the first 6 months of 2015, life was just making sure that everyone could be put back together again. I wanted to be sure my wife could walk and my kids were ok."

In spite of these setbacks, Steve and Hidden Beach continues to be a success. Steve released the eighth volume in Hidden Beach's critically

acclaimed *Unwrapped* series, in 2019. He says it's one of the best volumes they've done so far. "I probably have four albums of material spanning several years...." He describes the *Unwrapped* series as a "marriage between top jazz musicians playing covers of popular hip hop tunes." He takes a pause and begins to laugh when we ask if he feels like he has made it. "I don't think I've made it yet. I've definitely had benchmarks of success in regards to things that I strived for at any given time. When I recently found some of my essays that I wrote for law school, it's a little frightening to see how close I went down the path that I had espoused when I was young. I predicted that I would come out to California, get in the business and represent artists. I wanted to give artists representation. I thought that was what was needed."

When asked if there is any advice he would like to give to young entrepreneurs, he emphasized the power of the unknown. "A mentor of mine gave me advice that I pass on quite often.

BK FULTON AND NICHOLAS POWELL

If you can communicate all the steps that you need to take to get from point A to point B, then you're not dreaming big enough.

You know you're on the right path, in a lot of respects, when you have no idea of how you're going to get there. So a lot of dreams get stopped completely when someone says, 'Oh, I want to start a label or I want to do this or that, but I don't know how to do it or I don't know how to research it.' There are a thousand reasons why someone says they can't do something. The power of 'not knowing' is what I call it. We can use that uncertainty. If someone had told me that you're going to meet Stevie Wonder by calling his office everyday for five months and become great friends and have a 30 year relationship and have him sing at your wedding or be a godfather to your child, I would say you're out of your mind. Would I do that same approach now? I'm not sure. We are all born with so much innate ability and instinct. If you have a dream, you have to learn to tap the tremendous resources that everyone has inside them already. These internal resources can help us in achieving any dream we can imagine."

McKeever loves California. Very few places in the world afford such a wide range of activities that one can participate in. "I love travel but I am forever appreciative of living in California; so, I look out the window in awe on a daily basis. Just being around nature, especially the water, has always helped me to chill and relax. I paddle board and just a couple of years ago started surfing, which is the last thing I would have imagined doing, growing up in Chicago. I ski as well. Those are the things I do to relax."

When he looks back on his career and the future of his business, McKeever wants to continue grinding. "I'm forever appreciative of everything that I have—my family, the experiences in the industry, the wonderful things that I've been able to do and the people that I've worked with. I don't think I ever had that 'this is it' moment. I think it was Oscar Peterson that talked about the moment that you think you've made it, you should roll over and die."

Everyone has a
soul, except of them.

Linda Kenney Miller:
Strong Family Ties

The late Linda Kenney Miller's family history is filled with 20th-century innovators and disruptors. Through her stories, she hoped to lift up and inspire current and future generations. Her book, *Beacon on the Hill,* tells the story of her grandfather, John A. Kenney, M.D., a black physician who had a tremendous influence on opening the gates for African Americans in the medical profession. The Kenney family's success negates any harmful stereotypes used to make African Americans feel less than. They are the embodiment of excellence.

1912 POSTCARD

Linda grew up in Tuskegee, Alabama, during the civil rights era. "Tuskegee was an alternate reality to the pervasiveness of the segregation around us. It was like a little utopia in the middle of the chaos of Alabama." There were two sides of Tuskegee, Alabama: The black side called "Tuskegee Institute" and the white side, simply called, "Tuskegee."

According to Linda, they had all the tools needed to be a "separate, successful, independent and functioning society." Plumbers, electricians, and painters lived on the same street as doctors, lawyers and composers. They all worked together to make great contributions in their community. Linda admits she took for granted the array of talent in her small community. On her way to school, she would see the famous composer, William Dawson, and the "Father of Black Aviation," Chief Anderson, who once took Eleanor Roosevelt for a ride in the sky to prove blacks were just as capable of flying a plane as their white counterparts.

But things were different once leaving the racial haven of Tuskegee Institute and the community immediately surrounding it. Segregation was very real in the South.

We've all seen the pictures—"white-only" or "colored-only" signs above water fountains, restrooms, restaurants, and every part of public life. When she was 13, Linda and a few of her friends were sent up North by their parents to attend boarding school and to escape segregation. Her parents wanted her to be a part of an integrated educational experience. Reflecting on her childhood, Linda is grateful for everything she's learned. Those lessons influenced her work and life mission. "I know all too well the lifetime of emotional and psychological scars hate inflicts on its victims. That knowledge inspires me to write about it, talk about it and expose how it affects our lives today. It's my tribute to the ancestors who paved the way."

> "Tuskegee was an alternate reality to the pervasiveness of the segregation around us," she says. "It was like a little utopia in the middle of the chaos of Alabama."

Her father, Dr. Howard Kenney, was an early inspiration for Linda. "He was a revered doctor and director of the John A. Andrew Memorial Hospital, founded by his father (John Kenney) and Booker T. Washington in 1912." The hospital was a vital part of the school and community until 1967. He and his colleagues worked tirelessly to upgrade the health and longevity of the community. Some members of the community could only pay for their healthcare with chickens or eggs. It wasn't about money for Dr. Howard Kenney, but service to his community. "Like his father, service to his fellow man was his mission.

JOHN A. KENNEY, M.D

That was the mantra of so many of our black heroes growing up in that time: service to the race; service to human beings."

Ten boxes...that was the number of boxes her grandfather left behind after his passing in 1950. These boxes contained his autobiographical papers, papers that would end up being the source material for *Beacon on the Hill*. "He saved everything. There were even notes on napkins. Everyone in the family was going to do something with the boxes. My father and my uncle said they would do something with the boxes but over the years...ended up not doing anything with them." Linda took the boxes with her to Atlanta many years later. In between jobs, she made the decision to open them and see what she could find. "When I opened the boxes, I was stunned at the history my grandfather and grandmother were responsible for." She would write every day from sunrise to sunset. "It was an amazing project because I found letters and correspondence from some of the giants in 'negro medicine.'" She explains further, "There was correspondence from Dr. Daniel Hale

Williams, the 'Father of Open-Heart Surgery,' and Dr. Charles Drew, the developer of the first large blood bank. I also found correspondence from an ENT from Tennessee named Dr. C.V Roman. He was an amazing scholar, writer and orator. In the middle of a medical paper, he would wax philosophical on many topics affecting the black community and humanity in general."

Linda shared that she would love to someday write about Dr. James Arthur Kennedy and Cornelius Marion Battey. Dr. James Kennedy (her maternal grandfather) went from being a sleeping car porter to a pharmacist, then to a physician, ultimately becoming a general surgeon. He served in the 92nd Infantry Division in WWI. For his bravery, James was awarded the Distinguished Service Cross. The medal was placed on his uniform by General Pershing, himself. "During combat in France, Dr. Kennedy voluntarily moved his entire Aid Station from a protected dugout to an unprotected area nine miles from the front line and the Metz forts (German forts). In a partially wrecked shack with four of his

BK FULTON AND NICHOLAS POWELL

black trained assistants, he personally attended to and evacuated 360 severely gassed and wounded men of his Battalion! He worked 55 hours without food or water helping the wounded and wrapping and tagging those left on the battlefield for burial."

Cornelius Marion Battey, also known as C.M. Battey, was an influential photographer. Linda and her husband discovered almost 200 of his photographs while cleaning out her grandmother's attic. At the time, she didn't know who he was. They took the photographs back to Atlanta. A few years later, Linda visited the Tuskegee Archives to carry out research on Battey. They learned that Battey was one of Tuskegee's first photographers, initially doing independent photography for Booker T. Washington. After Mr. Washington passed away, President Moton of the Institute, hired him to be the official photographer for the school. "Battey started the first school of black photography with a grant from George Eastman (Eastman Kodak) at Tuskegee. He taught a number of esteemed photographers like P.H. Polk and photographers such as James Van Der Zee who followed him and mimicked his style and experimentation." He even captured the Grand Canyon in 1895 and 1896 – in all of its grandiosity. How he managed to do this perplexes Linda. With wonder, she shared, "How in the world did this man get to the Grand Canyon?" In those days transportation was difficult and dangerous for a black man. The nature and size of photographic equipment (required at that time) also would be problematic. Battey took portraits of some of the most influential men of his time, including Booker T. Washington, Frederick Douglass, W.E.B Dubois, and Paul Laurence Dunbar.

Linda's career as a writer started when she was over 50 years old. She quickly began to understand the impact and importance of words. "Early in my writing career, I realized how powerful the written word can be, especially in telling our history that has been too often overlooked," she explains. Linda saw how her words sparked the curiosity and creativity of her readers. Whether that meant telling stories of their own or unearthing the untold stories of African Americans throughout history, either way, it was inspirational to her. She was surprised her novel won four national book awards. "My effort to tell the story of my own family history, which I had only recently learned, was well received. The awards are humbling and the validation of my work means a lot."

When Linda is not working, she enjoys spending time with her family and traveling. "I have one granddaughter who is six years old who's teaching me as much as I'm teaching her. I love spending time with family, and traveling when I can is crucial." For those who would like to share their stories, she encourages them to just get started. She loves to pass on the little piece of advice her creative writing professor gave to her: "Don't die with that book inside of you." Even if you don't consider yourself a writer, get it out there. "It is very important that you tell your story even if you have to record it and have someone else write it. Whatever the mission is—put it down on paper so everyone can benefit from it."

> "My effort to tell the story of my own family history, which I had only recently learned, was well received. The awards are humbling and the validation of my work means a lot."

Her dream was to produce a documentary about John A. Kenney

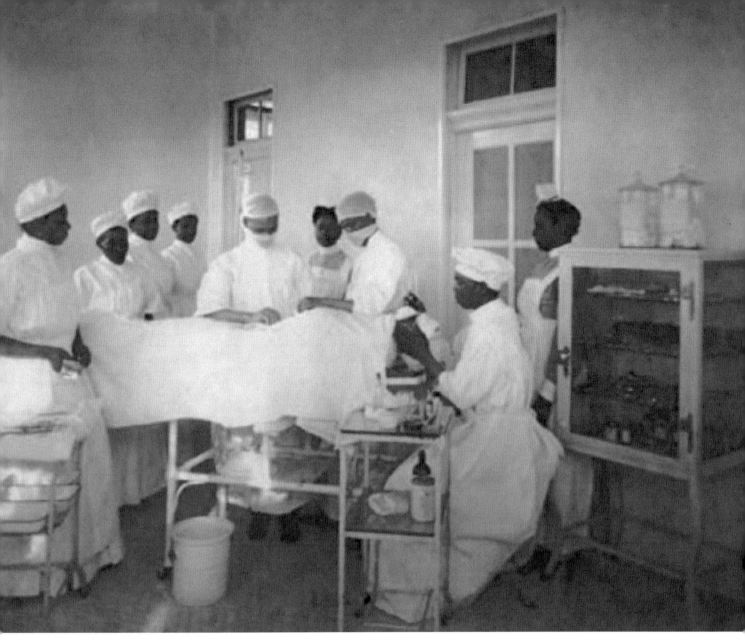

EARLY SURGERY FROM *BEACON ON THE HILL*

She also worked with Tuskegee University to make *Beacon on the Hill* required reading for incoming freshman. John A. Kenney's name is placed on the bioethics building at Tuskegee, yet very few students know his impact on the school and American society as a whole. Linda Kenney Miller does not want recognition or accolades for herself. She doesn't feel like she is quite finished with her mission. "I hope to feel like I've 'made it' when people of all ethnicities understand and respect the importance of our history and its integral role in making this country the most powerful in the world. My mission is to bring our history out of the darkness and into the light wherever I find it."

Vernā Myers:
Bringing Inclusion and Equity to Netflix

Vernā Myers, served as the Vice President of Inclusion Strategy at Netflix. She grew up on the west side of Baltimore, Maryland, during the wake of Martin Luther King Jr.'s assassination. It was a time of real social upheaval. "Baltimore burned like many other cities during that time, and I believe that instilled some kind of consciousness in me," Vernā explains. "I hoped to be what King had dreamed. I spent a lot of time in Baltimore until I was 18 and was the beneficiary of so many things that changed after King's assassination."

The federal government created Pell Grants and started to allow Black kids to attend schools with better funding and materials and advanced curriculums. They developed enrichment programs and other enhancements designed to give students a chance to succeed. "I got to go to schools outside of my neighborhood and that gave me a certain kind of access and social capital," she explains. "The new environments gave me an entrée into what was considered the 'A-course' of the time." During high school, Vernā applied to only one college because she didn't understand how the whole process worked. That school was Barnard College, Columbia University in New York City. She was going to be a writer, but as she began exploring her options (and was discouraged by her English professor who thought she was a B+ student), Vernā pivoted her focus to law.

She also wanted to have a skill that would allow her to make the world better and at the same time be financially self-sufficient. In her opinion at the time, it would be hard for a writer to make money. Accordingly, she enrolled in Harvard Law School. "I was going to change the world," she says. At Columbia, she was exposed to the history of her people. Cornel West was among the great minds to expand Vernā's worldview. While she was a student, Vernā was the leader of the Black Students Organization at Columbia University. As she learned more about her history, she became a little dismayed that she was not taught this history early on in life. Her parents instilled in her a go-getter mentality but did not talk much about the struggles of overcoming systemic and

individual racism and/or sexism. "I guess you don't want to depress your children, right?" Vernā says.

She mentions how detractors will use programs like affirmative action, which were created to close the gap between minorities and whites, to discredit the hard work, dedication, and sacrifice people of color had to make to have a chance at success. "It catches you a little flat-footed when you realize you're not just 'Vernā' but a 'category' to other people," she continues. "A category that they associate with being a little less capable even though you've made it to the same institution. They are not willing to cut you the slack." As she went through law school, she began to question who the legal system actually benefited. "I got to law school and started recognizing that the law is not how you change things, it's really how the people in power maintain their power. That was a very difficult lesson for me," she admits.

> "I got to law school and started recognizing that the law is not how you change things, it's really how the people in power maintain their power."

BK FULTON AND NICHOLAS POWELL

But she couldn't back out now. She was in debt and she needed to make something out of her degree. She landed a job at a predominately white law firm in Boston. She was the only black person there. "It was 1985 and I was breaking the color line," she comments. Then there was change. In the law sector, there was an awakening for more racial diversity. She was asked to be a representative for her law firm to a committee working on increasing the representation of people of color in law firms. This caught the attention of older black male lawyers who had gone on to start their own practices. They asked her to join them and she did. She was able to do more at the smaller black-owned firm than in the larger white one. "You're a cog in the wheel at most large firms and you're kind of learning a skill but for years you are not necessarily getting the whole picture, the opportunity to make major moves or feel any ownership," she explains. "I also realized I was working so hard just to make wealthy people (mostly white people) wealthier. That's fine for some folks, but it didn't seem worth it to me."

She recalls the small firm experience being very positive. The black partners invested in her success mentored her and gave her lots of opportunities to support black businesses and government initiatives to improve black neighborhoods. She was a mother and they were considerate and flexible with her schedule, but Vernā had a desire to be fully committed to motherhood and "...law is a demanding profession no matter what kind of clients you are serving or with whom you are practicing," she explains. She quit practicing law and started to look at new possibilities for herself. While taking care of her child, she began to read *Composing a Life,* by Mary Bateson. The book tells the story of how five well-known and successful women got to where they are. "The book gave me the permission to make my own choices because my life is a life no one has lived," Vernā says. "Knowing this, gave me so much freedom. That's what I started to do and that's what I've been doing ever since."

"You need to make choices that are right for you and be confident in where you are being led."

In the late 90s, Vernā founded The Vernā Myers Company (TVMC). The company helps organizations with their diversity and inclusion practices. Following her dream of changing the world, Vernā's diversity and inclusion work drives a global equity agenda. While Vernā believes she has made strides in her business, she will only see her work as complete when inclusion is the norm. "It is not inevitable yet," she says. "However, there are many people now pushing in the right direction."

As an author, Vernā finds a sense of accomplishment and success. She released her first book, *Moving Diversity Forward: How to Go from Well-Meaning to Well-Doing,* in 2012 and *What If I Say the Wrong Thing: 25 Habits for Culturally Effective People* in 2013. Her Ted Talk, *How to Overcome Biases? Walk Boldly Toward Them,* has been viewed more than 3 million times. TVMC has also created numerous learning courses. She says it feels good to have created resources out there in the world that can directly help others. Her business and books have rewarded Vernā with financial success, which she has used to help others. She recalls writing a "fat check" to a friend in need last year. It was a moment that felt different for Vernā. "It's a sign when you know that you can give someone that kind of blessing and not blink," she says. "It is nice to know that your gift is going to have a substantial impact on someone's life."

In January 2021, Netflix released their first-ever inclusion report. It was humbling for Vernā Myers to hear all the positive reactions to what we were doing. "I was like, 'What if it is true what people say? That my voice is really inspirational,'" she says. "I am almost always surprised when people say what you said changed my life." She says within and outside of corporate America, there are still real systemic issues. "We say that you can get a job if you work hard, but we know that just isn't true when we have substandard schools and underserved and troubled neighborhoods," she explains. "A person may say, 'I would love to work there too, but how in the hell am I supposed to get the experience or the understanding, or the education necessary if the opportunity is blocked systemically? Who do I know who can give me access?' Social capital isn't everything but it's a privilege that is not available to all, especially if they are first-generation in certain educational institutions or corporate workplaces."

In her position at Netflix, Vernā lead a team that made sure representation and inclusion are a priority in the entire employee life cycle (hiring, onboarding, development, promotion, compensation, etc.). "The vision of the Inclusion Strategy Team is to equip every employee at Netflix with the consciousness, competence, compassion, and courage needed to be a transformative force for inclusion and equity in all of the spaces that they inhabit," she explains.

Throughout her life, Vernā has achieved so much. However, it's the time when she stopped practicing law and felt uncertain about where she was headed that grounds her. "I said to myself, 'You know if anyone gets to live a life of meaning, it is the people who work hard and make good decisions," she says. "You need to make choices that are right for you and be confident in where you are being led. Yes, I have meandered a bit; but journeys aren't always linear. I was always pointing in the direction of MLK's dream — inclusion, equity, and justice — while having joy, spending time with my child, and getting a chance to experience new things that built on my best self. I am grateful." While there is still much work to be done, Vernā can say that she lives a great life of meaning. She is always thinking about how to make sure that all she has learned can help others to live their best lives.

> "Social capital isn't everything but it's a privilege that is not available to all, especially if they are first-generation in certain educational institutions or corporate workplaces."

To learn more about Vernā Myers and The Vernā Myers Company, visit vernamyers.com and follow them on Instagram and X.

Sophia A. Nelson
Challenges Us to Look Within

Sophia A. Nelson, Esq. remembers the day she stepped onto the 40,000-person campus of San Diego State University and saw a melting pot of cultures. She was a small-town girl from South Jersey (Camden County off exit 3) whose high school classmates were the same as her kindergarten class. "I only knew Black and white people growing up," Sophia says. "I had never met anybody who was Latino. I had never met anybody Asian. And that was pretty much my view of the world."

Sophia's mother, a nurse with an associate degree, was adamant about her eldest child and only daughter going to college. She wanted her to make the most of her time here on Earth. Neither of her parents attended a four-year college, but both had two-year Associate's degrees. Sophia was a military baby, born in Munich, Germany in 1967. Her father was stationed at Checkpoint Charlie, the most famous Berlin Wall crosspoint during the Cold War, and then resettled in South Jersey in 1968. Sophia's childhood household was turbulent. Her father was a heavy drinker and at times verbally, emotionally, and sometimes violently abusive towards his family. Sophia's mother wanted better for her. Her mother gave Sophia two options: be a doctor or be a lawyer. Sophia wanted to become a journalist, but that wasn't something her mother felt was a true profession with stability. So, she chose the law instead.

In many ways, Sophia is her mother's dreams manifested. "I think she was really clear that there was something better beyond the life we had growing up," Sophia says. "I think she was very clear that she wanted better for us and she never wanted me as her daughter to be stuck in a situation where I had to endure what she did as a wife and a mother. She wanted me to be in a position where I could make my own choices. I guess she succeeded in that."

Sophia's high school Latin teacher, Ms. Joan E. Daniels, a white woman, was a Freedom Rider in the 1960s. She was an important person in Sophia's life. After Sophia's guidance counselor discouraged her from pursuing law

SOPHIA WITH OPRAH AND FORMER FIRST LADY MICHELLE OBAMA AT THE MAYA ANGELOU FOREVER STAMP UNVEILING IN APRIL 2015.

because there weren't many Black female lawyers in the 1980s, Ms. Daniels told Sophia, "You know she's a jerk. Don't listen to her. You got the goods and you can go as far as you want to go." Ms. Daniels made it clear to Sophia that breaking out of her social class would be tough and the system was designed for that to be so. "She was very inspirational in sending a lot of us working-class kids to college who might have not otherwise gone," Sophia says.

As a Black woman now in her 50s, seeing Black women in the positions of Vice President and Supreme Court Justice is a dream come true. "These are my age cohorts," she says. As a little girl, Sophia said she wanted to be a Supreme Court Justice and while this is not something that happened, she feels good about what she has accomplished. "The day I felt most proud was the day I got sworn into the bar of the United States Supreme Court," she says. "Being sworn into that bar in those hallowed halls was just like when my first book got published."

As a young woman in her twenties, Sophia would sit in Barnes and Noble and the now-defunct B. Dalton and dream about the day she would see her name on the front cover of a book. Her first book, *Black Women Redefined: Dispelling Myths and Discovering Fulfillment in the Age of Michelle Obama*, went on to win a 2011 Best Non-Fiction Book Award and was Pulitzer nominated in Letters. "Getting my books published by major publishers and being paid to do what I love—that's

BK FULTON AND NICHOLAS POWELL

something most people only dream about," she says.

"Very few people get to have the success of walking into a bookstore and seeing their book on the bestseller list or being interviewed by major outlets and having their book literally change people's lives."

But when is one's success enough? This is something Sophia thinks about when looking at our current culture. "I think that you begin to feel like you have made it when you can take the trips you want, buy the home you want, buy the cars you want and not have to worry about money or, that you have to keep climbing and striving," she says. "I think that in our current culture having enough is very difficult because the usual trappings of success are rarely enough, and that is a problem. Because there needs to be a point when one has enough things and when you realize you've turned out to be a good human being. That should be the truest measure of our success."

SOPHIA'S MEMOIR BE THE ONE YOU NEED: 21 LIFE LESSONS LEARNED WHILE TAKING CARE OF EVERYONE BUT ME (SIMON & SHUSTER/ HCI BOOKS)

In 2022, Sophia released her fourth nonfiction book, a summer memoir *Be the One You Need: 21 Life Lessons Learned While Taking Care of Everyone But Me (Simon & Shuster/HCI Books).* After reading Oprah Winfrey and Dr. Bruce Perry's 2021 bestseller, *What Happened to You?*, which talks about how to deal with our past traumas in a more compassionate way, Sophia seized on the key themes in the book, which is to shift from asking "What is wrong with me" to instead asking "What happened to me?" A shift that changed Sophia's perspective on how to address her own life traumas.

Sophia began to ask herself this question during the pandemic when she contracted COVID twice. "The first time I got COVID was February 2020 and I almost died from it," she says. "When you face your mortality, it makes you ask some hard questions." Sophia had a parent who was home sick with a disability at the time. She was the sole caregiver for her mom for two years. In her memoir, Sophia tells the reader to ask themselves three questions she asked herself: *What do I want? What do I need? And how do I feel?* "Self-care is something that

SOPHIA POSES WITH ALPHA KAPPA ALPHA SORORITY (AKA) UNDERGRADUATES IN HAMPTON, VIRGINIA. SOPHIA IS PROUD TO CALL HERSELF AN AKA. MENTORING IS A HUGE PART OF SOPHIA'S SERVICE TO HER COMMUNITY. PHOTO COURTESY OF SOPHIA A. NELSON.

I really had to get a hold of because I was taking care of everybody else my whole life but me and that is something, as Black women, we are particularly conditioned to do," Sophia says. "That dates back to slavery and how much we had to endure and just push it down and keep going no matter the trauma or abuse we endured." Sophia cites the fact that nearly 3 million women dropped out of the workforce during the pandemic. "It was huge because women had to make a choice between do I stay home with my kids or work or do I try to do both? Something's got to give. I am only human. I can only do so much," she says.

As a Generation X Black woman, Sophia admires younger millennials and Generation Z's openness towards mental health and self-care. "We can look at them and say they are spoiled and coddled because they are always talking about mental health or what they want. Or, we can see that we didn't express our feelings or deal with our issues, which was also unhealthy," she says. "We had a lot of things that we should have talked about and worked through and we did not." Her generation, like the Baby Boomers before them, often let these issues fester into conflicts in marriages and in relationships, inadvertently hurting their children and loved ones along the way. "We have to find ways to talk about these issues by taking care of ourselves first and not having that be a bad thing or a negative thing. Because if I don't put my mask on first, then I can't save you." Sophia continues, "I can't be a good sibling, a good daughter or a good mother because if I die or if I'm not ok or have a breakdown, then what happens to everyone else? That is a discussion we need to have."

SOPHIA WITH HER MOTHER AND YOUNGEST NIECE, WHO IS ON ACTIVE DUTY IN THE UNITED STATES ARMY. PHOTO COURTESY OF SOPHIA A. NELSON.

Sophia is an opinion columnist who writes for major outlets such as *The Washington Post, USA Today, NBC* and is a contributing editor at *theGrio*. When it comes to being a columnist and on-air pundit for CNN and MSNBC who speaks on the political issues of our time, she consistently asks herself how she contributes to the public square. "I think that one of the challenges of our times is that opinion has become fact and has been deemed journalism," Sophia says. "And it is not. Journalism is when I am doing a story and I am looking at facts, timelines, and the players involved. I try to write objectively (as any of us can be) as human beings. We all have biases, but as a journalist, you have a code of ethics." As an opinion columnist, she must fight for her voice and firmly stand by what she has written. "I have to battle daily with my editors because sometimes my editor is very liberal and won't allow me to talk about certain issues," Sophia says. "And sometimes my editors are very conservative and don't want me to talk about other issues." Sophia pushes the envelope and doesn't hold back punches for anyone. "I don't just pick on one side or the other," Sophia says. "If it is wrong and I think it is wrong, then I am going to say it. If I think it is right, then I am going to say it." With each piece she writes, Sophia aims to inform and side with the opinions of the people. "I do my best to watch public opinion to see where the country is so that I can be someone who sheds light on unifying people and not dividing them."

To contribute to the political discourse effectively, Sophia created the *One America Podcast* based on the founding motto of America, E Pluribus Unum or "Out of Many, One". Sophia designed the *One America Podcast* as a platform where different viewpoints about American life—culture, sports, politics, and entertainment—can be shared freely. Sophia wants the actual discussion to be a staple of American life again. "I think the big failing of our country this time is that we do not want to have courageous conversations and we don't want to talk through things," she says. "We want to be offended at everything, to yell, we want to blame, we want to fight, and we want to be done and go to our respective corners. And that is breaking our country. If we don't watch ourselves, we are going to lose it."

Sophia is a woman who has built a global brand in the digital age. For Sophia, it isn't just about using the tools of our time. Building a brand is about your sensibility as a human being. "What kind of human being are you and how do you treat people? Do you have good manners? Do you say thank you? Are you a person of grace or are you out here saying all types of things that divide and hurt people?," she questions. She advises young people to be careful about the images they put out into the world. "Unfortunately, companies now look at your social media footprint. I don't know how I feel about that. I don't know if that is fair," she says thoughtfully. As a proud member of the Alpha Kappa Alpha sorority, Sophia mentors young women who have ambitious dreams. She advises them to value community over self in that other people matter just as you do. "If you want to be a professional and have some kind of professional success, you should be a light in the world, be inspirational," Sophia says. "Spotlight that you are somebody making a difference. Be somebody that is doing something that is moving the world. Move your community and country in a positive direction. Be an inspiration. That is what is going to build your brand and get you noticed and get you to where you want to go and be in life."

For someone like Sophia who is paid to talk and share her opinions on the topic of the day, it is important that she has time to turn off the switch. "The people who truly know and love me and who are in my ecosystem, know that I am actually not at all like the public persona," she says. "I cook up a storm. I love to garden. I am kind of quiet and don't necessarily say a whole lot when I am with those I love and trust. I like to chill out." To get away from it all, Sophia heads down to her house in Charleston on the beach. She plans to settle down south later in life where her paternal family roots began in the 1700s.

To ease her mind from the rush of the news cycle, Sophia plays her acoustic guitar and drinks wine with her friends and family. But socializing with friends and wine isn't just a relaxing pastime for Sophia, it's also a serious pursuit for Sophia. She is a serious wine connoisseur, maker, and seller. She partnered with Breaux Vineyards to create Wine for the Woman's Soul.

For Sophia, no amount of success can compare to being an aunt to two now grown women. "They are like my children. I just adore them beyond words," Sophia says. "The greatest of all my accomplishments is being an aunt to those two once little girls and having the privilege to see them grow up, have spent time with them and have poured into their lives– to watch them turn into two beautiful, smart, successful young women."

Writing is the thread that connects Sophia's life. It relaxes her. She is proud to call herself a writer and will write two more nonfiction books before getting into fiction writing. Her first two books, *Black Woman Redefined* and *The Woman Code*, have been optioned for television, and *E Pluribus ONE* is being looked at as a spin-off series about the founding fathers. But one of her biggest revelations is that she plans to run for office in the Commonwealth of Virginia. "I am not going to say what yet or when, but I will do it before I am 60. That gives me about six years and if I don't do it by then, then I won't," she says.

Sophia wants to run for office in the Commonwealth because she is worried about the state of our democracy. She is worried about the state of our discourse. She is also tired of how, at the statewide level, mostly white men are in charge. "Nothing against white men," she says. "I like white men. They can lead, sure, but I would like to see some people of color and some different people generationally. I would like to see more younger folks get involved in the political process. And I would like to be a spark and a light for these changes. I think I would be good at it and I think I have been preparing for this my whole life since high school when I came to Washington as a congressional intern, then as a U.S. Senate intern in college, and ultimately, as the first black female Republican Committee Counsel staff in the House of Representatives in the late 1990s."

Sophia reiterates her bid for public office, this time with a more declarative statement. "Within the next few years, I will make a decision that either I will do it or I won't, but I'm leaning heavily in the direction of doing it."

To learn more about Sophia A. Nelson, visit iamsophianelson. com and follow her on Instagram and X @iamsophianelson

PHOTO BY ANDREW SAMPLE

Case for Diversity

"Don't be afraid to step
into the unknown."

Chi-chi Nwanoku has been creating music ever since she discovered the piano at a neighbor's home when she was seven years old. Long before she became a member of the Order of the British Empire (OBE), the eldest child of an interracial union—her father, Nigerian, and her mother, Southern Irish—Chi-chi was raised to know her worth in the midst of racism and prejudice. After suffering from a knee injury as a 100-meter sprint runner, she decided to pursue a career in music. Chi-chi started to play the double bass at 18 and went on to study at the Royal Academy of Music. From there, she studied with Italian double bassist Franco Petracchi. Later, she co-founded the *Orchestra of the Age of Enlightenment* where she was the principal double bassist for over 30 years.

She eventually garnered international attention that led to accolade after accolade. Chi-chi was appointed MBE (Member of the Most Excellent Order of the British Empire) as part of the 2001 Queen's Birthday Honours and in 2017, the OBE (Officer of the Order of the British Empire) for her services in music. If that wasn't enough, the British Broadcasting Network, the BBC placed Chi-chi at number 9 on their 2018 Woman's Hour Women in Music Power List (Beyoncé was No.1).

After witnessing the lack of diversity in the orchestra, Chi-chi started the Chineke! Foundation. "Chineke" means wonderful, great creator in Igbo, the native language of the Igbo people in Nigeria. Chineke! is a place where black and ethnic minorities (BMEs) can shine and thrive as classical musicians. Chi-chi Nwanoku sat down with SoulVision Magazine to talk about her early career, the origins of the Chineke! Foundation, and what it means to be a black classical musician in England.

Where are you from and what was it like growing up there?

I was born in London. When I was thirteen months old and my brother was two months old, my father received a telegram from Nigeria to say that his mother was dying. My father was Nigerian, and my mother was Southern Irish. He bundled us all up and took us to Liverpool, which was one of the ports of the historical slave routes between West Africa and Europe. In those days, that was the cheapest way to get to Africa from England (Liverpool, North of England). We made the two-week crossing to get to my father's country. I spent the next two years living in Nigeria. I was fluent in Igbo by the time I was three. We returned to London, England, when I was three. From there, we moved to Kent near Canterbury.

The village we lived in and the school my four siblings and I went to was basically all white. We were the only black family in the area and I must say, we were very welcomed in our community. I know for a fact that it was because my father was an extraordinary man. Our father was a very calm and respectable person with an aura around him. If he walked into a room, people would naturally gravitate towards him, whether they knew him or not. He was like a magnet to children. On the other hand, our mother was a fiery Irish woman. She was like a lioness when it came to anyone messing with her kids or her husband.

Her family told her never to darken their doorstep again when she married my dad. If they wanted to behave like that, then that was their problem because she was very happy with him. We were raised by our parents to never doubt ourselves. Our parents had a tremendous amount of trust and belief in their five children; so how could we ever doubt ourselves? They raised five strong black kids, living in a completely white area. It might have been a coincidence that we had such a tolerant, welcoming environment. I don't know, but I think a lot of it was how my father conducted himself . . . and Mom too.

Do you remember any moments in your childhood where you and your family faced discrimination?

I think because we walked out and went to school without expecting to be rejected (it was our world just as much as anyone else's world), we were mostly shielded from discrimination in our immediate community. But when we went into Canterbury, we experienced some unpleasant confrontations. Some people would be horrible to our father. People

BK FULTON AND NICHOLAS POWELL

would stand in front of us and block our way and shout abuses at him. It was very distressing as a child, holding Dad's hand and seeing that.

One day when I was about seven years of age and my brother was about six years of age, we were walking through the city of Canterbury, doing errands. A white English woman was walking towards us with her children. She was determined to block our way, forcing us to stop. She said what was bothering her by unleashing a fury of racial slurs. My brother and I were frightened. It was a case of, "What can we do? Why is this happening?" Dad just squeezed our hands a little bit tighter, just to say "Don't worry. I got you. We are fine." He just stood there calmly until she finished. He then said three words to her: "I pity you." It destroyed her. That's what he was like. Through him, we learned to always go higher. He didn't get into fights with people. What was the point? He taught us to not degrade ourselves by going down to their level.

Sounds like your parents were huge influences growing up.

My parents were incredible. I remember when my father died at the age of 93, my mother just started to go downhill. They had been married for fifty years and for a black and white marriage in those days—they met in the mid 50s—what they had to go through was no one's joke. They had to fight to be a couple.

One of the most valuable lessons our mother taught us was to always be curious. She went to a school where students were made to recite Latin. It was part of the educational system in southern Ireland to recite Latin because of the tradition of Catholicism. Every day she would ask, "But what does it mean?" and the nuns would beat her. You weren't supposed to ask any questions. You were only supposed to do one thing: shut up and do as you were told. But every day she continued to put her hand up and ask the same question, "What does it mean?" and every single day, she took a beating. She never put her hand down until one day, they explained.

She encouraged all five of us to ask questions and to be curious. She believed a curious child is a healthy child and a curious child is an intelligent child. She wanted us to go out into the world and find out the truth for ourselves. She explained to us that we will be taught some things from our teachers, but it was important for us to ask questions. Our parents gave us the strength and confidence to know that there is nothing we cannot do, as long as we had a strong sense of morals and we knew what was right from wrong.

Was there a lesson that you learned early on that shaped you into the person you are today?

We know that we have to work twice as hard to get half as far and that is still a fact. It is not a fantasy or anything; it is the truth. The times in which we are living, you know, it wasn't like this a thousand years ago and I doubt it will be like this in a thousand years' time. We are called the "minorities," but there is nothing in biological science that proves that the white condition is any less constructed than the black condition. We are all the same. It is insane.

In the black community, no matter how good you are, you can still get badly treated. My siblings would often get arrested. My nephews and nieces have faced discrimination from the police, driving in their own cars. Unfortunately, we have to teach our children to keep their hands in full view. This is a consideration that no white kid has to learn for survival.

Did you have difficulty initially starting and finding musicians to play for the Chineke! Orchestra?

Yes. I had to literally find people myself. We don't have a network like you all have in the States. As black people, we have not had the same shared experience as African Americans do in the States. There was slavery here, but it was more of individual families owning one or a few black slaves each; there were not whole groups of slaves together. Because of this, it has taken longer for us to come together as a support network or a Black community. I had to work very hard to find all the players. Ed Vaizey, the previous Culture Minister in David Cameron's administration of the British government called me into Westminster to ask, "Why do we only see you regularly on the international concert platform?" I was the only black person in my orchestra. I didn't know if there was anyone else, seeing as I was the only black person in the *Orchestra of the Age of Enlightenment* where I had been a cofounder and the principal double bass for over 30 years.

The only black people I worked with were three opera singers and a violist. You can't start a full orchestra with three opera singers, a violist and a double bassist. Anyways, the more we discussed it, the more I thought — "Where is everyone?" I started to focus on the fact I could not possibly be the only active professional black classical instrumentalist in the UK, and people now ask me, "Well why didn't you think of this before? Why didn't you create Chineke! ten years ago?" I've thought the same but ten years ago, it would not have been well received. England was not ready for it. It was the right moment when I did do it. Even now as I remember asking myself, "Why I had not talked about it before with my colleagues?" The answer is that I did not know how my white colleagues felt about having a black person in the orchestra. I didn't know who to start the conversation with. It was easier for me to simply not have the conversation, so I didn't. That changed of course and now it seems to be a topic of conversation all the time!

Every great organization has a culture. Can you explain to us, the culture of the Chineke! Orchestra?

We have a certain philosophy with the orchestra. We have a Chineke! Junior Orchestra and the professional Chineke! Orchestra. It was important to have two orchestras from day one: the professional Chineke! Orchestra would change perceptions and create a pathway; the Chineke! Junior Orchestra would be the pipeline. Therefore right from the very beginning, I spoke with all the conservatories around the country because they all have junior departments. I spoke with teachers and then went further and called parents and other initiatives that had been created to support black/ethnic minority children in music. I was able to bring children from all over the country together. You are familiar with one of them because you saw him play the cello at the royal wedding of Prince Henry and Megan Markle. We're very proud of Sheku.

The talent and ability is abundant in the Chineke! Junior Orchestra. Their inaugural concert was earlier on the same day as the professionals' first concert, and the same camaraderie and feeling took place amongst them as with the professionals—they developed an imediate sense of community and belonging when we walked into the same room surrounded by people who looked like us. This was a completely new experience in an orchestra in the UK. If you're a black classical trained musical child in Canterbury, or Ipswich or Edinburgh, you will probably be the only one. The first couple of days of rehearsals were kind of organized chaos because we all had to get used to playing together. But seeing as we were joined with a collective philosophy of spearheading an important initiative of "change and diversity" in the industry, we were very soon unified. I remember at the end of the first day of rehearsal, nobody wanted to go home. For the first time, everyone felt as though they truly belonged; for the first time, no one was the odd one out.

Even three and a half years later, it is like that after a concert. Members of the Chineke! Orchestra will be the last people to leave the foyer, bar or other social areas of the Southbank Centre, because we are all celebrating with our guests, friends and audiences. We don't want to leave each other, because we get so much from just being in each other's company. There is also no time or place for ego; we have too many lives to lift up. It doesn't matter how big you are, be you a world-class soloist or someone just leaving music college, everyone has a responsibility to pull the other up. In every Chineke!Junior project, there will be a Chineke! professional mentoring every section of the orchestra and overseeing the work. Typically there would be around ten professional Chineke! mentors dotted throughout the Chineke! Junior Orchestra. So, from day one, the juniors have someone that they can relate to because they can see that there is someone who looks like them that has professional status. Through seeing their mentor's success, they believe they can do the same. It's family and we have a responsibility to keep lifting each other.

I never had a mentor or a teacher that looked like me. The only person that was like that for me was my father. He sang in the church. He had a good ear. He loved music. My mother would also play the harmonica with her family in Ireland. There was music all around us, but I was the only one who actually studied music. I was meant to. It was my vocation.

What advice would you give to young black classically-trained musicians who would like to have a career in classical music?

If you think you've done enough practice, then do some more. Never give up. A "that will do" approach is not going to work; you must be prepared to go that extra step. It will be like this for the unseeable future. We are hoping to have an unbiased approach for auditions, for "blind auditions," behind screens. If it really only matters how well a person plays, why should it matter what you look like? If you're the best player and happen to be black, you've got a better chance to win the audition if there is a screen and without being seen. All of my black American colleagues who have won an actual position in the orchestra have won them behind screens. All too often when auditioned without screens, black people get eliminated. Some orchestras have called the reasons 'unconscious bias', but no, it must be called out for what it is: bias and discrimination. I maintain there is no such thing as unconscious bias. It's just bias, end of story. Make sure you give no one the option to turn you down due to your ability. With that being said, it goes without saying, expect to work very hard. As my mother used to tell me, hard work isn't easy.

HUGH PARTICIPATING IN MARCH IN COLUMBIA, SC, IN 2000 TO PROTEST THE CONFEDERATE FLAG FLYING AT THE STATE CAPITOL. PHOTO FROM NATIONAL URBAN LEAGUE (NUL) ARCHIVES.

"Always know what you are capable of."

— Hugh B. Price

The Civil Rights Movement would not have been a success without the sacrifices of the era's young people. After college, many of the "talented tenth" took their skills to help directly with the movement. This meant helping people register to vote, offering legal counsel, and organizing protests. Hugh Price is one of those figures. When he graduated from Amherst College, Hugh was a marshal at the March on Washington in 1963. After seeing the huge crowd, he was inspired to give up personal aspirations and live his life for the betterment of his community. He would eventually become the president and CEO of the National Urban League. Throughout his career, Hugh has championed civil rights and has influenced a young and courageous generation of activists. Hugh Price discussed with us in great detail his life story of unflinching service and exceptional sacrifice.

Where are you from and what was it like growing up there?

I was born and raised in Washington, D.C. My home town was a rigidly segregated town when I was a child. It was below the Mason-Dixon Line. All aspects of life were segregated—schools, movie theaters, restaurants, you name it. The fabled U Street was "our" downtown. You could buy clothes at the big department stores in the white people's downtown, but you had to try them on elsewhere.

I grew up in the orbit of Howard University. Both of my parents were graduates of Howard. Virtually, all of their friends were Howard graduates who had stayed in D.C. The ethos of Howard permeated our community. That ethos led to progress and success. We were prepared to go through the barriers of racism and segregation and not let those barriers mess with our heads and affect us.

Many of our neighbors were quite illustrious people in the annals of the African-American experience. Charles Hamilton Houston was a neighbor and friend of my parents. He was the architect of the successful school desegregation lawsuits. Also, on our street was the famous sports reporter, Arthur "Art" Carter, as well as the Hall of Fame sports reporter, Sam Lacy, who crusaded for the integration of Major League Baseball. Right up the street from our home on New Hampshire was Todd Duncan, the opera singer who performed as Porgy in *Porgy and Bess*. These were my parents' contemporaries. Culturally, it was a very rich neighborhood.

Who was your biggest inspiration growing up?

The most proximate people you can imagine—my father, my mother, and my brother.

My father was a very self-reliant person. His mother was widowed when my dad was three. She was trained as a school teacher, but she couldn't get a job in D.C. She worked as a maid for wealthy white women. As a child, my father lived with his first cousin. Dad was a pioneer when he became the second African-American physician to be certified by the American Board of Urology, the major certifying institution. He became one of the nation's foremost authorities on venereal diseases. Ironically, the first African-American to be certified was my father's first cousin.

His stepfather did not particularly believe in higher education. In order to pay his way through Howard Medical School, my dad would go to classes during the day and then he ran elevators in the apartment buildings of wealthy white people at night. He would study in between the runs of the elevator.

I learned the virtues of service and hard work from my dad. He had his own medical practice. He taught part-time at Howard Medical School as did many other graduates who stayed in the Washington, D.C. area. He also worked in the free clinics at Freedmen's Hospital. My dad would often be out of the house and at the operating table at 7 a.m. and wouldn't get back home until 9 p.m. Through all of this, he published articles about some of the major cases he had. I don't know where he found the time and energy.

He was a great provider. Even though he didn't make a lot of money, there were never conversations about finances. His patients were the working class. Sometimes he got paid with Smithfield hams at Christmas time.

He taught me the centrality of family. If there was ever a ceremony at school where my brother or I got some kind of award, my dad was always in the audience. Even though he was a reserved man, he had this unrestrained cheer when we walked across the stage. We always knew where he was because we could hear him.

He never worried about celebrity or social life. My parents were very much peas in a pod. He loved nature. He became a disciple of Henry David Thoreau. He collected first editions of his work. He and my mother visited Walden Pond. Nature was an outlet from all of the stress of his medical practice. He never aspired to be anybody other than himself. The whole idea of knowing who you are, being comfortable in your own skin and not worrying about what other people think about you, had a huge impression on me.

My mother was also an enormous influence on my life. My father was always focused on the medical practice. He was a

HUGH WITH HIS MOTHER, CHARLOTTE PRICE.

traditionalist. He didn't believe wives should work so my mother "got even" by volunteering 40-50 hours a week. She was very active with the League of Women Voters and campaigned to bring voting rights to Washington, D.C. Along with a number of her friends, including many in the neighborhood, she was very active in supporting the desegregation of Washington schools. I learned by looking at the footnotes of Charles Hamilton Houston's biography, that my parents were part of the group of neighbors and friends who gave financial support for the lawsuits Houston filed to bring down school segregation. She was determined to live in as much of an integrated world as she possibly could. For example, we were members of the All Souls Unitarian Church in Washington where people of all walks of life were welcomed.

I can't remember who organized it, but diplomats from all over the world would visit Washington for conferences and my parents would have them over for dinner. I would never forget sitting in our house with folks from Japan and Sweden. We learned from them and they learned from us.

My brother, who is five years older than me, is very smart and ambitious. However, he struggled in school because of his dyslexia.

As an undergraduate, he loved socializing. He would be on probation one semester and the Dean's List the next. It didn't matter, he always wanted to party.

It took him about seven years to get through college but when he graduated from Howard, he wanted to go to medical school. Some folks doubted whether or not he could handle it—including my father. All of the reading that goes with the early years of medical school is really tough, but he powered through it. When he got to the more practical, second two years of medical school, he lifted up and went into orbit academically. By the time he graduated, he had Georgetown University Hospital and Medical School after him to do his follow up studies and even become a faculty member.

My brother was always encouraging me. If there was ever a major challenge and I was deciding whether or not to make a run at it, he would always tell me to just go for it. The only thing they can say is "no."

BK FULTON AND NICHOLAS POWELL

What was the single most important lesson that helped shape you as you began the early phases of your career?

I was most impacted by my mother's work in the civil and voting rights space. She was active and was determined to do what she could do to help promote integration, school quality, and voting rights. She even testified before a congressional committee for higher minimum wages. She and other patriots were always trying to advance the rights of our people.

I observed this when I was little. It carried all the way to my teenage years. The summer that I got out of college in 1963, I participated as a marshal in the March on Washington. Both my mother and my future mother-in-law were at the march. There was a point of crystallization for me when I was in the midst of the crowd of over 250,000 people. I wanted to be of service and help black people get ahead and surmount the obstacles we faced in a segregated world.

Take us through the journey of your career.

I was fortunate to do well in school. Therefore, I was blessed to get into a terrific college, Amherst College, and into a terrific law school, Yale. I was around brilliant classmates and professors. I will not say that I was a scholar. I wanted to take the courses and do well. I wanted to play intercollegiate sports. I belonged to a fraternity. I met the coed who would become my wife of over 55 years. I tried to live college life to the fullest without flunking out.

Because I was able to get a job at the VA as a typist, I earned a pretty decent income during the summers. From 1959-1963, tuition plus room and board at Amherst College cost about $2500 a year. I earned $1200 a summer as a clerk typist. I made $100 a week. I was able to buy a brand-new Volkswagen Beetle for $1600 cash with my summer earnings. My parents were, fortunately, paying the cost of college. After having my car on campus my sophomore year, my grades slumped, and I got a letter from my father. In those days, your grades went home with the tuition bill. We were not liberated adults, yet. The letter read: "Dear Son, I just got your grades. I see you are having a good time. We have a two-car garage. One of the bays is empty. Love Dad." In other words, you may think you own that car but if the grades don't come up the next marking period, the car is coming home. I saluted and got myself straight. My grades went up. I was keeping my car.

At Yale, I encountered not only brilliant professors, but also people like Marian Wright Edelman and Eleanor Holmes Norton. They were two

HUGH MINGLING WITH THE CHILDREN AT THE "DOING THE RIGHT THING" RALLY ORGANIZED BY THE LOS ANGELES URBAN LEAGUE AS PART OF THE NATIONAL URBAN LEAGUE'S CAMPAIGN FOR AFRICAN-AMERICAN ACHIEVEMENT. PHOTO PROVIDED BY THE LA URBAN LEAGUE

or three years ahead of me. They were already legends. They went down South to help with voter registration and participate in the greater movement. This reinforced the impact of the March on Washington on me.

The 60s was a time when young folks who really wanted to be of service were going straight into the Civil Rights Movement. Many of them placed their lives on the line in the Deep South. I decided I wanted to be active up North and got deeply involved in the Anti-Poverty Movement. After law school I became a legal services lawyer in New Haven, representing poor people.

I came along in a time when people would take chances on folks who were bright, hard-working, and curious. They didn't necessarily require that you possess years of deep, specific experience in the field. They wanted to see what you were capable of. In 1967, New Haven had riots. The Black Coalition of New Haven was created to try to put the pieces

BK FULTON AND NICHOLAS POWELL

of the city back together. I was hired as the first executive director of the Black Coalition at the age of 26.

There I was in the middle of it all. I was their face and their ultimate advocate. I served on the defacto staff as director of the Hill-Dwight Citizens Commission on Police Community Relations. We dealt with groups like the Panthers. We dealt with the fact our organization was infiltrated by the police and we were wiretapped. It was an incredible professional growth experience.

In 1977, I got a call from out of the blue by a man named Max Frankel who was the editor of the editorial page at the *New York Times.* He told me that I was under consideration for appointment to the Editorial Board of the *New York Times.* And I said, "What? Is this a group you get together for lunch a couple of times a year to say how you are doing?" He said, "No, you write editorials for the *New York Times.*" I said, "Well I haven't written for anybody to speak of, so why me?" He said, "Well, you've written, but just not for newspapers. We would like for you to come down for an interview." I went down for the interview and wrote several sample editorials. They hired me. I did that for about five and a half years.

I then was approached by the head of the public television station in New York City, WNET Thirteen. They were looking for somebody to become the senior vice-president in charge of the Metropolitan division that ran the program schedule and on-air fundraising. I didn't know anything about television. In fact, in that pre-cable era, the signal was so weak outside the city, it was hard to watch. I was appointed head of the Metropolitan division and then after a year and a half, they made me the head of the entire national production division. All of a sudden, I was running the division of the WNET Thirteen, which was probably the largest production operation in all of public television.

I was running the division that produces *Great Performances and Nature.* Our terrific producers created new series like *American Masters and The Mind.* I was overseeing all of these amazing world-class productions and traveling around the world—going to Vienna and sitting on the beaches of Cannes doing co-production deals.

I would just look and say, what am I doing here? But the joke wasn't on me. I was the first African-American running the largest production operation in all of public television. I made a run for the presidency of the station in 1987 but wasn't successful. I didn't want to stay. I wasn't happy about how the search was handled. I thought they gave the internal candidates, including me, short shrift.

About that time a good friend of mine was appointed to be the president of the Rockefeller Foundation. I wrote him a letter congratulating him. I went on to suggest to him some things that I thought they might be interested in. He got the message that I was available and invited me to join the foundation as vice president. I got to originate a lot of new initiatives like the National Guard Youth Challenge Program which gives school dropouts a second chance.

Then, the National Urban League opportunity materialized in 1994. It was something that I had dreamed about my entire life. I had come of age professionally with people like Whitney Young, Vernon Jordan, John Jacob, Franklin Thomas, Roy Wilkins, and Clifton Wharton as my role models. These were brilliant, devoted professionals who were deeply committed to the cause and the advancement of black people. The National Urban League was then and now, a revered and indispensable organization that has been serving black people since 1910. It was truly a privilege to be considered, recruited and appointed to that position. That was a dream come true.

When I was young, I set out to have as much fun as I could professionally as long as I could get away with it financially. And by fun, I mean I wanted to pursue work that was fulfilling, of service and made me feel like I was making a contribution. I got married in the middle of my first year of law school. Our first child arrived in the middle of my second year. I had a family. I knew that whatever I was doing professionally, I had to provide for my family just like my father did for his. This balance defined much of my life. It's funny. When I didn't get the job as president and CEO of WNET Thirteen in New York, it kind of put me in a funk. I was sort of moping around the kitchen and our eldest daughter, who is very spiritual, came to me and said, "Don't worry about getting that job. You're being saved for something more important." She said that to me in 1987. I didn't know what she was talking about, but all of a sudden, the clouds cleared, and I started the job hunt. That's when the Rockefeller Foundation position happened. When I was appointed President and CEO of the National Urban League seven years later, the something that my daughter had foreseen had materialized.

Were you satisfied with the progress of the National Urban League's agenda during your tenure as CEO?

Yes, on a number of levels. One of my main objectives was building on the legacy, platform and contributions of others. The Urban League is almost 110 years old. We've only had eight CEOs in the organization's

HUGH'S MOTHER, CHARLOTTE PRICE PARTICIPATING WITH THE LEAGUE OF WOMEN VOTERS IN A VOTING RIGHTS RALLY IN THE 1950S IN WASHINGTON, D.C. SHE'S WEARING THE CHECK COAT AND SEATED IN THE BUCKBOARD SEAT. PHOTO APPEARED IN THE WASHINGTON STAR.

entire history. Each CEO builds on the legacy and foundation of the previous CEO.

I used to walk in the lobby of our headquarters every morning and say to myself, "We must build on what John Jacob, Vernon Jordan, Whitney Young, and Lester Granger created." We do not want, in any generation, to mess this up or weaken it. We have an obligation to build and evolve so that this institution can continue to be of service and has all of the skills and assets that it needs to be relevant. We must continue to be a leader and servant into the next century. That was what I had tried to do organizationally. I had no clue how it would happen. I just knew it had to happen.

We wanted to fortify our board and staff. We wanted to focus the organization a bit more programmatically. We wanted to create a very strong policy and research presence in Washington. We wanted to grow our endowment. We did what we needed to do to strengthen the affiliate movement. I used to say to folks in our organization, "The graveyards are filled with the carcasses and coffins of fabled nonprofit organizations and for-profit corporations that did not evolve." They

HUGH ADDRESSING THE CADETS IN THE PUERTO RICAN UNIT OF THE NATIONAL GUARD YOUTH CHALLENGE PROGRAM, WHICH HE ORIGINATED. PHOTO PROVIDED BY THE PUERTO RICAN NATIONAL GUARD.

did not assess where they stood in the grand scheme of things and therefore fell by the wayside. Our job was to make sure that did not happen to the Urban League. It didn't and still hasn't. The League under its terrific current president, Marc Morial, is stronger than ever. We wanted to concentrate heavily on education and that was my shtick. We believed achievement mattered and encouraged parents to be deeply involved in their children's education. We were a major player in education policy.

We were also very proud of the work we did in fighting against police brutality and unwarranted use of deadly force. This was long before Black Lives Matter. The League played an important role in getting President Clinton to pay attention to this issue with our press conferences. Leaders of our affiliates would come to Washington with the parents of young people who had just gotten shot by the police. We complemented the street protests, particularly of Al Sharpton and others, by working the policy front. I know we made a difference.

We were also involved in the battles to preserve and protect the principles underlying affirmative action. The horrific book called *The Bell Curve* came out, questioning the intellectual capacity of

BK FULTON AND NICHOLAS POWELL

African-Americans. We lit out after that book. We said this is scurrilous research and racist. We held a major press event with Stephen Jay Gould and Edmund Gordon and a number of other experts to attack the fundamental premises of the book. I feel very gratified about the contributions the League has made.

At what point in your career did you begin to feel you had made it?

Like I said earlier, I wanted to have as much fun as I could professionally, as long as I could get away with it financially. I was never bored a day in my life in any job that I held.

I moved around a lot, so I didn't have the chance to get bored. I was a professional explorer, but as someone who was committed to service. This defined my entire career.

I "made it" when I retired and had gotten away with it financially. I capped my career with the privilege of teaching at Princeton University. I worked with a remarkable generation of brilliant young people. The entire journey has been unexpected and thrilling.

My wife and I will be married for 56 years in December. We have three daughters and two sons-in-law who we love dearly. I worked very hard, but I also worked hard at being a loving and supportive husband and family man. I was all in career-wise, but I did not allow that to ruin the personal aspects of my life. The primacy of family which my parents instilled in me had an impact; it still does.

There were some disappointments. It would have been fun to be the first African-American president of the largest public television station in the nation. It took a while to get over it, but I was being saved for something more important and I can't imagine a more fulfilling job than being president and CEO of the National Urban League.

What projects are you currently working on? How do you relax?

I do not have any new projects on the horizon. I recently finished two major projects. I published a memoir titled *This African-American Life* in 2017 and have done dozens of events over the last couple of years to promote it. I served on The National Commission on Social, Emotional and Academic Development. It was a remarkable effort. They issued their big final report in January of 2019.

I read a lot. I read material that is very intense then I have to relax my brain, so I read something less heavy. For example, I went from reading a fabulous Frederick Douglass biography to reading the biography of Ernie Banks, a great Chicago Cubs shortstop. The next book I will pick up after that is a book called, *Putin's World.* I go in and out of relaxing the brain and ramping it up again.

I'm trying to be true to the fact that my wife and I are retired. I've entered the zone where if I get asked to do stuff, I'm really selective. My wife and I spend a lot of time doing activities together. Despite the expense of living in the New York City area, there is always something fascinating to do. My wife is involved with the Neuberger Museum. We recently went on an art trek to a place called The Brant in the Lower East Side. The Brant has one of the most remarkable collections of paintings by Jean-Michel Basquiat anywhere in the world including one that sold for $150 million. I stood two to three feet from it. We have a place up in the Berkshires, so we love going up there and relaxing. When we get the opportunity, we love visiting our sprawling family which is spread out all over the country.

What advice would you give to the next generation of activists who would like to make real change in their communities?

It is critically important to be grounded and to understand the way communities, people and organizations work. You miss a lot if you only fly at a very high altitude and assume that you know all of the answers. It is very important to understand the nature and frailties of people and institutions. You can proclaim that this should happen or that should happen, but often times it doesn't. You won't be able to change anything if you don't understand the vagaries of reality.

Understand that change can happen rather quickly and at times, rather slowly, but that doesn't mean you shouldn't organize and prepare. You want to be ready for it. Then, when the window of opportunity opens, you can climb through.

You look at how long it is taking to solve issues surrounding climate change and the resistance that we still must overcome. You look

BK FULTON AND NICHOLAS POWELL

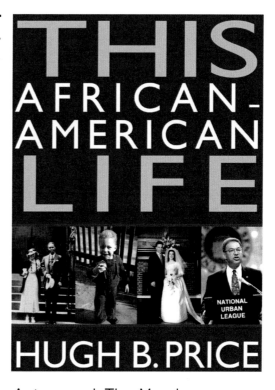

at what it took to get the Voting Rights Act passed. The March on Washington didn't yield a lot with President Kennedy. But after his tragic assassination, Lyndon Johnson was a very unexpected gift to the African-American community. Nobody saw Lyndon Johnson's liberalism coming. When he arrived on the scene and was ready for change, all the work that leaders of the Civil Rights Movement had put in bore fruit. Johnson was ready to giddy on up and get legislation passed. In a matter of a couple of years, decades of work crystallized in legislation. During my later professional years, I saw the opportunity structure open up and immensely talented people could find jobs and make careers in worlds where we never had a presence before. A lot of talented people gravitated to the private sector. We must always remember that despite all the ugliness and pushback these days, Barack and Michelle Obama have shown the world what is possible in America. I sense that there is a real awakening of commitment and activism now. The outpouring of young candidates running and succeeding during the last midterm election was spurred by grassroots groups who were doing world-class organizing. There is a renewed spirit of service and commitment to changing this country. Personal integrity is also important. We each have to be comfortable in our own skin about what we're are prepared to sacrifice for the sake of our careers. I was not prepared to give up family. That is a very personal judgment. I was telling my students, "You all have to figure out where you are along the spectrum and then live with it. You have to decide where you fit and then be at peace with it."

'Entrepreneurs are
the problem-solvers
of today.'

Marc Randolph:
Netflix Co-Founder Continues to Innovate

In 1997, Marc Randolph co-founded Netflix with current CEO, Reed Hastings. If his name doesn't ring any bells, don't be alarmed. Marc is a humble, but charismatic entrepreneur who isn't motivated by fame or fortune. By the time he started working on Netflix in the late '90s, he already had experience with five other start-ups. In 2003, Marc left Netflix to pursue other ventures. He admits his skills were more suited for the beginning stages of a start-up than later stages. He's just released a new book titled, *That Will Never Work: The Birth of Netflix and the Amazing Life of an Idea,* that serves as a mix between a memoir and a guide for anyone who wants to take a chance on innovative entrepreneurship. It's the story of Netflix and how it all began from an idea for shipping DVDs in the mail to a streaming video service that changed how the world watched TV and movies. Even with success, Marc has not lost track of what is important in life.

Marc grew up in Chappaqua, New York, which he describes as an affluent community. As a youth, he quickly learned from an early age that enormous wealth does not bring happiness. "They are two different things," he says. His parents were always supportive of what he wanted to do. He is appreciative of his parents' open-mindedness for entrepreneurship. "I happened to grow up in a family where anytime I came up with a crazy idea, they encouraged me to go for it," he says.

In his final year at Hamilton College, one of the bigger advertising firms arrived on campus to recruit for an account executive position. Marc knew he wasn't necessarily qualified for the position, but applied anyway. He passed the initial interview and was flown down to New York City for a follow-up interview. He aced it! Eventually, he made it to the final rounds. Marc was now competing with three other candidates. After going through an entire day of interviews, he was told he did not get the job. Marc was disappointed, but he immediately took action. "I thought to myself, I don't get this. What am I missing? I'm going to write every single person I met with and ask them what I can do differently the next time."

After he sent out the letters, he received a response to come back down to New York City to meet with the firm again. He ended up getting the job. "Now, here is the amazing part: They didn't offer the job to any of the four finalists," he explains. "They wanted to see which one of us wouldn't take no for an answer. It's a lesson I've taught my kids and young people I've mentored, that in a business context, no does not necessarily mean no."

Marc does not name them specifically, but there were three entrepreneurs who inspired him early on in his career. He says that it was from sheer luck that he got to work so closely with them. He does note, however, one entrepreneur who mentored him and gave him an opportunity to work with him on the U.S. edition of *MacUser* magazine. Even though he had an "entrepreneurial bent," Marc never before had the opportunity to see it done by someone who had real skin in the game. "I paid attention to the way he made decisions, who he hired, what he invested in, how to test things," he says.

He soon learned the lesson of being a *doer* instead of just a *dreamer*. "The people who were getting things done were not the ones who took their ideas and then went back to work on a business plan," he says. "They were the people who did things and learned from that experience. The entrepreneurs who are successful have this predisposition for action."

BK FULTON AND NICHOLAS POWELL

He recalls a famous story of him and Reed Hastings bouncing ideas around in the car and he came up with the crazy idea of video rentals by mail. There was no driving back to the office and working on a business plan or a pitch deck; instead, they bought a CD and mailed it to Reed's house. It worked. Instead of planning, they tested their idea and when it worked, validated it. "That's the kind of thing you want to see in people and that was an incredibly timely and important lesson for me to learn pretty early," he says.

Marc looks at the early days of Netflix as a moment in his life where he was enjoying himself as an entrepreneur. "It was fantastic. I felt I had made it because I was running my own company," he says. "We were doing great and fun things. I had these great people around me." However, if you looked from the outside looking in, things did not seem all that great. "My take-home pay was pitiful. We were losing money. We weren't anywhere close to a scalable business model," he says. "But that wasn't what I was aiming for. I was aiming for a chance to have all these pieces come together. I've achieved that quite a few times in my life." But, he admits that Netflix isn't his biggest personal success. "It was more of a realization that I have had a lot of entrepreneurial success. Netflix was my sixth startup. Looker Data—the startup I've been mentoring for six or seven years—in some ways, is going to be a bigger personal success for me than Netflix."

Marc says his life is motivated by balance. He doesn't think too hard about the superficial aspects of success. Instead, he is conscious of how much time he is giving to his family, himself, and his business. "Am I balancing all of the right pieces of my life? Am I giving the right attention to my family? Am I giving the right attention to myself? And do I have the right intellectual engagement in a way that can earn me a living?" Marc's greatest success is the fact that he was able to do seven companies and still remain married to the same woman. "She's still my best friend. My kids have grown up," he says. "I've grown up knowing them and them knowing me and the best I can tell, they like me. That's what I'm proud of."

Throughout his career, Marc has seen startups come and go. He states there are two reasons why startups are not successful: not taking action and a lack of focus. "They get this idea and they leave it in their head," he explains. "They love their idea and have built it up in their head so much, that it becomes a castle in their head, but too hard to manage in reality. They end up never getting it off the ground. Instead, they should just start."

Marc emphasizes the road to being an entrepreneur isn't easy. "There are a hundred things that are conspiring against you and that you have to have the skill to pick the one or two things you have to get right and if you get those one or two things right, all of the rest of them won't matter."

> "If people get into this business because they love the experience of sitting around a table with really smart people and solving really interesting problems, then they are in this for the right reasons."

When Marc is hearing pitches from eager young startups, he runs into what he calls the "selling the T-shirts" dilemma. "Rather than wasting time thinking about all the things you'll do once you are successful (like selling T-shirts), you should be spending all your time thinking about how you are going to get there in the first place," he explains.

When asked if he feels the landscape for TV and movies are in a much better place than 10 years ago, he enthusiastically agrees. "I love what's happening now. I mean there are so many amazing things to watch and that's because of the competition," he says. "Netflix is great, but so is HBO, Amazon Prime, and Hulu. I think it is great for consumers that we have all these spaces and I think it's great for the industry that we have these choices."

He thinks it's never been a better time to be a content creator. Creators are no longer restrained by commercial breaks and narrative restraints.

"The creative restraints that used to be on television were ridiculous and now, of course, you can do what you want. One episode can be 29 minutes and the next 60 minutes," he explains. "Now, you can have the story arch run across four episodes before it concludes. I mean it's spectacular."

Marc criticizes the modern glorification of entrepreneurship. If they are only in it for the money and fame, then they are in it for the wrong reasons. "After dreaming about those things, you'll be disappointed," he says. "But if people get into this business because they love the experience of sitting around a table with really smart people and solving really interesting problems, then they are in this for the right reasons."

In his life, he is at peace. He finds happiness in mentoring "early-stage entrepreneurs and sitting around the table with them to help solve their problems." He chooses these companies based not on technology, but on the people. This approach gives Marc an opportunity to be a part of technologies that are new and exciting. One such technology is a robotic dishwasher that eliminates the burdensome (and gross) task of restaurant kitchen workers having to clean the dirty dishes. "It's the worst job in the kitchen, so, we're building a robot that automates that job," he says.

When Marc is not stimulating his intellectual compulsion to solve problems or working or spending time with his family, he is busy "feeding the rat." The phrase was coined by 20th-century British mountaineer Julian Vincent "Mo" Anthoine. "It's that feeling of needing to go out and be an adventurer," Marc explains. "Ever since I was a kid, I've been a climber, a skier, a mountain biker, surfer, and kay-aker." Being outdoors and active makes him feel whole. The feeling of being dependent on himself or a small group relaxes him. "That's my release."

To learn more about Marc Randolph, visit his website marcrandolph.com. You can also follow him on Facebook @thisismarcrandolph, Instagram @ thatwillneverwork, and X @mbrandolph.

Daphne Maxwell Reid
Isn't Finished Yet

PHOTO BY TIM REID

"Learn about it before
trying to be about it."

Daphne Maxwell Reid

Actress, fashion designer, photographer, and former model Daphne Maxwell Reid isn't finished yet. There is so much more she wants to achieve in her career. Working in front of the camera is just one of them. "Daphne Style is how I express my design passion with all custom pieces," Daphne says. "I want to be known for all the creative things I do in my life. I continue to strive to fulfill the ideas that come to me." At 73 years old, Daphne Maxwell Reid appreciates where she's been and is optimistic about where she is going.

Daphne grew up in Manhattan, New York, and was raised in the Amsterdam Houses. "They were called the projects," she says. "It was a multicultural environment full of multicultural things to do. I had a wonderful childhood. I had a mother, father, two brothers and lots of friends." Even though they were poor, Daphne and her brothers didn't know it. Her parents instilled in her an appreciation for education. After graduating from the Bronx High School of Science, she enrolled at Northwestern University, receiving a National Merit Scholarship.

She graduated with a Bachelor of Arts in interior design and architecture. Throughout her life, she was the first of many—first African American on the cover of *Glamour* magazine, first Black homecoming queen at Northwestern, and co-owner of Virginia's first full-service film studio. "I think my favorite first was being my mother's first and only daughter," she says jokingly. "But I've been breaking down barriers since I was in the fourth grade." She was the only Black child in advanced placement classes in the fourth through the ninth grades. At Northwestern University, she was 1 of only 36 Black students in her freshman class.

Her time at Northwestern was tough. Daphne was called the N-word by a potential roommate after they found out they would be rooming with a Black girl. Daphne chose to room on her own. There were no Black sororities on campus back then and the white sororities didn't accept her. After a former high school teacher submitted her picture to *Seventeen* magazine for their "real girl" issue, that photo was placed in *The Daily Northwestern* newspaper for the homecoming queen competition. Daphne was a finalist along with four white women.

When she was crowned homecoming queen, the president at the time didn't look her in the eye. After the photo op, he just walked away. No one applauded her. Northwestern didn't include her crowning in the yearbook because they deemed it unimportant. This was 1967 Illinois.

DAPHNE MAXWELL REID'S FIRST PUBLISHED MODELING PHOTO IN SEVENTEEN MAGAZINE (JANUARY 1967). PHOTO COURTESY OF DAPHNE MAXWELL REID.

DAPHNE MAXWELL REID BECAME THE FIRST BLACK HOMECOMING QUEEN AT NORTHWESTERN UNIVERSITY. PHOTO COURTESY OF DAPHNE MAXWELL REID.

"I certainly was not looking to be crowned but things fell into place and it happened," she recalls. "It wasn't a pleasant experience but hey, some things aren't and you just have to keep on moving." But Daphne kept climbing. In 1969, Daphne became the first black woman on the cover of *Glamour* magazine. Upon reflection, Daphne doesn't believe being the first has a special meaning to her personally. "It only has meaning in hindsight because when I am doing something, I am doing it because I want to," she explains. "I am moving forward towards a goal and if I happen to be the first to do it, then so be it." After not returning to Northwestern for decades, Daphne returned to the university in 2006 to be awarded the Hall of Fame Award by the Black Alumni Association. In 2008, she returned to Ryan Field to crown the homecoming queen. Currently, all of her archives are now available at the library of Northwestern University.

While Daphne was in college, she was a model for the Eileen Ford Agency. She would model until the early 1970s before getting into

BK FULTON AND NICHOLAS POWELL

IN 1969, DAPHNE MAXWELL REID BECAME THE FIRST BLACK WOMAN ON THE COVER OF *GLAMOUR* MAGAZINE. PHOTO COURTESY OF DAPHNE MAXWELL REID

DAPHNE MAXWELL REID EXPRESSES HER PASSION FOR DESIGN AND CUSTOM PIECES THROUGH HER DAPHNE STYLE FASHION LABEL. PHOTO BY MICHAEL HOSTELER

acting professionally. Daphne got her first big break from actor Robert Conrad. In 1979, she was cast in his shows *The Duke* and *A Man Called Sloane*. In 1980 she first worked with her now husband, Tim Reid, on his show *WKRP in Cincinnati*. And then in 1987, she worked with Tim again on *Frank's Place* as Hanna Griffin. The two would later create another show called *Snoops* in 1988. In the late 90s, Daphne and Tim founded New Millennium Studios, the first full-service film studio in Virginia. Several scenes from Steven Spielberg's *Lincoln* were filmed at New Millennium before the couple sold the studio in 2015.

Her most well-known role was her role as Aunt Viv on *The Fresh Prince of Bel-Air*. In 2020, Daphne Maxwell Reid was asked by Will Smith to be part of the *Fresh Prince of Bel-Air Reunion*. The cast was flown out to Hollywood and stayed in separate hotels to make the reunion even more special. "We all had not been in the same place at the same time in over 27 years," she says. "So just to see each other all together on the old set was such a kick. It was a joy. It was a warm and very moving experience. We

DAPHNE MAXWELL REID IS MOSTLY KNOWN FOR PLAYING AUNT VIV ON *THE FRESH PRINCE OF BEL-AIR*. FROM LEFT: DAPHNE MAXWELL REID AS VIVIAN BANKS, WILL SMITH AS WILLIAM 'WILL' SMITH, THE LATE JAMES AVERY AS PHILIP BANKS.
PHOTO BY CHRIS HASTON/NBC/NBCU VIA GETTY IMAGES.

were all glad to be there together because the love that we have for each other is evident."

In 2022, Reid starred in the film *Trophy Wife*. Daphne says the film was shot in Virginia and Maryland and she will play the grandmother of Toni Carter. Audiences can also expect to see Daphne in *The Business of Christmas* series.

Daphne says breaking into the film industry isn't easy. "You have to understand that showbiz has two words: show is one of them and business is the other," she says. "If you are going into the film industry, find out how to be self-employed. Find out how to best support yourself until they call you." Daphne emphasizes the importance of understanding that the business is much more than acting or directing or writing. "To make a proper film, it generally takes about 100 different people and they

BK FULTON AND NICHOLAS POWELL

THE FRESH PRINCE OF BEL-AIR CAST TAKES A SELFIE IN 2017. THE
CAST OFFICIALLY REUNITED IN 2020 FOR *THE FRESH PRINCE OF BEL-AIR
REUNION*. FROM LEFT: WILL SMITH, TATYANA ALI, ALFONSO RIBEIRO, KARYN
PARSONS, DAPHNE MAXWELL REID, AND JOSEPH MARCELL.
PHOTO COURTESY OF DAPHNE MAXWELL REID.

really have to work as a team. If you want to be a director, which most
young people do, you have to know what the other 40 departments
are doing and know that they are doing it well." Simply put, Daphne
believes that ". . . experience in the field is helpful, but if you want to be
in the film business, learn about it before trying to be about it."

Daphne is an avid traveler. This is documented through her
photography books of doors she has taken from around the world.
Daphne is currently offering a limited edition tote bag made from
custom fabrics that feature her door prints.

Daphne is a creative force, a mother, and a grandmother of three. She
loves her family. "My greatest accomplishment was raising a group of
very fine people: my children," she says. "Because when it is all said and
done, all we have is family."

**To learn more about Daphne Reid, visit Daphnemaxwellreid.com and
follow her on Facebook and Instagram.**

David L. Robbins: The Foundation of a Writer

"Whatever you are
writing about, you want

David L. Robbins, the son of WWII veterans, went through boyhood with the feeling of otherness. This resulted in a profound sense of him wanting to do good by others. Growing up in the small town of Sandston, Virginia, David was tall and talkative but ethically and culturally different than his peers. He and his family were the only Jews in town. "My skin's white, as white as theirs, but I was different," he recalls. "Growing up in East Richmond in the late 50s and early 60s and going through my boyhood was an education in how to navigate differentness and otherhood. I have not ever forgotten those lessons and sympathies."

Towards the end of WWII, his Dad developed multiple sclerosis. This led David to question the very notion of what masculinity is. "My father was a strong, powerful dude. You didn't want to mess with him," he says. "But because of his malady, he needed courage beyond being a father and husband." David never saw his father run, only limp. No matter the circumstances, his father got up in the morning to work multiple jobs and provide for his family. "Strength exists when it is tested, right?" David says. "You don't know how strong you are until you pick something up. You don't know how strong you are until you face a challenge." To this day, David believes his father to be the "most consistently strong man" he ever met.

These moments of courage and strength surface in his novels. "My early life taught me to admire big thematic human characteristics," David says. He isn't interested in exploring the base desires of men— money, love, or fame. Instead, he writes about the kind of courage that someone needs to get through war or disease. In his own words, David describes himself as a "writer of themes more than plots."

When David was beginning his writing career, he was offered the back pages of *Style Weekly*, Richmond's alternative weekly culture and arts newspaper. He was appreciative but didn't find much satisfaction in writing for a newspaper. "I wanted to see my name sideways on the spine of a book, and I was not going to settle seeing my name horizontal anywhere." In 1999, when David's first book, *War of the Rats*, was published, he felt like he'd made it. That was his goal, "to do nothing more than write stories for the rest of my life." David has become much more than a *New York Times* best-selling author.

All of his success would be in vain if he did not give back. Service is a theme that came up frequently in our interview. "I believe my greatest achievement is getting off the merry-go-round of self-interest," David says. With his platform and successes, he hopes to make an impact that outlives him. "I had an epiphany, and the epiphany led me to understand I don't have spare time," he says. "Everything in my life can be directed towards a goal. When I'm done with my work, writing, editing, and teaching, what's left over is not something to waste. It's a resource of time and money and heart that can be dedicated to the welfare of my community. It's not excessive to care about the people in our community."

"My early life taught me to admire big thematic human characteristics."

David is well known for his work within the Richmond community. *The Richmond Times-Dispatch* named him 2017 Person of the Year honoree. In December of 2014, David read an online article about a writing program in upstate New York for military veterans to study writing with a college professor for a weekend. David thought he could create his own program that better served veterans. "These cats put on uniforms and trained hard and sometimes went overseas to do difficult things, and they just get a weekend?" He met with the executive director of the Virginia War Memorial to create a project that would go on for 12 weeks, similar to a college semester. David was already teaching creative writing at Virginia Commonwealth University (VCU). After talking to the Virginia War Memorial Foundation's board, the project was a go. "Now, I had to do it."

Now in its sixth year and impacting over 150 veterans, the Mighty Pen Project has not only been a success for David, but a cathartic experience as well. As David sits around the table with these veterans, he sees them tapping into their own hearts and bearing witness to each other's experiences. He never tells them what to write. He says it would be wrong to do that. "It's a self-guided tour—the healing is theirs, the stories are theirs, the catharsis is theirs. The writing instruction is mine. It's really beautiful to see them band around each other and understand what each other has gone through. I couldn't have anticipated that. I fully intend the Mighty Pen to outlive me."

In 2019, David was having dinner with a friend, a former chair of the Richmond School Board, when an African-American police officer entered the restaurant and greeted her. She began to "gush" over the success of the Mighty Pen to the officer. Impressed, he said he would like to have a program like that for police and other public safety

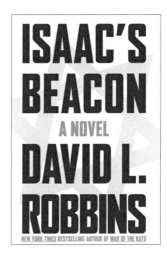

employees. David says, "Then I put my head in my hands and said, 'I don't have the time or the patience, resources or desire to do this. But dammit, now I have to.'" In April of 2020, David started Frontline Writers —a writing program similar to Mighty Pen for police, fire, and emergency services essential workers. "These people live traumatic, adventurous, and dangerous lives," he says. "The writers share remarkable stories of human empathy and courage. You can just see the heads nod around the table. A cop will tell a story and a fireman will go, 'Yeah' and a fireman will tell a story and an emergency medical tech will go, 'Yeah.' They terribly need this program." In the coming years, depending on resources and support from the community, David hopes to expand the Frontline Writers program to other professions of public service, people who might also deal with traumatic circumstances as part of their working lives, including nurses, teachers, social workers, even emergency room staff.

Before he starts to write, David does a lot of prep work. "The absolute last thing any writer should do is touch a keyboard," he advises. "So much should come before you put words on the page. When I prepare, I don't think about the plot first, ever. I always consider the theme. If you have a story you want to tell, you must isolate that part of the story first—like loss, grief, loyalty, courage – something your reader can recognize and share, something human and common, and often powerful." He compares theme to a lighthouse. "If you have a beacon that tells you what your stories are truly about, you won't ever get out of your path when the story gets foggy. It'll help you make the right choices."

Most of David's stories revolve around moments in history. For research, he will read and notate dozens of books, scan the internet for images and testimonies, go to libraries and archives, always digging in the hope that his characters and the story's smaller moments will emerge from the research. He recalls a time when he was on a panel with other historical writers and someone in the audience asked how much of what they've learned made it to the page. David asked the other two writers to write down what they thought that percentage was. All three wrote 10 percent. "You research to inform your character, not so much about what your character does or says but to fully create the world your character moves in." Many of David's novels revolve around the grand events of the mid-20th century. He will look through newspapers of the period for details like the price of pork or savings bonds or the most popular car of that year.

"I believe my greatest achievement is getting off the merry-go-round of self-interest."

David also advises writers to travel, to visit the places they write about. "I've gone to some of the coolest, exotic, and weirdest places in the world just to sit on a hill and imagine a tank battle." In fact, David literally did this when he sat on a hill in the middle of the Russian steppe that overlooked a sunflower field. "The Germans came from over here and the Russians came from over there." This would be where the climax of his book, *Last Citadel*, which dramatizes The Battle of Kursk, would take place. "You wouldn't know the sunflower field was there unless you actually went there," he says. "It's an incredible scene. There is this beautiful juxtaposition of armor and men dying and struggling, blinded by these tall stalks of golden sunflowers."

After the writer does all the heavy lifting, they're then ready to write. David uses the example of a juggler to create an analogy about the role adequate research plays. "A juggler might have 10 items in the air but is only touching two at a time, while the others stay in his orbit," he explains. "He knows where they are, but they're free. That's how research should work. You have to stay out of the way and only touch those bits of the story you need when you need them. But you must have it all there, ready to fall into your hands. That only comes from preparation, the reading, note taking, travel, interviews. Time spent with your chin in your palm."

BK FULTON AND NICHOLAS POWELL

David doesn't write stories simply for the reader's pleasure. He hopes readers can actually learn something that they didn't know before. "If somebody wants to learn about Stalingrad, they'll read *War of the Rats*. If they want to learn about the fall of Berlin, read *The End of War*. If they want to learn about Kursk, there's *Last Citadel*. By the time they're done, they know a helluva lot about the Eastern Front of World War II."

"I had an epiphany, and the epiphany led me to understand I don't have spare time."

Looking back at his work, David is proud of the oeuvre he has put together for readers to digest. "I feel like I've written a handful of definitive books," he says. "I feel like the one I'm writing now could well be another. I accept that may be a literary pretension of mine, but I don't want to write books that are easily disposable, as so much modern fiction tends to be. Historical novels give me the best chance of that."

His latest, *Isaac's Beacon* (released in 2021), is about the creation of the State of Israel. "I always wanted to write about this moment in history," he says. "I'd read *Exodus* by Leon Uris, but I didn't feel it aged well. It was written in 1959. I don't think *Exodus* captured enough about the contemporary mindset of the short history of Israel. It's truly a beautiful place, but it's a hard land and people, and their story is really morally complex." *Isaac's Beacon* focuses on the Deir Yassin and Kfar Etzion massacres, both taking place in 1948 just before the creation of the State of Israel. "If you look at Deir Yassin, it was a vicious act on behalf of the Jews. They just went nuts on an Arab village. Then, weeks later, the Arabs did the same at a place called Kfar Etzion where they mowed down a couple hundred surrendering Jews. The story of *Isaac's Beacon* revolves around the leadup to these two events."

When asked if he had further advice for aspiring writers, David stresses the importance of having tough skin. Learn to coexist with the word 'No,' and tell your story no matter what. "Don't be dissuaded because of how difficult or hard it is. Trust me, little compares to somebody telling you they love your writing. It can sometimes be even better than saying you love me. To quote Henry David Thoreau, 'Madam, you are holding the best of me.' That's what I try to put on the page. And when I'm done, what I try to bring to the rest of my day. That's the best of me."

If you are interested in joining the Mighty Pen Project, sign up at https://vawarmemorial.org/mightypen/. If you are interested in joining Frontline Writers, sign up at frontlinewriters.org

'Be the bridge between
the young and old, the

Victoria Rowell:
Leader, Advocate, and Power Player

Victoria Rowell is poised and elegant in her speech. Over the years, Victoria has become an important voice for those in foster care. While her career has reached far beyond the 60-acre farm she grew up on in Lebanon, Maine, Victoria has not forgotten the woman who made her the person she is today. She knows she owes a debt to her late foster mother, Agatha Armstead. Agatha helped Victoria develop discipline and a love for the performing arts. "She had a love for music. She had studied at the New England Conservatory of Music. Through my exposure, I developed a love for classical ballet. Occasionally, she would let me stay up to watch the *Ed Sullivan Show* to see the June Taylor Dancers," she says. Agatha was a "Rosie the Riveter" during the war (WWII). For $2,000, Agatha used her hard-earned resources to purchase the farm Victoria would call home. Agatha was a scrupulous businesswoman. "She was a woman of faith and principle," she says. From Agatha, Victoria learned the power of prayer and service. After all, Agatha was in her 60s when she took in a two and a half-year-old Victoria. "To quote the great John Lewis, 'find a way out of no way,'"

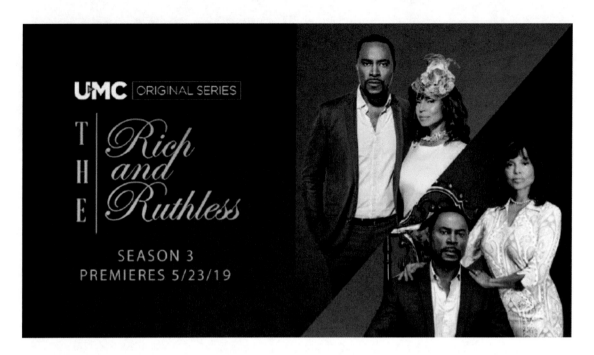

Victoria says. "There isn't a day that goes by without me thinking about her. Because I feel she is with me," she says. "She was my long term mentor. I am the beneficiary of Agatha Armstead's wisdom."

Our conversation steers towards Oscar winner Hattie McDaniel and her activism in Los Angeles. Even though she later grew critical of her role as a "Mammy" in *Gone With the Wind,* Hattie used the money she earned to help her community and fight housing discrimination in Los Angeles. Her strategic advocacy laid the groundwork for the creation of the Fair Housing Act. The women who helped raise Victoria came from the same cloth as Hattie. "Agatha had three sisters who I called my aunts. Aunt Ruthie was the first black executive assistant to a United States governor, Governor Paul A. Dever of Massachusetts. Josephine Baker sent her a telegram telling her that she was a pride to her people," she explains. "I now own this telegram from Josephine." Her Aunt Marian was a church organist. Her Aunt Theodora often referred to as "Aunt T" was a school teacher for 35 years. "Their father was a self-taught violinist. He never went past the fourth grade but taught himself the violin. Not only was he a talented violinist, but the neighborhood math tutor as well," she says.

Her book, *The Women Who Raised Me: A Memoir,* is a love letter to these women and her foster mother. "I wrote the book as a homage to these extraordinary women," women," she says. Victoria emphasizes the importance of being grateful for those who have helped you in your journey to becoming the person you are today. This is the lesson she wanted people to learn after reading her book. "Recognize and

BK FULTON AND NICHOLAS POWELL

value those people. Practice reciprocity. Go back to your first-grade teacher or college professor and thank them. It matters that they know we've utilized the knowledge and wisdom they have shared with us and passed it forward to the next generation," she says.

The impact of the novel has been real and humbling to Victoria. "Because of my work, I have become a support line. Social workers have told me that the book has made a difference. It's in libraries across America. The youth want to read it. I am very proud that it has affected people in a positive way," she says. "It has been translated in braille and it is in our National Library in Washington, D.C." Victoria gave a speech at the National Court Appointed Special Advocate Association's national convention in Atlanta last month to an audience that included former FBI Director James Comey and his wife, Patrice, who introduced her. "I was very honored. Politics aside, the Comeys have been foster parents for years, and I appreciate and respect what they have been able to do with children in social services," she says.

"I know I am in a window of my life that is going to be spectacular."

At age 60, Victoria Rowell feels like she has reached a new chapter in her life. "I know I am in a window of my life that is going to be spectacular. All of the knowledge and all of the work is going to culminate into expansion these next 10 years. Even though I've achieved a lot, my greatest achievement has yet to come," she says. When she thinks of success, she believes those who are successful never quite say "they've made it" because they continue to have more and more "success" to experience and share. "We who are successful don't rest on our laurels," she emphasizes. "We have a sensational appetite to create, to be successful, to share, and to teach, so it's ongoing. The 'making it' is the continuation of manifesting it," she says.

"I was blessed with Agatha and other women from different disciplines who banded together and raised me."

Her reality show, *The Rich and the Ruthless,* is a play on daytime soap operas. It's a "dramedy" with influences from meta-styled productions like *30 Rock* and *Anchorman.* In other words, it's self-aware, making humor out of its absurdness. She thinks there is more room for this kind

of humor in the digital age. The fans and critics love it. "I think people today want levity. They want drama but they also want levity too. I've provided this Emmy-nominated show. We just won 'Best Assemble Cast' (two years in a row) and 'Best Lead Actress' for the Independent Series Awards," she says. "There is an audience that wanted to watch programming that offered soap opera, that offered behind the scenes, that offered comedy, calamity and cause. I was able to deliver that with a nice dose of drama. And by virtue of just launching our third season on May 23, I know there is an audience out there that appreciates this kind of content," she says.

Victoria is staying with one of her foster sisters in her Plum Beach house in Newburyport, Massachusetts. The night before, she was sitting by the fireplace with one of her younger guests. He asked her about the entertainment industry and the purpose of having an agent. She explains the agent has to believe in your potential and ability enough to work hard for you. "That's rare," she says. "You can have an agent for agent's sake. You can have a manager for manager's sake and they will take the 10, 15 or 20 percent, whatever the negotiation is. But you better be ready to do 90% of the work."

She explains you have to stay relevant and have a diverse portfolio. "You have to be open to lecturing, writing books and scripts, and directing," she says. "You have to study all of this. This way you are able to teach what you have learned. You are going to have to be willing to work on your communication skills so that you can talk to people in the room and they know that this is a person who they want to do business with," she explains. If there were a group of young people around the fireplace, she would tell them that discipline is a must for success in this business. "Whether they are ballet dancers, or jazz musicians, or going to the UK to study Shakespeare or actors, writers, camera people, you name it . . . discipline is non-negotiable.

BK FULTON AND NICHOLAS POWELL

You have to have the discipline—the ability to do the required work and craft practice—and it has to come from somewhere," she says. "Unfortunately, there are many young people who were never taught discipline. I was given a gift. It fell out of the sky for me. I was blessed with Agatha and other women from different disciplines who banded together and raised me," she explains. "For example, consider the discipline of gardening. You have to be disciplined to be a great farmer.

"You have to be prepared to do the lion's share of the work."

The discipline of classical ballet requires uber discipline, professionally. The discipline of being an actor is important to me because when I talk to young people I want them to get what I have learned through work and paying attention to the details."

"The entertainment industry is about selling choice in fantasy, inspiration, and education. The contradiction of the whole thing is that entertainment is often smoke and mirrors," Victoria explains. "We create this atmosphere of allusion and aspiration but behind the Oz's curtain is a real business. Unfortunately, what aspiring artists often see is a lot of show and no business. I really like to have a frank conversation with young people. I did that with our house guest. The young man's eyes looked like they were going to pop out after I was finished," she says with a chuckle. "You have to be prepared to do the lion's share of the work."

Victoria's free time is spent on maintaining good health and strengthening the bonds of friendship and family. "To relax I take Bikram Yoga. I took Bikram Yoga this morning. I walk, I listen to music I love, I write and I spend time with good friends and family. I try to honor myself. I eat good food and I laugh," she says. Her calendar is full with projects in the pipeline. "Expect a Christmas movie opposite Sherri Shepherd. It is titled, '*Twas the Chaos Before Christmas*. It should be on the small screen so check your listings," she says. "I am working on editing the *Woman Who Raised Me* script. I have a new lifestyle show, *Trash vs. Treasure*. I'm getting ready for the future and the opportunities and blessings to come."

To keep up with Victoria Rowell and her various projects, you can follow her on X @VictoriaRowell, and Instagram @victoriarowell.

"Believe in the
relevance of your
story."

Misan Sagay: Telling Stories Through the Colorblind Lens

Misan Sagay is one of the most brilliant screenwriters of our generation. Her stories give life the panoramic view it so desperately deserves. Misan migrated with her parents from Nigeria when she was five. "I am Nigerian and I was born in Nigeria but I came to England at the age of five and lived in Cambridge for most of my formative years," she explains. "I would say I'm partially from Warri, Nigeria and Cambridge, England."

Her father was an academic. From her father, she learned the value of holding herself up to her own standards. "You measure yourself against the best that you can be," she says. "It wasn't about competing with other people. It was really about competing with the best of you. You will know when you are falling short," she says. Because of this, Misan had the motivation to succeed academically. "My father had this profound love for learning," she says. "Approaching learning with joy is an amazing lesson and legacy to leave a child."

Her father's emphasis on learning instilled discipline into a young and bright Misan Sagay. As she recalls it, she loved "learning for its own sake." Before her start in film, Misan always had plans to become a doctor. Her love for reading and learning helped her appreciate and push through the rigor of the medical field. "I grew up as somebody who read widely and voraciously with great enjoyment," she says. "I think the ability to read and to read with joy is something that is very useful in anything you do. It gives you focus and concentration and wider life experience that you might otherwise not have. My love for reading served me very well in medicine," she says. Even though she isn't in the medical field anymore, she considers it to be one of her greatest achievements.

The modern-day film industry is in the midst of a renaissance. Big budget film companies like Disney are banking on talent of color. "Having the opportunity to write for a studio in a profession that has been dominated by white male writers is also a great achievement.

It's unexpected but I'm excited," she says. Her screenwriting journey started in, as she says, a "rather strange way." She was working as a doctor in the A&E (Accidents & Emergency) department of Charing Cross Hospital. The biopic of British politician and abolitionist, William Wilberforce, *Amazing Grace*, was playing at the local theater. "I remember the hunger people had for any film that might have relevance to one's experience," she says. "I knew it was a film about slavery, so I wanted to watch it. I remember walking out of the film and found myself sympathizing with the tears of a white woman because her husband didn't come home for supper," she says. "It showed how structurally disruptive slavery was for her social life. Looking at slavery as evil through that lens left me with an unimaginable rage."

She used her free time to work on her screenplay in the A&E. "In the A&E you have busy and quiet time. So when there was quiet time, I sat down and wrote this story. I was going to write this story with a black woman lead," she says. "This was the first story I had ever written. I had sent it to the British Screen, which works as a government film agency, and they wrote back and said, 'We want to make your film.' They had sent it to Jeremy Irons who had just won an Oscar. He loved the script and he said, 'I will help you raise money and we're going to make this movie together.' I was very lucky that the first thing I made was produced into a full-length film. That film was *The Secret Laughter of Women*," she says. After *The Secret Laughter of Women*, Oprah Winfrey caught wind of her work and hired her to write an adaptation of Zora Neale Hurston's classic novel, *Their Eyes Were Watching God,* for Harpo Films.

"My early years were quite easy. It was harder to move to the next level. That was where I found it difficult," she admits.

> "This was the first story I had ever written. I had sent it to the British Screen, which works as a government film agency and they wrote back and said, 'We want to make your film.'"

Then Misan created her next film, *Belle*. But the inspiration for *Belle* came much earlier.

BK FULTON AND NICHOLAS POWELL

in her journey. Misan was attending a party at Scone Palace in Scotland while a student at the University of St. Andrews in Scotland. She was wandering around the house and stumbled upon a secluded bedroom. In a back corridor off of the bedroom, she found herself looking at a face similar to hers. "I had this extraordinary moment where I came face to face with another black person," she says. "At St. Andrews, I really was the only black person for miles. Seeing this portrait was quite an amazing moment." The portrait was of two women—a black woman and a white woman. Under the portrait, read the caption, "the lady lives with Murray." Misan found this funny. The black woman wasn't mentioned by name but just as 'lady,'" she says. "I wondered about the identity of this woman. Who was she?"

Years later, she went back to the palace but the portrait had been moved out of the bedroom and into a more public place. The caption had been changed. It read: "The Lady Elizabeth Murray and Dido, the housekeeper's daughter." This didn't make sense to her. The clothes were too striking and regal to belong to a housekeeper's daughter. Misan had her story. She got in touch with the family in Scotland and did weeks of research. "The two girls in the portrait were, in fact, of equal relationship to Lord Mansfield at the time he lived in Scone

Palace," she explains. "His descendants still lived there and that was the beginning of finding Dido's story and then making the film."

> "I think the ability to read and to read with joy is something that is very useful in anything you do."

When the conversation turned to diversity in film, Misan had an alternative take on what makes it difficult for people of color to break through. "The difficulty—in my opinion—isn't about racism as much as it is about visibility," she explains. "As a black person, if I walk into a room as a black person or look at a work of art or anything, I see me and therefore I assume they see themselves and in seeing themselves, perhaps they don't see me. But if I go in to pitch a project, first of all, I have to pitch that black subjects are interesting before I pitch myself as a writer or the actual story," she says. "Every time you go in, you go in with this monumental task. Not just pitching the story but pitching of one's own relevance."

There is a blindside in the industry that Misan feels needs to be addressed. "I think the reason why black films are made through the lens of a white character, is because that is the only way they can capture the attention of the person they are pitching," she says. "I didn't do that nor am I going to do that. When I was pitching *Belle,* I would come in and say I wanted to make a film about Dido Elizabeth and people in the room would say, 'Well why would you want to make a film about her instead of Lord Mansfield?' To pitch relevance that anyone would want to see it is hard when you're pitching to someone who might not necessarily be the audience you want to engage with," she says. Her point being, that the industry needs more people that look like the person who is pitching. "Listen to what I have to say because I know my audience," she says. "I shouldn't be forced to tell it in such a way that people who are not particularly necessary to the story are brought to the forefront as cream in the coffee. I think we have to be comfortable with straight black coffee when we tell our stories," she says.

"I think the reason why black films are made through the lens of a white character, is because that is the only way they can capture the attention of the person they were pitching."

For young screenwriters, she advises before approaching any door to "make sure you have done everything that you could possibly do to deserve to go through that door. If it requires study, you study. If it requires hard work, then you work hard. If it requires meeting people, meet them," she advises. "But once you get to that door, you let nothing stop you. You can then storm those gates because you came prepared and you know you'll have the right to be there."

Misan Sagay feels like the doors that once were closed for minorities are being increasingly pried opened. "I am working on several new projects including writing a studio movie," she says. "The message is coming through that we make better films when the people making them are diverse."

She's been researching the history of Islam in Europe. "There were 800 years where Islam was the major religion in Western Europe and in much of our art," she says. "We came out of the Dark Ages because of the Moors being there." A movie about the Moors' influence? That could be a possibility. She's watching her children grow and spread their wings. "As they get older, you have to learn how to let go and let them fly," she says. This prompts her to consider the motivations of why she does the work that she does. "Curiosity, that's what it is. If you remain endlessly curious, you will never be bored. You will always find something to do in your spare time."

"The message is coming through that we make better films when the people making them are diverse."

"Let the universe
lead you."

Coviello Salinès
Take's First Place

Coviello Salinès knows he's on to something big. His product and brand, Amour Genève, is more than just wine with an "electric blue" hue. It is an inspiration for those dreamers to keep going. His work is a gleam of hope in the midst of tragedy. He has taken first place by creating something the world has never seen.

Coviello's parents migrated from the Caribbean to the South Bronx, where he spent much of his early childhood. "They were rarely home," he says. "They worked around the clock to provide us the life they never had." His dad was a serviceman. His mom, a correctional nurse at Bellevue Hospital. When his father had the time, he used it to teach young Coviello the wonders of neurology. He wanted his son to become a neurologist or neuroscientist. "He wanted me to be like the early Ben Carson, so he would bring home large brain books for me to study," he says.

Life changed for Coviello when his father was deployed to Tobyhanna, Pennsylvania. "My life changed very drastically when dad got deployed. I was put into a school that was predominantly white," he says. "This was around age 9 or 10. So, throughout my compulsory education, I was always around white kids. This was initially a very trying and traumatic experience for me. The area was very traditional in views and not accustomed to cultural change at all."

> "As beautiful as the world is, there is so much destruction in it. It's important to be observant and steadfast. I've learned to be passive towards negative energy and to passionately embrace positive energy."

His new community did not know much about his culture and he knew little about theirs. It took a while to get acclimated. Sports kept him sane during this time. "I did a lot of track and cross country. I wrestled and played soccer," he says. "I had a lot of great coaches that would keep me on the right track through my high school career. They became my family since I had no family in the area." Because his parents were busy working, they didn't have time to come up with a strategy to help him adjust to his new neighborhood and school. "You start to lose your identity and it took me a very long time to figure out who I was at a time when I thought I already knew who I was," he says. "But bouncing back and forth through different demographics and geographies had some lifelong benefits. It allowed me to understand what it is that makes the world tick." This moment in his life made him come to the realization that people are more alike than different. He admits this experience was important to his long-term personal development. "If I didn't go through that period of disruption, I would not have been as original as I am today," says Coviello.

Aside from his parents, Coviello's grandmother, Sarah Rosario, was a big inspiration for him growing up, especially after his parents got divorced. "She raised me when my parents were gone. She was known as the woman who would never turn away a child in need," he explains. "I was always intrigued by the way she carried herself and the way she kept us all in line." She was fundamental in developing Coviello's discipline and common knowledge. Around this time, his creativity and entrepreneurship grew. "I was always interested in luxury and fashion. I was inspired by many designers and started to sew and create Miskeen-inspired art apparel as a child," he says. "I was quite a creative child without even knowing it." He likes to say that he was raised by families of many cultures and backgrounds: Italian, Puerto Rican, Black, and many more he cannot name. He was a child of the world.

As an entrepreneur, Coviello has learned the hard lesson that not everyone has your best interest at heart. Similarly, you have to find people who are willing to support your vision. "It is very rare that you will find people who really understand everything that you're doing, let alone accept it," he continues, "either from them not being able to do it themselves or them seeing you in a certain light. There were a lot of people that would look at me and say, 'Ok you can't do this but wouldn't explain why,'" which to him, wasn't very helpful or worthwhile to his entrepreneurial journey. "It is very important to know your own mind and your own story," he says. "Because people can use their version of you against you. As beautiful as the world is, there is so much destruction in it. It's important to be observant and steadfast. I've learned to be passive towards negative energy and to passionately embrace positive energy."

During his childhood, he was taught to ski by his parents who enjoyed the sport in their better years. "My father used to share stories with me about his travels to Europe. He was in love with the nature of the city Genèva," he explains. "We planned to go there one day but it never came to fruition." Amour Genève was inspired by this trip that never came to fruition. Coviello says Amour Genève means "the love for Genève" in French. "I wanted to make sure this rare and original blue wine was something that was created around my father," he says. "The love that he had for Genève and the love that I had for my father created this." If you look at the illustration on the bottle, you will see a picturesque view of the city of Genève.

Coviello's outlook on his business opportunities is nothing short of forward thinking. He knows his wine brand and other innovative ventures. He's not looking for the approval of others, but seeks understanding. He reflects on some of the most renowned innovators of their time who pushed on, regardless of public opinion.

"Elon Musk didn't look for approval when he was constructing Tesla. Albert Einstein wasn't looking for acceptance and approval when he was calculating his formulas and theories," he says with enthusiasm.

"What does it matter what the industry thinks? If the idea is pitched correctly and with authenticity, the work can drive the idea forward into reality."

"I wanted to make sure this rare and original blue wine was something that was created around my father. The love that he had for Genève and the love that I had for my father created this."

We ask if he thinks there will ever be imitators and whether he has experienced negative feedback. "It's funny because I don't have too many naysayers these days," Coviello says. He understands not everyone is a chemist, engineer or in medicine. They will not understand the more technical aspects of wine creation. That is where proper branding comes into play. "I have to share our story. I know I have to share the whole aspect of what this product is. I have to help people to understand the methodology and process behind my product. Knowing how much to share and what to keep is the key," he explains. He admits he isn't reinventing the wheel. "I'm just creating something that people have never seen before. If it drives creativity, it drives creativity," he says. "I'm going to continue being me and doing what I do. People don't always embrace creativity as they should and greed can be overpowering, but there is always an open space for creativity."

One of Coviello's proudest moments was the day the European Union and the Alcohol and Tobacco Tax and Trade Bureau (TTB) sent him a letter of clarification for his formula. "It was a validation of what my father would always try to put into my head," he says. "When I was young, I didn't understand it. Now I see that this is all bigger than me." He recalls when his father would watch National Geographic and the Sunday morning news. He was particularly a fan of programs detailing the lives of the Indigenous people. His father explained to him that if you really look into someone's eyes, you can feel their passion and story. "Now, when I look into people's eyes and share my story with them, I can tell if they really understand it. That's how I know my wine is bigger than me; how I figured out that I had made something special—the first naturally blue wine in the world. It's the most rewarding feeling."

"My greatest achievement is actually doing this—creating a wine product that has never been done before," he says. "I'm a firm believer in the idea that things are brought to us for a reason. This was something I felt I had to do. So, this has been my greatest achievement—sticking with a process after more than 300 attempts and creating Amour Genève." Coviello often wonders why it was him. Why was his product chosen to be approved? "This is the universe speaking," he concludes.

Coviello believes anything is possible. "It takes persistence, being true to yourself and not listening to the negatives," he explains. "I truly believe you can do whatever you feel like you want to do." He dismisses what he deems as the "cookie-cutter shape of presuppositions" when society speaks about paths to success. He feels the educational system needs immediate reform to better prepare students for the trials of entrepreneurship. Art can liberate minds for greatness.

He's a skier and a golfer. With humor, he admits people wonder how he has time to do these things. "Networking and connecting with people has always been my strong suit," he says. "That is something I've always loved

BK FULTON AND NICHOLAS POWELL

to do. It keeps me balanced." To be a successful entrepreneur, Coviello emphasizes the importance of being present and not glued to the phone or computer screen. "To be a successful entrepreneur you have to understand all aspects of life, aspects of many cultures, and understand how to pivot," he says. "Pivoting is very important."

He continues to ponder the mentality needed to be a successful entrepreneur. "Understanding what direction to take at any given time—when to move, where to go, and how to time your movements is very important," he says. "You have to learn patience. Relaxing can help that; whether it be meditation or just going on walks." For a brief moment, he reflects on one of his father's favorite pastimes: walking. "My father would go out in nature and relax. I find myself doing that a lot now," he says. "It's crazy. You can't deny the gene pool," he laughs. As an entrepreneur, Coviello has a few projects in the pipeline including logistics applications and dealing with the important issue of mental health. "I'm working on a few interesting projects with some colleagues of mine. Most of them deal with mental health. Being a black entrepreneur in America can sometimes be very trying. I appreciate those in the industry who are keen on mental health and ask me how I'm feeling. 'Where is your mind?' 'How are you?' 'Where are your levels of stress?' I think those are questions we don't ask each other enough." This is an issue that hits close to home for Coviello.

In 2010, Coviello lost his father. "I lost my father very tragically. We still don't know what happened," he says. "Mental health is what sent him down a destructive road. I always wondered in those moments of his life, where was he? Nobody had ever asked him how he was doing; how was his mind. He never really discussed it and I wonder if it was something I could have changed." With his father's memory in mind, Coviello says he will continue to carry on his legacy. He looks to the universe to lead the way, after all that is what got him here in the first place.

To learn more about Amour Genève's blue wine, visit their website amourbluforever.com or follow Amour Genève on Facebook @ Amourgeneve and Instagram @amourgeneve.

"The metaverse is an opportunity to upskill economically stressed individuals into relevant new economy careers."

Marcus Shingles

Marcus Shingles Bets Big on the Metaverse

Marcus Shingles has always been a step ahead of everyone else. He started his career at the Kellogg Company. He quickly got into management and consulting, where he became an executive and partner at Deloitte, and Bain & Company, where he led practices that focused on business innovation and emerging disruptive technologies. Recently, Marcus was the CEO of XPRIZE, a nonprofit organization that uses incentive competitions to solve the world's most complex problems. He currently sits on the board of a host of mostly educational nonprofits like Stanford University's Disruptive Tech and Digital Cities Program and the World Economic Forum's Expert Network. He also is collaborating with the United Nations' International Telecommunications Union (ITU) agency on its Metaverse for SDGs Global Prize and VR Competition.

What he calls his current "day job," Marcus is the Chief Innovation Officer at MultiCORE International, where he is responsible for leading initiatives to design and build "smart cities" in Chiang Mai, Thailand; Cambodia, and other regions of the world. In the last seven years, Marcus has focused on what may be his most important job yet: mentoring youth and adult learners from primarily low-in-come and under-resourced communities. His educational nonprofit Exponential Destiny—a team of youth leaders from South Los Angeles—is preparing students for another disruption that is happening right now, the "metaverse". Marcus and his cofounders at Exponential Destiny believe the metaverse— an immersive 3D experience using augmented, mixed, and virtual realities —is a positive innovation that can be used to create a more immersive and experiential learning environment. This learning environment incorporates educational pedagogies around "edutainment".

Marcus and his leadership team at Exponential Destiny have been working with school administrators and underserved students in the public school systems of Los Angeles, Chicago, and Florida to experiment with leveraging this new technolgy.

Recently, Marcus Shingles took the time out of his busy schedule to talk to us about his nonprofit work, the metaverse, and what he hopes he and his team can accomplish within the next few years.

EXPONENTIAL DESTINY PRESENTING AT THE UN GLOBAL YOUTH SUMMIT IN KIGALI, RWANDA.

How did you get into working with and supporting young people in under-resourced communities?

I thought the education system was not contemporary and progressive. It was very linear versus thinking exponentially and staying up to date with what was relevant. My daughter was a biology major at a private university and I remember asking her if the professors had introduced the notion of CRISPR gene editing and she said they hadn't. I was just astounded by that. I didn't understand how you could get a degree in biology without an understanding of genetic engineering, especially CRISPR gene editing. If my own children are having challenges with getting current science through their paid education, then I wondered what an under-resourced kid in South Los Angeles was getting.

I went to Jefferson High School in South Los Angeles, which I originally read about in an article in the *Los Angeles Times*. The school got so scorched earth that they literally put out a request for proposal to get bids from people who could help reinvent it. The team that won the bid for the proposal was actually a group of parents and teachers from the community. They created the Nava College Preparatory Academy within Jefferson High School.

I said that I was consulting Fortune 500 corporate teams on the type of labor they would need down the pipeline; I was interested in sharing topics that would be relevant in teaching students how to be, what I called, "exponential entrepreneurs." The principal was receptive. So long story short, I went down and met with him and the superintendent

BK FULTON AND NICHOLAS POWELL

and we bonded. They were completely enthusiastic. We took what was a business elective and designed a curriculum that focused on upcoming technologies and innovations like AI, robotics, blockchain, 3D printing, and biotech. This was in 2015 and most of the students were sophomores. I am happy to say that the students who started the program have graduated and several are now running their own businesses. They are very successful. So much that I co-founded Exponential Destiny in 2020 with one of those students, Marco Vargas, to do something similar but at a grander and broader scale.

EXPONENTIAL TEAM ON AN "ADVENTURE TRIP" IN WYOMING.

Can you tell us why you are so excited about virtual reality and the metaverse as a potential leapfrog opportunity for schools, particularly those in under-resourced communities with limited budgets?

A little back story — I had the opportunity to speak at an executive summit with Fortune 500 executives. I was paid to talk about spatial web (what we now call the metaverse) and suggested to this community of executives that I would help advise them on a proof of concept for their business using virtual reality. We would then show the other executives their experiences in virtual reality at the summit three months later. The point was to see if we were able to create value.

I had my team at Exponential Destiny sign NDAs and had them on every call with the CEOs. These were twelve-week projects. After about week eight, the young people were the ones leading the projects. They realized they didn't need to be experts in business. They just needed to ask the right questions and be experts in how you build out these environments.

That is amazing. From a technical standpoint, how easy was it for your team to learn the software?

Virtual Reality Training & Education: 2020 Efficacy Study

VR Learners Were:

4x
Faster to train than in the classroom

275%
Improved Confidence - Acting on Issues: More confident to apply skills after training

3.75x
More emotionally connected to content than classroom learners

4x
More focused than their e-learning peers

Source: PwC VR Soft Skills Training Efficacy Study, 2020

https://www.pwc.com/us/en/tech-effect/emerging-tech/virtual-reality-study.html

This group wasn't the most technical group. Out of the twelve members of the team, maybe only three were somewhat technical. They were mostly liberal arts majors. The kicker was that the software was like learning Powerpoint in 3D. You didn't have to code anything.

Think about what that means. It doesn't matter what skill set you have. If you are determined and want to learn and have a creative mind, you can go into these spaces and build. This was like teaching someone how to build a website back in 1991 when the demand for building a website became part of every organization's internet and broader business strategy. This is history repeating itself, but this time, we have an opportunity to upskill individuals from low-income public school communities. We must do so proactively, versus teaching them how to code websites 30 years too late.

After we were finished with the first round of projects, we realized we were on to something and I said, "Let's do another seven projects. But this time you guys aren't shadowing me. You guys are the leads." And so we did another seven or eight projects. So at that point in early 2021, these young people were the most qualified metaverse designers probably on the planet, in terms of having projects under their belt that helped companies create value. You couldn't find a lot of examples back then because we were on the leading edge. We were giving software requirements for the leading software players, too.

And then there was a pivot.

We decided that this software is so effective that we thought it was best to bring it to schools. We started seeing statistics from an efficacy study by PwC in 2020 that showed how VR could help in not only learning hard skills but soft skills as well. Employees were divided into a classroom cohort, an online learning cohort, and a virtual reality cohort for training. The results of this study were significant. VR learners were 3.75 times more emotionally connected to the content and said they

BK FULTON AND NICHOLAS POWELL

could act on what they learned.

There is no surprise that there is a positive effect when you are experiencing it versus just reading about it. This doesn't mean VR replaces other methods. It just means you can do so much more.

EXPONENTIAL TEAM WITH LOS ANGELES HIGH SCHOOL FOR METAVERSE TRANSFORMATION.

Can you give a example?

When you are in these environments, you are dealing with digital real estate. If teachers want to talk to kids about how to live, eat, and stay healthy on a budget, they can build an entire supermarket, gamify it, and have kids walk through the store and purchase items virtually. This eliminates teachers from spending money out of their own pockets by bringing groceries into a physical classroom.

What was the first school district Exponential Destiny worked with after this pivot?

The first school district we worked with was Broward County, Florida, the sixth-largest school district in the United States. We worked with the chief administrative officer, the teachers, the principals, and the students on a six-month project that was funded by Verizon. I did the work pro bono and used the funding to pay the young people on the team a respectable $45-60k per year. They were the ones delivering these projects. We could have done this in two months, but the schools were busy. The students were busy. The teachers were busy. We really wanted them to commit to one hour a week. And if we spread that over six months, we could do a lot. We created educational pedagogies that the schools could adopt to improve learning and education around topics that were not successfully taught with traditional techniques, whether classroom or digital.

What other school districts are you working with?

We just finished a big project on the Westside of Chicago, in a school that is dealing with significant urban trauma and other social issues. We are fortunate to have worked with an exceptional principal there.

EXPONENTIAL TEAM WITH LOS ANGELES HIGH SCHOOL FOR METAVERSE TRANSFORMATION.

The school chose Social and Emotional Learning to Cope With Urban Trauma as their topic in VR. We also just finished a project with two schools from South Los Angeles.

When we work with a school, not only do we help the school to be self-sufficient and have this built into their curriculum as a new way of training and education, but we also deliberately try to attract any graduating senior into this project. They get upskilled and then our goal is to hire these seniors as one of the leads for our next school project. It is a way to get people employed but also into a professional salary.

What advice would you give to young people who would like to be entrepreneurs?

My advice to entrepreneurs, especially those in an economically stressed situation, is to find a technology that is starting to emerge and one that doesn't require a significant amount of technical degree to master, like the metaverse. It is not as technical as it sounds and it is something that is going to be in high demand. If you want to be an entrepreneur, there are going to be plenty of opportunities for you to be entrepreneurial in this space, especially if you adopt early.

I would also suggest learning all the tools in your toolbox. You don't have to be an expert at AI or robotics or quantum computing or biotech or 3D printing or virtual reality. But if you generally understand these innovations, as well as crowdsourcing or the sharing economy, you have a much broader mindset about what adds value to a business or a

BK FULTON AND NICHOLAS POWELL

nonprofit organization. Most people can't speak that language yet. Most people can't walk in and have a general understanding of what all these technologies do. And if you know all that, you are going to be more equipped to connect the dots and figure out the solution to problems.

Where do you see all of this work going and what are the team's ambitions?

This year my team and I were asked to do a keynote at the United Nations' ITU in Geneva. The ITU is the specialized agency of the United Nations that focuses on information and communication technologies. We did a 30-minute keynote on how the United Nations' sustainable development goals—zero poverty, economic stability, good work for everybody, and so on—can be affected by web 3.0 (the next version of the internet) and the metaverse. There is some real potential here.

I poked fun about how the metaverse is getting hijacked by commercialism and hype. You see NFTs being sold for $25 million at auction. With all of these headlines, it is really going to overshadow the real potential of the metaverse, which is to drastically transform how we educate and teach our citizens, and how we get people into a new skillset from every community.

With the support of the ITU and United Nations, we announced the Metaverse for SDGs Global Prize and VR Competition.

How can people sign up? What can they expect?

Teams can sign up at SDG Metaverse Prize. Teams of 2-6 people have 10 months to pick one of the UN's 17 sustainable development goals (SDGs). We will coach them over the next six to seven months on how to get into these environments and create spaces that bring empathy and awareness to these SDGs. We are raising money from different groups. In June of 2023, we will fly in the 17 top finalists and will have an overall best of show award at a United Nations' ITU collaborated summit for the Metaverse for SDGs Global Prize and VR Competition.

You have a lot on your plate. What is relaxation to you?

I recently bought a place out in Jackson Hole, Wyoming. I spend the majority of my year there, where I am kayaking down the Snake River, mountain biking or snowmobiling or snowboarding with a little bit of fishing here and there. That is how I find peace and tranquility—when I am just pausing for a minute.

CHRISTINE SIMMONS WITH HER SON
CHRISTIAN. PHOTOS BY APRIL JOHNSTON.

Christine Simmons:
Academy Trailblazer

In Rancho Cucamonga, a suburban city in San Bernardino County, California, Christine Simmons's mother raised her and her three sisters as a single mother. Her mother was independent, strong, and had all the love in the world to give her girls. "I watched her make the impossible possible without the help, raising us while working three or four jobs at a time," Christine says. "She did that for us and still does to this day. Even in retirement, she is the strength of our family. Because of her, we evolved into the women that we are today." As the former chief operating officer of the Academy of Motion Pictures and Sciences, Christine Simmons helped to evolve the structure of a nearly 100-year-old institution.

Christine is a big proponent for using your network of relationships for the greater good. She uses the term "social capital" to explain this critical social skill. When Christine had just graduated from UCLA, where she was premed, she met Los Angeles Lakers legend Earvin "Magic" Johnson. She asked Johnson about the health clinics he was beginning to open. They talked and found they had similar opinions about athletes and their transitions for making a living off the court. Christine and Johnson kept in touch and he became her mentor. "I checked in to see if he and his family were doing well over the years," she says. When she was the supplier diversity & sustainability manager at Disney World, Christine helped Mr. Johnson gain the opportunity to compete for a contract for his foodservice and facilities maintenance company, SodexoMagic. "I came to the relationship with something to offer," she says. "Even for someone as well regarded as Magic Johnson, it's important to have something to offer." He hired her to be vice president of strategic alliances for his company and eventually, executive vice president of Magic Johnson Enterprises. Social capital doesn't necessarily mean networking with famous people. You can also call on your friends from college. "It is so important to nurture relationships with your peers who you are coming up with," she says. "You keep nurturing these networks and social capital, so you can advance and be successful together. I think that is key, and this is how business has been for quite some time."

"What people should or shouldn't do in their careers is being challenged, and it is a beautiful thing to watch."

Christine appreciates the direction popular culture is headed in. Mainstream culture has defined who can create, who can get funding, and who can get exposure. "We are now reconciling with our past, whether it be in film or society," she says. "We are now breaking down the systemic infrastructure that has put people in these hierarchical positions that weren't always necessarily merited." The culture of work has changed as well. Employees are now venturing out on their own or moving from company to company for better opportunities. However, people looked at Christine funny when she moved from company to company, specifically after working in high-level positions. "People wondered why I didn't just stay and collect a pension," she says. "What people should or shouldn't do in their careers is being challenged, and it is a beautiful thing to watch."

After #OscarsSoWhite in 2015, the Academy created the A2020 initiative. The initiative addresses the criticism of the Academy's lack of diversity in its nominations and voting process. The goal was to double the number of women and people of color in the Academy's membership. Christine says they have met their goals and, in many ways, exceeded them. After the murder of George Floyd, Christine says the Academy doubled down on diversity and inclusion. To further its progress, the Academy created Aperture 2025 that details new standards for the film industry. "We chose the word aperture because we want to broaden the lens through which excellence is recognized," she says. Aperture 2025 includes several internal strategies for the Academy that address inclusion issues. The Academy has made unconscious bias training mandatory for its board of governors, branch executive committee members, and staff. They are looking at their investment portfolio. They are looking at HR and marketing and red carpet press. "All of these are tangential things that we as an organization can do," Christine says. "And that is on top of the talent, diversity, and development programs we have that are nurturing the next generation of filmmakers." The Academy has also made it a priority to target these groups in their Academy Gold programs, "a global talent development and inclusion initiative."

Aperture 2025's most significant change is the new inclusion standards for Best Picture. The measures won't go into full effect until around 2024. The inclusion standards center around four categories: in front of

BK FULTON AND NICHOLAS POWELL

the camera, behind the camera, internship/training/work opportunities, and marketing/publicity/distribution. Hollywood studios must make sure they include underrepresented racial/ethnic and identity groups in these categories. "We still need to do a lot of work in the Latinx community, the LGBTQ community, and the Indigenous/Native populations as well," Christine says. "These are all areas we have to shine a light on. There are so many beautiful and brilliant artists in these groups who deserve to be celebrated. We can do this and continue to lift our Asian and black brothers and sisters, women, and those with disabilities in the arts." The Academy Museum of Motion Pictures opened in late September of 2021. In 2022, *Regeneration: Black Cinema 1898-1971* will explore African Americans' history and their roles in cinema. "If you want to research the history of black cinema, you can do so in our library and our archives," Christine says.

> "If we can expose young men and women from all different backgrounds to all things that are possible, then you don't have those limits that society teaches them."

Advising those who would like to be in the industry, Christine recalls the advice of a colleague who suggested staying until the end of a film and watching the credits. Why? Because the end credits represent a giant listing of all of the jobs in the industry. "Some folks may want to be a studio exec, and that's great, but some folks may love technology or coding," she says. "Maybe they like dressing sets and location scouting. There are so many phenomenal opportunities for careers in film." She also recommends internships. The Academy has its Gold Rising Program. This program includes internships with the Academy and production and media companies like Jordan Peele's MonkeyPaw

BK FULTON AND NICHOLAS POWELL

Productions and Warner Media. Christine recommends networking and getting on set for those who would like a career change. "You may have to take a step back and be ok with that if you feel that is where your passion is," she says. Christine recommends that creatives just go for it, even if it is outside the traditional career path for filmmakers. "Tyler Perry did it," she says. "Ava DuVernay did it. Tons of folks are just starting out on their own. And that is beautiful too. You don't have to work within the system." She also suggests using iPhones to capture content. "Technology has helped democratize that a bit for us. Just do it and don't ask for permission," she says. When it is all said and done, Christine is excited about the Academy's work. She wants people to know that they don't have to be in Los Angeles to be part of the industry. "There are so many opportunities to meet our amazing members who are excited to welcome each new class of Academy members and create amazing movie magic together," she says.

While Christine has garnered many accolades and earned prestigious positions in the entertainment industry, motherhood takes the top spot. Her son, Christian, sees his mom as a leader. Accordingly, women in power have become second nature to him. She recalls when Christian was three and attended his first Sparks game when she was president and chief operating officer of the Los Angeles Sparks. The Sparks were his favorite team. "The guys who would ask him his favorite basketball team, when he would say the Sparks, they would say no, your favorite basketball team," she says. "I would have to pause and look at Christian and say, 'They mean men's basketball, my love.' He would then reply with 'Oh, the Lakers.'" Christine believes that exposure to women in traditionally male spaces can suspend some ingrained biases from childhood. "If we can expose young men and women from all different backgrounds to all things that are possible, then you don't have those limits that society teaches them," she says. Christine believes she is making a significant contribution to society by mentoring young people and teaching her son progressive values at home. "I love mentoring and empowering those who are coming after me; hopefully, they will outshine me and arrive sooner and bigger and faster than I did," she says. "I see myself building future leaders of tomorrow; ultimately, that is what we are put on the planet to do."

To learn more about Christine Simmons, you can follow her on Instagram.

'Know a good story when you see one'

Ron Simons: The Maestro of Broadway

Growing up in Detroit in the late 60s and 70s, Ron Simons was yearning for a way to get out. His family was blue collar like many during that time period. "I had a couple of ideas of how I was going to get out," he says. "Not atypical for most families, I was thinking doctor or attorney. I thought either of those goals might get me out of the poor neighborhood and on track to buy. I was really ready for change." His grandfather was a sharecropper in the South. He was part of the Great Migration. He didn't have more than a third-grade education but taught himself how to read. "I don't know how one does that." When he arrived in Detroit, his grandfather learned the skills required to get a job as a mechanic fixing cars. "It wasn't the worst paying job. It actually paid well back then, close to what people made on the assembly lines," Ron says. "I felt like that was an inspiration to me because it said to me that if you believe in what you are wanting to do and you work hard, you can achieve your goal."

In 1982, after graduating from Columbia University with a degree in computer science and English/theater arts, Ron had two choices: follow his dream as an actor or put his computer science degree to good use. He had put applications in at various technology companies and at the same time, he applied to the Yale School of Drama. He accepted a job at Hewlett-Packard. A week later, Ron got a phone call from the head of admissions at the Yale School of Drama. "The deadline has passed, but we were so enthusiastic about the package you sent in that we are going to extend the deadline for you," Ron recalls the voice at the other end saying to him many years ago. Ron was perplexed and began to think of every dilemma in his life: *How would I pay for it? Maybe I can get a loan, but you are already deep in debt from undergrad. And then when you get out of college, actors don't always make the most money. Your mother is about to retire, and your grandparents are already retired.*

After Ron rambled on about his concerns to the head of admissions, they wished him the best and ended the call. "I came to the conclusion that I was not going to pursue getting into the Yale School of Drama," he says. "I was going forward with my corporate plan because I needed to support my family. That did not change due to the Yale call but what did change was my focus and reassurance that acting and entertainment was where I was supposed to be. I felt like it was my destiny. That was the universe telling me that maybe not today or tomorrow or even five years from now, but somewhere down the line you are going to become an actor. Nineteen years later, I did."

"All of the places I've been in my life and the dedication, focus, and tenacity I had to learn folded into making me a better producer."

BK FULTON AND NICHOLAS POWELL

Even though Ron began his journey as an actor after graduating from the University of Washington with an MFA in Acting (2001), he soon became a little disgruntled with the projects that were being greenlit and the characters he was being asked to play. "I just thought they were mediocre," he says. "And I was like, you know what? I think I can do mediocre by myself. Matter of fact, I can do way better than mediocre." In 2009, he began to produce his own plays under his own production company – SimonSays Entertainment. He was in his late 40s. Notwithstanding this ostensibly late start, in 2012 his first production, *Porgy & Bess*, won a Tony Award for Best Revival of a Musical. This would be the first Tony of many for Ron.

In life, we don't always know which skills will be of the most use during particular phases of our careers. For Ron, he believes every degree he has earned and every job he has worked helped him to become a better producer. When Ron was studying at Columbia Business School in 1989, he took a course on managing personal and group dynamics. The course taught him how to deal with stress in his job and how to lead a team. His time as an actor taught him what makes a good story. "I don't know everything as a creative producer, but I do know a good story when I see one," he says. "So, when I find something, I leverage everything. All of the places I've been in my life and the dedication, focus, and tenacity I had to learn folded into making me a better producer."

When scouting for new productions to get behind, Ron looks for three characteristics. "The project must not only have a great story but must have commercial viability, artistic integrity, and it needs to focus on or support the stories of underrepresented communities," he says. His new Broadway play, *Thoughts of a Colored Man,* has all three. *Thoughts of a Colored Man* is the story of seven African-American men who discuss the issues that affect them the most. The play takes place over the span of a single day in a gentrifying Brooklyn neighborhood. "The characters speak about their truths in very authentic and raw expressions and words," Ron says. "It is the first time that I have heard a play that was totally devoted to the inner life of the African-American male. I have never seen that before." Ron says this will be the first play that was written and directed by African-American males, starring an all African-American male cast and produced by a majority of black men. "That has never happened before on Broadway," he says. "And part of that is because there are not enough black producers to go around. At last count, there were like six or seven of us."

Regardless of a lack of diversity in Broadway, Ron is grateful that he is providing opportunities for new black talent. "I get the chance to help give Keenan Scott II, a talented African-American writer, his opportunity to premiere on Broadway with his first play," he says. "It gave me the chance to provide an opportunity to give Steve H. Broadnax III, a talented African-American director, his Broadway debut. And at the end of casting, I realized we had a number of actors who were making their personal Broadway debuts." Wherever Ron goes, he wants to open the doors for more diverse voices to play a role in the larger picture. "I think that this piece contributes significantly to the American canon and diversifies and updates that canon, so there was just no way I could turn it down," he says.

"There are not enough black producers to go around. At last count, there were like six or seven of us."

Because his route to producing on Broadway was so unconventional, Ron doesn't recommend anyone following in his exact footsteps. "I woke up one day and wanted to produce," he says. "I hadn't read a book. I hadn't had mentors. I didn't take a class." He recommends pursuing educational opportunities like The Commercial Theater Institute, which has a comprehensive program for emerging producers. The program has a placement for 27 participants every year. He also suggests reading books like *Producer to Producer: A Step-by-Step Guide to Low-Budget Independent Film Producing* or *The Commercial Theater Institute Guide to Producing Plays and Musicals.* "There are so many ways that you can educate yourself," Ron says. "The reason why you want to educate yourself is twofold. First, you need to learn the vocabulary. You need to know what people are talking about so that you aren't in the dark trying to catch up. The other thing is if you can find a good course, you can find a good mentor who can advise you." Ron still calls on his professors from the University of Washington for advice.

"Whether it is in academia or a mentor or a working professional who is already a producer, you can sidestep some of the main traps that I have fallen into," he says. "If I had done it a different way and had learned more early on, I could have saved myself some heartache that was unnecessary." Regardless of these hurdles, Ron has gotten himself back up every time.

In 2022 Ron revised Ntozake Shange's *For Colored Girls Who Have Considered Suicide/When the Rainbow is Enuf. It* was led by acclaimed choreographer, Camel A. Brown. "This was the first time in over 65

Change the World: Tell the Untold Story.

years that an African-American woman has served as a director and choreographer for a Broadway show," Ron says. The first of a new genre called choreo-poem, this will be the first time *For Colored Girls* will be performed on Broadway in years. *For Colored Girls* and *Thoughts of a Colored Man* resonate so deeply with Ron because he sees his loved ones in the characters. "In *For Colored Girls*, I knew those women. My auntie is in there, my momma is in there, my cousin Rachelle is in there. In *Thoughts of a Colored Man*, my granddaddy is in there, my uncle is in there, my best friend is in there, my neighbor is in there." Ron is proud to present a revival play all about black women in the same season as a new play about black men. "If there are any Tony voters who are reading this, look out for both," he says. With four Tony Awards under his belt (the most for any African-American producer in history), Ron shouldn't worry too much.

> "I think that *Thoughts of a Colored Man* contributes significantly to the American canon."

Note: Ron Simons passed away on June 12, 2024. We will miss his genius.

"Always be ahead
of the curve."

Stacy Spikes

Stacy Spikes:
Disruptor-In-Chief

The means of how we see films is a rapidly changing process that no one can predict. Stacy Spikes is responsible for some of this disruption. He is an entrepreneur like no other. He developed the Urbanworld Film Festival in 1997—the premier festival responsible for bringing more diverse voices to the big screen. Ava DuVernay, Issa Rae, and Tiffany Haddish have all premiered work at the festival.

Stacy has an appreciation for films and works to make sure everyone can join in on the fun. "I am from Houston, Texas. I specialize in promoting the seeing and attending of movies via subscription or advertising services," he says. He's always had a passion for cinema. Streaming cannot replicate the magic feeling of seeing a movie in theaters. Stacy wants to preserve that feeling.

"We are working on some exciting brands that we will be partnering with around some exciting movies that people will get to see for free. We are thrilled to start to have customers use the service."

Now, Stacy is building something even more exciting and potentially more lucrative—PreShow. Stacy describes the service as "a next-generation platform that allows customers to see movies in theaters for free by using a proprietary ad platform." As of this writing, the Kickstarter campaign for the service has surpassed its campaign goal by more than 450 percent. Recognized as one of the top African Americans in technology by USA Today, Spikes has a talent for identifying what audiences want to see and putting it out into the world in an easily accessible package. "We are working on some exciting brands that we will be partnering with around some exciting movies that people will get to see for free. We are thrilled to start to have customers use the service," he says.

When one door closes, another opportunity usually presents itself. That opportunity may not come from someone else, but may come from within.

For more information on Stacy Spikes and his book, Black FounderThe Hidden Power of Being an Outsider visit www.stacyspikes.com.

"Diverse stories
are global."

David Steward II and Carl Reed: Intersectionality on the International Stage

David Steward II and Carl Reed are the co-founders of Lion Forge Animation, an Academy Award-winning animation studio based in St. Louis, Missouri. It is one of the only black-owned animation studios in the Nation. After winning an Academy Award for the short film, *Hair Love*, a story about a black father styling his daughter's hair for the first time, it was off to the races for the extremely talented David and Carl.

The son of a successful and pioneering entrepreneur, David Steward II saw first-hand the trials and tribulations of stepping out on your own and being one of the first to do something, but he also saw the success of what happens when you don't give up. In 2011, David partnered with Carl to launch Lion Forge Comics with the intention to push diversity in the comic book industry. Towards the end of the decade, David wanted to expand. In 2018, he created the holding company Polarity to house his many creative endeavors and ambitions. The next year, Lion Forge Animation was established.

Lion Forge Animation most recently inked a deal with Starlight Media (known for financing *Crazy Rich Asians* and its director-focused business model) to bring animated shorts and feature films to international audiences. The two studios are collaborating on an adaptation of the Chinese folktale *Journey to the West*. Diversity isn't just a measure of good faith but is ingrained in Lion Forge's business model. In our interview with the two creatives, we discuss the trials of entrepreneurship, what makes Lion Forge unique in the animation industry, and what it means to be a black creative today.

Where are you all from and what was it like growing up there?

David Steward II (DSII) – I grew up in St. Louis, Missouri, and that is where we currently are now. I was born and raised here, then spent a little bit of time in the Washington, D.C., area attending American University. I lived there for a couple of years and moved to LA for a short stint and then moved back here to St. Louis. It is one of those places that keeps drawing you back.

Carl Reed (CR) – I am also St. Louis raised, and I think there are not many places like St. Louis. I think we have, like everywhere, our scars. I lived right on those scars before they started healing up. Even in those places, there is a sense of community and a sense of being a part of something meaningful.

What was the most important lesson you learned in the early phases of your careers?

CR – One thing that I learned very early on, which I think helped me focus and continue to move quickly, is that we have a lot of control over the trajectory of our lives. You need to be single-mindedly focused on your goal. If you put in extra work, you are going to be on top from a position of skill. When Dave and I first met, we both had these agencies and merged them into a bigger agency. When you are creating a new business, you have to work in every role and learn how everything works. You have to dive in and learn from the pain points early so that you can experience the pleasure later.

DSII – Carl said it right when he said that it is important to become a jack of all trades and doing everything and understanding all aspects of a business. It is not just about doing what is fun. Before we became this creative agency, I took up photography. I had to do so much more than get behind the camera and take pictures. I had to do the sales, the marketing, the accounting and the business planning. Winning requires all these things that go around it. You start a business and it sounds all glamorous but, you know, 80 percent of what you are doing is business and 20 percent is working on the product or service that you are delivering. Because the business side makes it successful and puts you in the position to be able to do the work.

BK FULTON AND NICHOLAS POWELL

At what point did you begin to feel you all had made it?

DSII – I don't think we've made it. I am definitely not in that mindset. We are always hungry for more. We are always hungry for more success to grow bigger and better. Winning the Oscar was great for us, but it was really just the start. We see ourselves being the size of Dreamworks and beyond. We see ourselves being able to change the landscape of what the animation industry looks like in terms of diversity and black participation in particular. Diverse voices and portrayals on-screen happen because of the work. There is a lot of work that needs to be done and every success is a stepping stone to get to the next level.

CR – I think we would start to feel like we've made it when we are able to be a source that people can go to for authentic content and we are able to immediately say you know what, the world needs to see this and we have the ability to make it happen. That is what we are trying to do and what we are working towards.

Greatest achievements?

CR – That Academy Award win and the ability to be able to get on that national stage was huge. But from a greatest achievement standpoint, there was a time, I can't recall the name, when we published a children's book. We brought the book to my kid's kindergarten class to read. It was like this is what we are doing it for. It was not only a great achievement to experience but a great way to set the tone for what we wanted to do going forward.

DSII – Building on what Carl said, our greatest achievement so far is having a recognized presence in both the comics industry as well as the animation industry. And for those industries, that is something significant for a studio in the Midwest. These are hard industries to get into. It is hard to get people to work with you and return your phone calls. There is something to be said about breaking in and being able to make a phone call and people know who you are and what you stand for. We have the opportunity to really talk about doing meaningful business.

What characteristics do you all look for in projects that end up getting the green-light?

CR – We have a pretty strong and focused mission. We create content that challenges expectations and reflects the diversity of our audience. Those are our core two tenants. On one side: we challenge expectations. This means that there are no new stories. What are the unique perspectives that come out of this story? What is exciting about this?

On the other side: The diversity of our audience is directly correlated to our work because it defines what our characters look like, what the creative team looks like. How is it different in the market? Diversity directly affects those expectations because sometimes you have a different viewpoint. You are from a different community or culture, which will often challenge mainstream expectations and bring something new to the genre or the story.

Lion Forge Animation teamed up with Starlight Media for a joint picture partnership. You all are currently working on *Journey to the West,* which will highlight a Chinese folktale. Why was this partnership so important?

DSII — For us, it is really an extension of the work we started as a comic book company. Our company and all of the companies under our umbrella stand for diversity in all senses of the word. It is especially relevant when it comes to us being African American and how we know what it feels like to be overlooked and minimized in media representation. And so not only do we want to tell authentic African American stories, we also want to provide opportunities and be able to help aid and produce stories from other cultures that have been overlooked.

CR — And we couldn't have found a better partner than Starlight. They helped bring *Crazy Rich Asians* to the forefront. Who would have thought that a film with an entirely Asian cast would do so well in a traditional mainstream sense? Traditional Hollywood too often relegates productions with a majority-minority cast as not a mainstream thing. What they miss is how good these stories can be. So building upon that, I don't think we could have found a better partner to create something that focuses on Chinese folklore and we are looking forward to adding our perspective to something so deeply ingrained in Chinese culture.

DSII — In addition to *Crazy Rich Asians,* Starlight also funded *Marshall,* a story about Thurgood Marshall. They also have been cross-cultural in their support of movies. They are a true partner with us in authentic storytelling.

We hear a lot about the promise to be more diverse and more inclusive in the entertainment industry. As black creators/ executives, what specific changes do you want the industry to make?

DSII — I think they have just taken the first steps. In 2020, we have seen a proliferation of black executives that have gotten into influential positions in various companies. There is one thing to get the position and the title but what is going to be truly meaningful is if that person has the power within those companies to be able to really affect change, to be able to green-light projects, to affect who gets opportunities with and within these companies.

How those projects are received is vital as well. In the past, you had a lot of situations where diverse content would get greenlit but as that content is moving through the studio system you had non-diverse executives looking at the content and changing it based on what they thought that culture was. These executives were not relying on an authentic voice in these portrayals.

Based on stereotypes.

Right. Remember the movie, *Hollywood Shuffle*? There is a scene where Robert Townsend has to play a gangster and they say he has to be "blacker" and he's just like what?

BK FULTON AND NICHOLAS POWELL

It was a joke but that really happens. Hopefully, they embrace these executives and really embrace what they bring to the table and not only create opportunities but also help to make sure that content and voices are coming through in a real meaningful way.

What advice do you all have for young people who would like to get into production and animation?

CR – We live in a completely different time and it is crazy that even one generation ago our grandparents had to deal with media that consistently diminished who they/we are. Now we are in an even more unprecedented time where we can directly create something and put it out there immediately in our true voice. We don't have to get beat up or stumble as much as we used to, so I would encourage people, particularly the young, to create now. Fight for what you believe in. As you grow and your skills improve and your audience grows, you can then talk to people in positions of power with a level of confidence that evens the playing field a bit.

DSII – The best thing you can do, especially for breaking into this industry, is to invest in yourself. Investing in your own personal education, knowledge, and ability to do things. The more you can do and the more you can do on your own, the less you have to rely on other people to get it done. So if you have a vision that you want to put out, you can achieve that on your own.

You are also not limited by what might go wrong in the process as well. There are times where you might be collaborating and something gets halted and stalled. You have the ability to jump in and fix it if you have the skillset.

The ability to teach others is also important. One thing that we have been able to do effectively is to build teams. We are able to teach those teams how to engage on the different aspects of production and come up with ways to do it more effectively and efficiently. I cannot underscore enough the importance of internal knowledge when coming into this industry.

To learn more about Lion Forge Animation, you can visit lionforgeentertainment.com.

"Expose yourself to what is
beautiful about this world."

Adriana Trigiani

Adriana Trigiani's
Hope for Humanity

Adriana Trigiani is a proud Italian American, prolific fiction writer, screenwriter, director, playwright, and former TV writer and producer. She's from Big Stone Gap, Virginia, located in the region where Virginia meets with four states: North Carolina, Tennessee, West Virginia, and Kentucky. She calls her hometown the "enchanting part" of the mountainous region. "I'm a very proud Appalachian," she says.

Early on in her writing career, Adriana worked on *A Different World,* a popular sitcom that aired for six seasons in the late 80s and early 90s. This is where she learned three lessons as a young writer: make your deadline, be persistent and have a message. "You got to know who you are and what you're writing about," she explains. "You have to have a sense of clarity about your message and that leads to excellence." Because Adriana has lent her talents to film and television, she understands who is "king" in each medium. The writer is king in television while the director is king in film.

Giving insight into her creative process, Adriana Trigiani sees herself as a writer who takes it day by day. "There are people who will create one thing that is perfect," she says. "Then there are people like me who are workaday journeymen who have to keep working at it to get better." She finds it impossible to be sitting at a desk writing a novel for long periods of time. She says she may come up with an idea or do research for long periods of time, but once she starts to write, it is off to the races. "I could not be entertained by something for 10 years on a daily basis," she says. "I could not be engaged in that because I would be focusing on one thing for too long."

Writing and directing the film *Big Stone Gap*, based on her novel of the same name, holds a special place in her heart. "We filmed in my hometown. I'm not going to tell you for one second that it was easy," she says. "It was very hard but joyful." She admits working with a crew and different personalities were part of that difficulty. Sometimes you just don't get along. But Adriana knows how to stay focused on what's important. "You can't let them get to you. You just have to roll over them and keep it moving," she says jokingly. "You continue to

PHOTO BY TIMOTHY STEPHENSON

work with the people you love and stop working with the people you don't." She understands all working relationships aren't equal. "Learn to work with people who will appreciate your gifts," she says. "Maybe I didn't?"

Even though Adriana lives in New York City now, she still finds similarities between the big city and the place she grew up. "I lived here most of my life," she says. "The neighborhoods are like small towns." Even though there are similarities, Big Stone Gap has an edge over New York City for Adriana. "I always said that if you want to understand street smarts, then come to Big Stone Gap, don't come to New York City," she asserts. "They are sharp as tacks where I'm from and they know what they are talking about." With that being said, she does appreciate the diversity of New York City. "There is every color, nationality, and gender. We got it and we flaunt it," Adriana says proudly.

> "I would argue in the United States of America, we still have not had that watershed moment for black people and other people of color."

Back when Adriana was a theater major at Saint Mary's College in South Bend, Indiana, she learned what it takes to put on a production. Anything can happen and you must know what avenues to take to keep it going. She applies this early lesson to her directing. "I got excellent training but all training does is reinforce what you might do," Adriana says. Adriana explains the perspective you must have when creating a film. "You have to have a very visual sense of the world," she explains. In order to be successful, you also have to be flexible. "Yes, it's all about experience, but it has to do with your flexibility as a creator. You can't get calcified in your thought process ever. You have to be open and you have to listen to your audience."

BK FULTON AND NICHOLAS POWELL

Adriana also focuses on the business side of the entertainment industry and how you must be on your p's and q's. "You have to know when people are playing you. That's on the money side," she says. You also have to be resourceful. "You are going to have to figure out why a certain costume didn't show up on set or where to find the money if the person raising the money cannot find it," she says.

ADRIANA TRIGIANI WITH CHRISTINA GEIST. PHOTO COURTESY OF ADRIANA TRIGIANI.

While xenophobia, racial bias, diversity and inclusion, in general, come up in our discussion surrounding media and America, Adriana is also reminded of the prejudice and discrimination Italian-Americans experienced in the first half of the 20th century. She acknowledges Italians who migrated to America were not always welcomed, especially before World War II (WWII). "Prior to WWII, no white person ate spaghetti above 14th Street in New York City," she says. "Nobody mingled with the Italians. The Italians were persona non grata. We were associated with crime and this and that." Things soon changed when Italian Americans began to be more visible in the media after WWII. Beacons like Sophia Loren, the Italian haircut and the rise of people and groups like Vic Damone, Frankie Valli, the Four Seasons, and Dion and the Belmonts helped to change minds about Italians in America.

Adriana also gives credit to the draft during WWII for ushering in a newfound acceptance of Italians. "All of these young men—the rich, poor, and the in-between . . . had to go fight," she says. "You had Christians, Jews, and Muslims fighting for a united cause." As they were stationed in Italy and began to eat the food, the threat of the Italian-American began to dwindle. "When they returned, they were busting over to 14th street to go to Little Italy to eat. It became a thing," she says. Italian culture was now mainstream. She reminds us of the canned spaghetti and meatballs called Chef Boyardee created by Hector Boiardi becoming a popular choice for supper in American homes. She says this moment has yet to happen for other ethnic groups, particularly black people. "I would argue in the United States of America, we still have not had that watershed moment for black people and other people of color." But she believes that moment is coming soon.

Adriana reflects more about identity and race. She recalls attending Diahann Carroll's memorial service. She heard Lenny Kravitz give his speech honoring her and talking about her being like family. But what stood out for Adriana was how he mentioned his mother and the influence she had over him. His speech made her think about identity and being proud of who you are. She says in order to be proud of who you are, you have to be proud of what you have accomplished. For people of color to be liberated, their accomplishments must be addressed by those in power. But with that acknowledgment comes a sense of responsibility for past wrongs. "It is a consequence to tell people the truth about our history," she explains. "We got to tell the stories. That's important and they have to be repeated and they have to be in our school books."

"Learn to work with people who will appreciate your gifts."

Adriana has a few creators and writers that she really admires and would love to work with. Writer/actress/producer Lena Waithe is the first person that comes to mind. "She has a show called *Twenties* on BET. A beautiful woman of color named Susan Fales-Hill is her showrunner," she says. "Lena Waithe is just putting a lot of great product out there." She also mentions the novelist Lauren Groff (*Fates and Furies*) and poet Ben Lerner. "I think he's terrific," she says. She also mentions Jean Kwok (*Searching for Sylvie Lee: A Novel*—a mystery identity novel). "She grew up in Brooklyn, worked in a factory and went to school at the same time. I think she's fantastic," she says. Nodding to our previous discussion about diversity she says, "There's some color up in there."

For young writers, she suggests to simply start putting pen to paper. "How do you do it? Write something every day and what will emerge is the kind of writing you will be doing," she says. "Maybe you like to research and write about what you have found. Maybe you're a non-fiction writer or a poet. If the pages are filled with dialogue, then you may be the next great playwright. Now get into the theater!"

"Things will never be the same. It will be an adjustment, but change does not always mean misfortune."

BK FULTON AND NICHOLAS POWELL

Her message for parents is simple as well: Expose your children to culture and the arts. "For your children who you think are creative, take them to museums, shows, and to plays. It doesn't matter what they see specifically, just take them," she says. "Let them see the world on the stage. Take them to concerts and expose them to all kinds of music even if they think they hate it. It's nothing like taking a kid to opera. They will be either mesmerized or bored, but there will be something."

She says all of these art forms are available in communities, you just have to look. She also mentions the importance of reading and taking children to the library. "Make reading a pleasurable experience for kids. Let them read actual books," she says. "Take away that iPad for a little bit." She emphasizes, children who read go on to make the world a better place," she says. "I don't think it is time for doom and gloom. I think it is time for action." We conducted this interview before COVID-19. As we work our way through this global pandemic, her words are more prescient than ever. "Things will never be the same. It will be an adjustment, but change does not always mean misfortune." Adriana's words ring more urgent now than when they were first uttered to SoulVision Magazine a few months ago. We must take action to change our world for the better. We have the power to make change a good thing. Thank you, Adriana, for doing your part.

To learn more about Adriana Trigiani and her projects, you can visit her website adrianatrigiani.com and follow her on Facebook, Instagram, and X.

ADRIANA TRIGIANI WITH KATHIE LEE GIFFORD (LEFT) AND HODA KOTB (RIGHT). PHOTO COURTESY OF ADRIANA TRIGIANI.

"Keep yourself centered

Tobias Truvillion
Has Arrived

Tobias Truvillion is grateful for the progress he's made in his career. When Tobias is on screen, he is natural and charismatic. A standout in his role as Greg Jeffries in the romantic-comedy, *Love Dot Com*, Tobias started out on the stage at The National Black Theater of Harlem and trained under the auspices of the late great Tundé Samuels. On stage is where he garnered the prestigious AUDELCO Award, a theater award bestowed among some of the finest African American actors like Denzel Washington, Wesley Snipes, Ossie Davis, Ruby Dee, and other icons. He eventually ventured into the soap opera world where he played Vincent Jones on ABC Daytime's *One Life to Live*. Now, he's had roles in major television shows like *Empire* and will star alongside legends like Jill Scott, Malik Yoba, Anthony Mackie, Vince Vaughn, and young stars like Kristen Stewart and Zazie Beetz in upcoming projects. Tobias sat down with us to discuss his biggest inspirations growing up, the lessons he's learned so far in his career and his works on deck. After more than a decade into his career, it feels like Tobias Truvillion has arrived.

Where are you from and what was it like growing up there?

I'm originally from the Flushing, Queens area of New York City. We lived in a place called "The Ville." The Ville was this little pocket of black middle-class families. My grandfather, who was West Indian, arrived from Barbados. He met my grandmother who was from Virginia in New York. They eventually settled down in Flushing and had five children.

Flushing was a very competitive place growing up. There was a lot of style and a lot of swag. I think of people who grew up there. Julius Erving and Rap and Hip-Hop icons that Big Daddy Kane and Salt-N-Pepa. It was a town that influenced a lot of people and culture. Unfortunately, it also took out a lot of people.

Growing up in the late 80s and early 90s, there was a sense of brotherhood in the culture. It was just a beautiful time. We played sports. Everybody around the way was into either football or basketball. It's crazy to think about how long ago that was, where we are today, and remembering those who aren't with us anymore.

Who or what was your biggest inspiration growing up?

My biggest inspiration growing up was my football coach, Kenny Wolf. When you're a preteen, you are trying to figure out your place in the world. You aren't quite a teenager, but you're headed there.

Playing football was my number one passion. I was always a starter. Kenny would hold you responsible for your actions. I remember getting off the bus in Alley Pond Park for warm-ups. As a warm-up, you had to

BK FULTON AND NICHOLAS POWELL

SIGNED STAND-IN PHOTO FOR MICHAEL JORDAN'S "SIX RINGS" CAMPAIGN. COMPARED SIDE BY SIDE. PHOTOGRAPHY BY DAN WINTERS.

run laps around the park and come back and do calisthenics. After seeing everyone get off and leave to run, me and a couple of the guys decided to stay back. We were like, "Ok, we'll run over there when we do the calisthenics." But little did we know, Kenny could see us from the bus stop. He comes running over to us and he looks at me and looks at the fellas and he says, "Guys, what are you doing over here?!? We're a family. Toby (what people called me back then), you're a starter. Come on! Get over here!" He was a solid, blue-collar kind of guy. Kenny was a great man.

He also formed a great team and helped me to develop my character. That was really my first lesson about teamwork—setting yourself apart, but being selfless and a part of the team. I thought about him my entire life. Twenty-five years or so later, I saw his wife, Susan, on Facebook. We reconnected. I could not wait to talk to him. I had tears in my eyes.

What has been the most important lesson you've learned so far in your career?

Two things were key for me. First, you can't put yourself above the work. Second, you have to be who you are. It is important to know about your ancestry and family history and be involved in your community. At times, it feels like the media machine has been turned against us. It can be hard to find your way in this industry as an artist and as a man.

In this art, knowing who you are will protect you, as long as you keep God first and keep yourself centered. I really believe those are the things that give you the courage and strength to push through. Always check in with yourself. When I was a youngster, I remember when the drug epidemic divided the community. Through culture and how we pulled together, we were able to push past that. Right now, our culture still has a great influence on the economy and in this world. We also have some stuff to push through, especially self-doubt.

Do you feel like you have made it?

Absolutely not. I'm still growing as a man and in my career. I look at the early part of my career and compare it to today. I'm working on projects that are totally different. I'm always staying true to myself, learning to be more vulnerable, and more open to opportunities that allow me to continue to grow in my craft and as a human being. I have had a long career and I'm now getting into a space that allows me to be able to stretch a little bit more.

When you're playing supporting roles, you're placed in the story in a certain way and you try to put on your best performance. When you're in leading roles, you get to create a different kind of art. I am grateful to be in this place in my career. I'm getting leads.

BK FULTON AND NICHOLAS POWELL

What would you consider to be one of your greatest achievements?

One of my greatest achievements was when I was asked to host the Harry Belafonte, Martin Luther King Tribute Ceremony. As I strive to serve through philanthropic efforts in my community, it was an honor to contribute to this event as it acknowledged another amazing historical figure. It was one of the most humbling experiences for me. I also had an opportunity to recite the speech that he wrote for Dr. King, "Kind of Man."

I also had a chance to work with the GOAT of basketball, Michael Jordan. I was the stand-in model for Michael Jordan in one of his videos. It was for his sixth ring campaign. When you're a stand-in, they come in and adjust the lights so that when the stars come in, they only have to be there for less than fifteen minutes and can leave. The day before, they came up with all of these ideas. Mike comes in and I get the chance to wear all six of his rings and meet the greatest baller of all time. He signed one of my Polaroid's from the shoot. That was pretty cool.

What was the biggest challenge working in the film world compared to the soap opera world?

Soap operas are actually a good training ground because soaps move so fast. There is actually more work in a soap than there would be in a film. Soaps are more intense because there is a lot of dialogue and dramatic scenes that take time and energy. It's grueling. You can't mess up. You only get one or two takes. When you're in a film, you can stay with a character and build out the role for as long as it takes to get it right.

In *Love Dot Com*, you play the urban planner Greg Jeffries. What attracted you to the role? What lessons do you hope audiences will learn from your character?

There are things in my life that lead me into that moment. It was an opportunity to play a leading man and play alongside the beautiful and talented Brave Williams. I met some great people in Washington, D.C. I love D.C. That's what made me want to do the picture. I wanted to channel the vibe of the city with my role.

I think Greg was a good man. Just like in D.C., there are people in my city that are in politics and redevelopment. They are also supportive of the community. I lived that life. Playing Greg Jefferies was like being somebody I already knew. It was natural. It was familiar. It's a black love story and we have to do the work to change the way we are portrayed and what we portray on screen. *Love Dot Com* points out the importance of eating better, living right, and loving right. It all was authentic and that's cool to me.

You worked with Rodney Gilbert, Artistic Director of the Advantage Arts Program for Youth at the Dr. Marion A. Bolden Center. What has been the most rewarding experience you have had working with the youth in the program?

Putting people above yourself is part of our legacy. It's not that you have to know everything and be the best, but you do have to get in where you fit in. We have an obligation to each other. We're in a crazy world and I'm so happy that I'm blessed to do the work that I do and have an impact on the next generation. I hope my work and my story helps young artists believe that their dreams can come true.

What advice would you give to young actors trying to make it in the entertainment industry?

I think about Nipsey Hussle's message about never quitting—running the "marathon." You have to endure a lot to be in this game and you have to be able to give it up. What I mean by "give it up," is that you have to give it up to God. You have to know who you are when you step into this industry. The movie machine can be very unforgiving. At the same time, it is a beautiful place where you can work and build your fortune. Did I mention it's a lot of work!? It's not a hobby. The industry is built on the labor of a lot of talented people that paid dues before you got here. So get in, do the work and make your dreams come true.

My favorite producer, Tundé Samuels, says, "You always hear me say I'm in the game, still playin'." That's how you have to be. You've got to be in it and if you're in it, you have to pull your weight. No one owes you anything. You have to pull people up with you—lift as you climb."

What projects are you currently working on?

Love Dot Com was released in 2019. We love D.C.! Up next was *First Wives Club* in the same year on BET. It's with Malik Yoba, Jill Scott, and Michelle Buteau. *Equal Standard* is an independent film released in 2020. I also did a Christmas movie called *Holiday Heist*, and a true crime series on TV One called *Love to Death*. In the very near future, I would like to produce projects of my own.

How do you relax when you are not working?

I love to cook. I'm on this new health tip. I make all kinds of food and now I'm on this vegan/vegetarian lifestyle, so my recipe book is expanding. I've always tried my best to live a healthy lifestyle—taking care of myself physically, mentally and spiritually. People don't know I also do a lot of photography in my free time.

But the best thing to do when I'm not working is to be still. When you are on and off the road in different cities and you have been working 16 hours a day for three or four months, you just want to chill at home. I'm going to sit back and mind my business. I get to listen to my classic soul on Saturdays while cleaning the house. If I don't do that, I will lose my mind. That's the main thing that helps me keep my sanity. Once I get my energy in order, I like to travel and see different cities on my own time. Traveling helps me replenish my thoughts and spirit so when I do the work, I can pour all of my energy and new experiences into it.

MAX TUCHMAN, CEO AND CO-FOUNDER OF CARIBU, AN INNOVATIVE VIDEO-CALLING APP. PHOTO BY MICHELLE CITRIN.

"Early childhood literacy is integral to the well-being of us all."

Max Tuchman's
Devotion to Literacy

Max Tuchman is the former CEO and cofounder of Caribu, an innovative videocalling app that connects kids with their families to read and draw together over long-distances. A child of immigrants, Max was born in the beautiful city of Miami, FL and always knew the value of education and self-worth. When she looks back at her Miami upbringing, she appreciates the radical diversity she was a part of. "I was born and raised there," she says. "It is like New York City, where you grow up around a ton of diversity—socioeconomic, racial, ethnic, and religious—and everything and everyone." She believes diversity is helpful to the city's evolving reinvention of itself. While growing up, she saw how people who migrated to Miami worked their way up to the top and into the C-suite. "Miami inspired me to be whoever I wanted to be because I saw it," she says. "I'm '305 ride or die' like Pitbull. I'm really proud to be from here."

Her family had to endure immense tragedy and wars to get to a place where they felt secure. Her paternal grandparents survived the Holocaust. Her maternal great-grandparents survived the Bolshevik Revolution. Both families ended up in Cuba. "When you grow up with that type of history where your grandparents, your great-grandparents, and parents were constantly having to flee, you grow up with a sense of education being the most important thing. It is the only thing you can take with you and nobody can take away," she continues, "You can sew your silverware and jewelry into your coat, but at a certain point what you have in your head is the greatest asset you can take with you to the next country because it gives you the opportunity to succeed there."

Max attributes her work ethic to her family's history of struggle and achievement in spite of the obstacles. "I'm an overachiever because I feel like I can never repay my family for their sacrifices. Nothing is enough. Getting into Harvard (She earned her M.P.P. from the Harvard Kennedy School of Government and an M.B.A. from the Harvard Business School) and into the White House Fellows program was not enough," she says. She wants to do more. She gives back to her community and wants to continue to extend

MAX TUCHMAN AND KIDS HAVING FUN WITH THE CARIBU APP.
PHOTO BY SONYA REVELL

a helping hand to anyone who needs it. "I know so many people who reached out a hand and gave my parents and grandparents a lot of resources and opportunities," she says. "It is my obligation to pay it forward."

Max lives by the golden rule of treating everyone the way you would like to be treated. In business, she says it is important to treat everyone like you're equal, no matter their position in the company. "I feel you should treat everyone well from the most senior people to the most junior people, including those who clean the offices and/or do security because everyone is a human being and has value," she says.

As a "minority" in a leadership position, Max believes unity between women and all so-called minorities is vital to success. According to Max, you should ask yourself two questions when walking into a room: *Whose voices are not being heard? and Who's not even in the room?* Beyond just race and gender lines, Max says we need to look at other types of diversity like people's abilities. As a businesswoman, she believes diversity can do more good than bad for business. "Believing and practicing diversity makes you a better leader," she says. "If you don't take diversity into account, you are not serving all people and it is important for you to make sure your product is actually solving people's pain points."

When Max was beginning her career, she taught government and economics for Teach For America in a high school in Liberty City, FL. The majority of the school's population was black—African American, Haitian American, Jamaican American, and Nigerian American. Most of the school's population did not have the opportunity to go out of their neighborhoods and explore the Miami she knew and loved. Max had an assignment for them: research religious winter holidays that were not Christmas. They came back with Hanukkah and Diwali. The assignment eventually expanded to other holidays that did not fall on the traditional U.S. holiday season, like Ramadan. One of Max's students worked as a candy striper at the local hospital. She wanted to make a sign that showed respect to all of the different holidays. But she wanted to make sure she had the correct spellings of each holiday, so she texted Max and asked, "Can you help me with spelling the holidays correctly?" "I was just so proud at that moment because she saw everybody," Max says. "All of a sudden, her world was expanded. She wanted to be kind and considerate to every patient and let everyone in the hospital know about all of the holidays that were being celebrated there."

"Believing and practicing diversity makes you a better leader."

While teaching government and economics at the high school, she received a grant to buy and teach the lessons in *Rich Dad, Poor Dad for Teens*. They also received a game called the CASHFLOW Board Game as part of the grant. "It was all about showing kids that you're going to live paycheck to paycheck unless you invest, buy assets and think about ways you can save your money," she explains. She remembers one of her students—Oluremi—saying to her, "You know Miss, the Miami Arena is up for sale and I think it's a good asset and I think I should buy it." Her work was figuratively done. "All you want as a teacher is to make some kind of impact—hopefully long-lasting—on a kid's life," she says.

"For me, I could see his prospects in the world being so different, because he knew the difference between an asset and a liability, and he was already thinking about investing in real estate."

In 2015, Max, and fifteen others were appointed by former President Obama, to serve as White House Fellows. This was during his last year in office and Max was given the opportunity to work for the US Department of the Treasury. In her teaching days, she worked with students on financial literacy, but it was not at this scale. "Here I was thinking about not only financial literacy but inclusion and ensuring every American had an opportunity to be banked and that students weren't being crushed by their student loan debt," she says.

"It is unfair to children if we allow them to graduate from school and they can't read a job application or even read for pleasure."

Max says every Tuesday and Thursday, Fellows had the opportunity to sit with the President, First Lady, and members of the Cabinet for lunch. "We would sit and talk and ask any questions we had," she says. "They gave us advice and let us know their mistakes as well as the lessons they learned that lead to the successes in their careers." She remembers talking to former Secretary of State, Colin Powell. He let her know he was also a former White House Fellow and his experiences outside of being in government. "It was mind-blowing. You can't recreate that anywhere else," she says.

Max sees Caribu as a vehicle for advancing early childhood literacy. She refers back to her time as a 12th grade teacher. It was then that she realized how the education system failed her students who could not read at grade level. She had 180 days to get them to the point where they could be productive in the world. "It is unfair to children if we allow them to graduate from school and they can't read a job application or even read for pleasure," she says. "This is unacceptable." When she was a White House Fellow, she met the former Secretary of Education, Arne Duncan. She asked him if he had unlimited funds what would he put a majority of his focus on. He said he would focus on early childhood education. She says he believed it could change the world.

Through her research, Max understands quantity and quality are two factors that help in early childhood literacy. "There are two components to learning to read: there's quantity of reading and quality of time reading. We do both, but we really focus on quantity," Max explains. "From 0-3, kids should be reading a minimum of 20 minutes a day and should be hearing 30,000 unique words every day, and that is hard." What makes Caribu different from services like Skype and FaceTime, is the ability to play games, draw and most importantly, read from a library of over 1,000 books in-app with a caring adult who might be located anywhere in the world. It's very cool and easy to use.

The idea for Caribu came from a photograph of a soldier trying to read to his daughter through a webcam. The team at Caribu wanted to know how they could make this exchange more fun and engaging. It also inspired the team to partner with *Blue Star Families*, a non-profit that helps those in the military, to donate Caribu to active duty military families. With Caribu, consumers have access to over a thousand titles

BK FULTON AND NICHOLAS POWELL

in eight languages. While Max understands not every family can afford $6.99 a month, she believes the service is affordable for most and costs less than one hardcover book.

For Max, Caribu solves some of the problems she saw while she was the executive director of Teach For America Miami-Dade. They would have students, including football players (who the kids idolized) to spend time reading with the elementary school kids across the street. After the readings were over, the children could take the book home with them. She recalls one girl in second grade running up to her sister and screaming with excitement, "Look, I have a book. It's going to be the only book in our house! It's going in my room!" Max was shocked. "I couldn't believe it, but that is the reality," she says. "For me, it is about high-quality access and making sure that kids have access to a library of high-quality books."

"If you are constantly trying to surprise and delight your customers, you will always win."

For young entrepreneurs, Max advises them to chase the customer and not the investment dollars. "Fundraising is not why we build companies," she says. "We build companies because we found a problem customers have and we can solve it better than anyone else." When a young entrepreneur is focused on thinking about the customer, they will always be successful. "If you are constantly trying to surprise and delight your customers, you will always win," she says.

Max sees Caribu becoming a household name. She wants everyone to have the chance to experience Caribu. "I want every child to have a way better reading experience with their parents and grandparents no matter where they are. I also want kids to read a lot more," she says. "I want them to have a fun time with long-distance families. I want them to enjoy art, coloring, and reading stories of faraway lands with people who may look like them and some who don't look like them. When we have fully accomplished that for every child, it will bring me the greatest joy."

All seven books of the Mr. Business: The Adventures of Little BK series are available on Caribu. To learn more about Max Tuchman and Caribu, you can visit caribu.com and follow them on Facebook, X, and Instagram.

PHOTO COURTESY OF CARIBU.

"Do something great
with your gifts."

Ed Welburn

Ed Welburn:
Master of Design

Before "graduating from his last corporate gig," Ed Welburn designed cars for a living at General Motors (GM). In fact, he was a trailblazer and innovator, known to be the highest-ranking African American in the automobile industry. Ed recently spent some time with SoulVision to reflect on his career. "I've never had one of those jobs where it was just work," he says. "I wouldn't even call it a job. It doesn't quite fit. My work has always been and continues to be fun, fulfilling, and rewarding."

Even at 19 years old working as a tow truck driver at a Chevy dealership during the summer, Ed didn't think of it as work. "I have a big smile on my face thinking back to those days," he says. In this next phase, he relaxes at home and enjoys making creative playlists driven by the mood he is in. He spends time in his office sketching like he did when he began working as a designer many decades ago. "I see no value in sketching what everyone else is doing," he says. "You need to look at what's next and what is different."

One of his latest projects is founding the Welburn Group, which houses Welburn Media Productions. He is currently the design advisor for Usain Bolt's *Bolt Mobility*, a micro-mobility company that specializes in e-scooters. He's developing athletic shoes as well. His film company is currently developing *Eraced*, the story of Charles Wiggins, a great African American race car driver during the 1920s and 1930s.

Ed always knew he wanted to design cars. "My inspiration came from the great automobiles of the time," he says. From a young age, he was focused on automobile design. "I've been drawing cars since I was 2 and a half," he says. "By the age of 8, I decided car design was what I wanted to do."

> "My whole mission was to become a designer for GM. I never even thought about working for another company... never."

Ed remembers being a child at the Philadelphia Auto Show with his parents. "The auto show was my Disney World," he says. He remembers seeing a concept car that "just blew [him] away." He would later find out the concept car was a Cadillac Cyclone. As a child, Ed had difficulties with reading. His mother placed him in special programs that would help him with his reading, but they did not improve his reading. She knew he had an interest in cars so she bought young Ed a subscription to *Road & Track, Sports Car Graphic, and Autoweek.* "It was in those magazines where I found the company that designed the Cadillac Cyclone and I wrote them a letter at the age of 11," he says. That letter ended up in the hands of Milo McNaughton, head of personnel and design. The letter revolved around information about careers in the industry. That initial letter led to ongoing communication with Mr. McNaughton through Ed's middle and high school years. "My whole

BK FULTON AND NICHOLAS POWELL

mission was to become a designer for GM," he says. "I never even thought about working for another company...never."

After graduating from Howard University's School of Fine Arts, Ed landed a job as an associate designer at the Advanced Design Studio of General Motors. He was the first African American to be hired into this position. "I didn't realize I was a trailblazer when I walked through the doors of General Motors for the first time," he says. "I was simply thrilled to reach this lifetime goal of mine to be a designer for GM." Thinking about that time, he says he was aware that how he carried himself would affect those who came after him. He also knew that his performance would reflect on his alma mater. He was determined to have an impact. In design, designers would display their autographed work for everyone to see and critique. It took Ed a while to learn how to take constructive criticism. "One of the other designers might have told me my sketches would look better here with a little bit of blue on the highlights of the finders," he said. "It might be another month or another year before I would implement that advice. Taking input from others is something that is really important. It is not easy to do sometimes."

Ed was definitely a trailblazer and after a long 30-year journey and a lot of hard work, he eventually became the first African American VP of Design. "The journey was very rewarding," he says. Ed was only the 6th person in the history of GM to hold that title. He held this position for 13 years. He felt like he was still learning and growing until his eighth year of the position. By then, he had evolved the job into a global operation. "I had taken what had been regional design and created this global deal," he says. "I felt like our responsibility in design was more than designing the cars; it was the aesthetic of everything in the company." This led to working with Michael Bay on the design of the cars in *Transformers,* including the Camaro.

"I didn't realize I was a trail-blazer when I walked through the doors of General Motors for the first time."

The Camaro is Ed's favorite. He and his team were developing the new Camaro styling before it appeared in the first *Transformers* film in 2007. After connecting, Ed took Michael to the secret location where they were designing the Camaro and he instantly knew the Camaro would be Bumblebee. "We then developed this whole plan that we were going to build a silver one for the auto show and a yellow one for the movie. It all worked in harmony," Ed says. Michael and Ed formed a lasting partnership that led to a brief speaking role by Ed in *Transformers: Age of Extinction* in 2014.

One of the last projects that Ed worked on at GM was the now wildly popular Corvette C8 Stingray. "For at least 60 years, people like me and other car designers have dreamed of creating a mid-engine Corvette," he says. "We never thought it would happen." When it came time to develop the C8 Corvette, there was a bit of nervousness. Ed and his team needed to deliver. They had to distinguish the car from other mid-engine sports cars. "I emphasized to the design team that we had to accentuate the brand character of Corvette," Ed explains. "We need to give it that Corvette look, feel, and smell." He explains that the design calls back to the '59 and '63 Corvette Stingrays. "What makes a Corvette a Corvette is the hard edges, the nose of the car, the way it is shaped in plain view, and the way it comes to a crease at the center where other cars don't," he explains. On his last day at General Motors, he had the final review of the Corvette C8 and was given a farewell blessing from his team.

Young people interested in following in Ed's footsteps must first consider if they are truly passionate about automotive design. "Don't do it because it just seems like the cool thing to do. I've seen designers think it was cool and not realize the commitment that was required," Ed says. Ed also wants young people to know that it is never too early to start thinking about schools and building out a portfolio. "It is very competitive to get hired at one of the car companies. You need to go to a school with a very strong program in design, particularly one that is in automotive design. To get into these schools, you need to develop a portfolio of your work."

With all that he has accomplished, what is most important to Ed is his relationship with his family. "I feel much closer to my children and my grandchildren," he says. "They are my world."

To learn more about Ed Welburn, you can follow him on Facebook, Instagram, and X.

Matthew Whitaker:
The Great Jazz Hope

When 20-year-old jazz prodigy and multi-instrumentalist Matthew Whitaker takes the stage, audiences are in for a spectacle of improv, familiarity, and mastery. He was born three months premature, weighing 1 pound and 11 ounces. The oxygen that he needed to save his life damaged his retinas, rendering him blind. He is often compared to Stevie Wonder, but when asked how he feels about that comparison, he humbly says that "there is only one Stevie Wonder." He hopes one day he will have the opportunity to collaborate with him. He was three years old when he taught himself to play the piano after his grandfather bought him a Yamaha keyboard. He was nine years old when he won the "Child Stars of Tomorrow" competition as part of Amateur Night at the Apollo. When he was just 10, he was the opening performer for Stevie Wonder's induction into the Apollo Theater's Hall of Fame. Because of these life-changing moments, the Apollo is a special place for Matthew. "I've been going back there ever since. It is always a good time playing there. They have really become my extended family," Matthew says.

Growing up in Hackensack, New Jersey, Matthew spent time in New York City. "I always end up going back and forth from New Jersey to New York," he says. "I've played a lot of venues and shows there. You never know what you are going to get into." Even at his young age, Matthew is jotting down mentally what he has already learned. "I would say less is more, especially when it comes to playing music," he says. "You don't have to play everything that you know all at once. The music really speaks for itself."

In 2020, Matthew released *Connections*. The album connects the past to the current. It is an album that was created during the issues we are dealing with right now—the pandemic and the continued fight for social justice. The album also serves as documentation of where he is in his life. On songs "Stop Fighting" and "It Will Be Okay," Matthew composes what sounds like reassurance in the midst of upheaval.

For this album, Matthew called on friends like musician, bandleader, and television personality Jon Batiste; violinist Regina Carter; drummer Alvester Garnett; trumpeter Steve Oquendo, and more to compose

PHOTO BY TAYLOR BRANDT

PHOTO BY RAHIL ASHRUFF

alongside him. He covers songs from musical forebearers, Thelonious Monk, Stevie Wonder, and Duke Ellington, among others. "This album is very important to me, not only because I am paying tribute to my heroes but also the musicians who are on the album," he says. "These are people who have been in my life for a very long time. Everyone is special." When Matthew is in these sessions, he lets the music guide him. "The more you play the music, the more the ideas come out," he explains.

When composing, Matthew loves the tactile feedback and control he gets when he plays the organ or keyboard, or drums. Particularly, he loves the experimentation the drums afford him. "You can put different materials on top of the surface. You can use brushes, mallets, multirods, and so on," he explains. "There are so many possibilities. For me, it is always about the sound."

For those who dream big, he has a few simple pieces of advice: "Continue to grow and be yourself. Trust your gift, follow your dreams, and always have fun," he says. Just like his friend Batiste, Matthew is interested in creating film scores one day. He has already been tapped for a documentary with The WNET Group's ALL ARTS, a multimedia

BK FULTON AND NICHOLAS POWELL

PHOTO BY TAYLOR BRANDT

platform devoted to engaging with numerous artistic genres. Matthew will be a part of their artist-in-residency program. He is billed with director, Jonathan McCrory, multimedia artist, Don Christian Jones, and interdisciplinary, Le'Andra LeSeur.

There isn't one medium that Matthew Whitaker limits himself to. He even rock climbs when he is free. When thinking about those who inspire him, he thinks of two particular figures who have been with him from the beginning. "My biggest inspiration would have to be my dad. He was the one who really made sure that I remained grounded," he says. "But musically, before he passed away last September, my mentor, Dr. Lonnie Smith, was a strong inspiration." Like the jazz greats before him, Matthew Whitaker is using his music to express the emotions we feel every day. Dr. Lonnie Smith would be overjoyed.

To learn more about Matthew Whitaker, you can visit matthewwhitaker.net and follow him on Facebook, Instagram, and X.

Brave Williams:
Golden Heart

Brave Williams is just getting started. She's a singer, spoken word artist and now an actress. Most importantly, she's a good soul. She's young, vibrant, and a bright smile in a room too often full of frowns. She's somewhat of a homebody, satisfied with sitting at home, lighting some candles and getting lost in a good book. But she is also a planner in moments of solitude. She writes down her plans and how she will carry them out. Audiences will see her play Shelby Quinn in the indie film, *Love Dot Com*. The movie has mass appeal, mostly because of Brave's natural talent on screen. A few years ago, she was on *R&B Divas: Los Angeles*, but she was destined to do much more than reality television. Brave's body of work and her work ethic will inspire generations.

She grew up in Baltimore, Maryland. Because of her mixed-race heritage (Czech and black), the kids at school would bully her. "My sister and I experienced a lot of bullying and situations that tested our courage. At the time it hurt: however, it later taught us strength and helped us to develop an enduring mind frame. I wouldn't have changed it for the world," she says. The name 'Brave' did not come from this moment, but instead in another display of strength. When she was 13, she spoke at an open mic in Baltimore. She was speaking a truth way beyond her years. The audience called her "Brave" for saying what everyone else was too afraid to say out loud.

"My sister and I experienced a lot of bullying and situations that tested our courage."

Spoken word was where Brave felt most comfortable artistically. She could speak her truth and people would listen. She would write and rap. She didn't find out until much later that she had the gift to sing. She would listen to an eclectic group of artists for inspiration. "It was a lot of Tupac,

Maya Angelou, and Jill Scott. When Jill Scott came out, that changed my interest in music and made me want to turn my poetry into songs. When I first started in music, I was a rapper. I was constantly rapping and doing poetry. It wasn't until I turned one of my raps into a song, that I discovered I could sing," she says. She still considers herself to be a poet and is in the early stages of writing a book. Like anything, she wants to take her time to make it right. Publicists want to write it for her, but she believes writing it herself will give her more time to make it perfect.

> "The entertainment business is multiple marathons. In order to get across your first finish line (whatever that is), working hard, focus, and prayer are the needed tools..."

In the late 2000s, Brave created the R&B vocal girl group, RichGirl.

While the group was short-lived, Brave received the blessing to go solo. She started her own label and ended up securing a distribution deal with Empire Records along the way. "It was important for me to have my own label because as an artist, it gave me the power and control to create my destiny," Brave says. The digital revolution has changed the relationship between record labels and artists significantly. Brave not only has artistic freedom, but the ability to gain more widespread visibility of her music in the digital space via her distribution deal. Brave has learned to be patient with her career. She believes what is for her will be for her. "Nothing in life is a sprint. The entertainment business is multiple marathons. In order to get across your first finish line (whatever that is), working hard, focus, and prayer are the needed tools. Your mind is your greatest enemy and asset," she says.

"Everything that is meant for you will attract to you as long as you do your part."

Acting is a fairly new category for Brave. The biggest challenge has been letting herself go to be in the present. "Acting challenges me as an artist because it forces me to be authentic as my character. I have to turn off my mind and ask, what would the character do? Being an artist can be tough as we often overanalyze, overthink, and simply try to control our immediate situation. Acting releases that," she says. While playing Shelby Quinn in *Love Dot Com*, Brave found similarities between herself and her character. "I related to her stubbornness. It was hard for her to not get out of her own way and appreciate what was in front of her," she says. "That used to be a trait I excluded often growing up. Being a Taurus, I have to

work on not being stuck in a particular mindset, as life is forever evolving and you have to be willing to keep an open mind."

Early on, it is important for young artists to carve out their own paths. Brave struggled with her confidence early in her career. "Your journey is sincerely your journey. You have to make sure you don't get distracted by someone else or things you see or from the images you click on. You have to make sure you aren't chasing an idea of what you think you should look like, sound like, or act like. You need to hone in on who you are and simply give that because everything that is meant for you will attract to you as long as you do your part," Brave says. "I wish someone had told me that. As an artist, we're like sponges. You build

BK FULTON AND NICHOLAS POWELL

on the idea in your mind that, 'When I meet this person, I'm sure they are expecting me to look and act like this or the song needs to be this as opposed to what I really want to sing in my heart.' So, I got to a point where I was able to find my own voice and confidence in who I am. I put my foot down and said, 'You don't have to be someone you're not.'"

In the age of social media, it can be hard for young artists to find their footing and become their authentic selves. There is the constant lure of following the pack to stay relevant. "In 2019, I feel like it is much harder for you to be an individual. Girls want to look like the Instagram models they see and want to start doing those type of things to gain attention," Brave explains. "It's not even who they are—they are just doing it because the next girl is doing it. I would simply say: find out who you are, be confident and show the world that person."

> ## "I used to be all about my work, and I still am, but I am now open to the idea of finding that special person."

Brave is busy finishing up her debut album, Brave Williams, and in 2020 filmed, *Available Wife*, which made us ask if she was dating anyone. "I have opened myself up to the idea. I used to be all about my work, and I still am, but I am now open to the idea of finding that special person. The energy you put out into the universe will come back to you. There was a long period of time where I wasn't putting that energy out. It simply wasn't important to me. But now I have graduated to another level. If "Prince Charming" happens to hit my shopping cart in Whole Foods, I'll take it." As cliché as it may sound, being yourself is never a bad thing. Your life becomes more joyful in the process of finding the authentic you.

CREDITS

Stylist: Sinceré Armani

Makeup: Jamaya Moore

Photographer: Paul Greene

Editor: Year 2139 Corp

.#BRAVEWILLIAMS

"You can't get a win unless
you are willing to lose."

Gordon Williams

Commissioner Gordon Williams:
Music's Architect

Producer and engineer, Commissioner Gordon Williams, has been in the recording sessions of some of the most celebrated albums of all time. He worked with Lauryn Hill on *The Miseducation of Lauryn Hill*. He worked on Santana's *Supernatural*. He worked with Amy Winehouse on her debut album, *Frank*.

He grew up in the Bronx, New York, the birthplace of hip hop. His parents split when he was in elementary school and even though he and his younger brother grew up in a single-parent home with their mom, Gordon was surrounded by love. He had "surrogate dads" in the neighborhood who looked after him. One of these men was his uncle Peter, who recently passed away. Gordon was inspired by his uncle to express his creativity. Uncle Peter was an avid comic book collector and one day while 9-year-old Gordon was sitting around his grandma's house, his uncle plopped a box of old Marvel comic books like *Spider-Man* and the *Fantastic Four* at his feet. "I'm talking about from the 60s," Gordon says. "First of all, I hadn't really seen a comic book. On top of that, a comic book during those days was 12 or 15 cents. He inspired me to read and draw."

His uncle also was a guitar player. Gordon would see his uncle play around with the guitar in his room. That's when he heard Bob Marley

  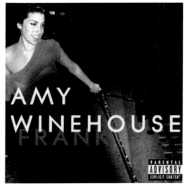

SOME OF COMMISSIONER GORDON WILLIAMS' MOST CELEBRATED PROJECTS: LAURYN HILL'S *THE MISEDUCATION OF LAURYN HILL*, SANTANA'S *SUPERNATURAL*, AND AMY WINEHOUSE'S *FRANK*.

for the first time. "From hearing Bob Marley, that was the sound and the person that made me feel like, 'Ok. I want to do this. I want to do music,'" he explains. Gordon would eventually connect with Marley's descendants. He would work with Marley's sons Damian and Stephen Marley and record at Marley's Tuff Gong studio during *The Miseducation of Lauryn Hill*.

Gordon was given the Commissioner moniker by KRS-One, with whom he would develop a working relationship. It wouldn't have mattered to Gordon if hip hop didn't become mainstream because it was something that touched the youth in his neighborhood. "It was fun," Gordon explains. "It wasn't about making a record. We came in around the second generation, so we watched the first." The figures of the first generation were Grandmaster Flash and the Furious Five, the Cold Crush Brothers, DJ Jazzy Jay, and others. In the late 70s and early 80s, hip hop was very much a local phenomenon. "They were stars to us," he says. "We didn't know that the outside world didn't know who they were."

When Gordon visited his grandmother in Brooklyn, he would bring his cassette tapes of his favorite MCs. Kids in the streets would ask him what he was listening to. He couldn't believe they didn't know. "To us it was like everyone knew, but they didn't," Gordon says. "It wasn't about any kind of industry play." He doesn't think any of the original artists thought that hip hop would have made it this far. Now, Grandmaster Flash and the Furious Five have been inducted into the Rock & Roll Hall of Fame. The first generation was focused on community and not any kind of mainstream success, Gordon believes. "I think it was more about what we were doing at that moment and the urgency and importance of participating in creating with each other," he says.

In the early days of his music career, Gordon was a member of the house music group, Touch. They were signed to the independent record label, Supertonics. Their record, *Without You*, became a dance hit and afforded Gordon a production deal with Motown Records. At

BK FULTON AND NICHOLAS POWELL

COMMISSIONER GORDON WILLIAMS IN THE STUDIO WITH AMY WINEHOUSE WORKING ON HER DEBUT ALBUM *FRANK*.

Motown, Gordon developed as a producer and mixer working closely with Timmy Regisford, the head of A&R. His achievements at Motown opened new career doors and led to Gordon meeting Benny Medina and Quincy Jones. "Meeting Quincy literally changed everything," Gordon says. "Every conversation with Q was a treasure chest filled with knowledge I still use to this day. Eventually, Quincy's interest in my group's material led to a huge production deal with Tommy Mottola and Sony Music. It was really one of my first lessons in managing money and managing people. I was inexperienced at both. Just because someone has the ability to make great art doesn't mean they are a great person." Taking responsibility for his failure, Gordon says he "salvaged" his deal with Sony when Mottola asked him to stay on as a staff producer and senior director of A&R at Columbia Records. "You have to take responsibility for your losses just as much as your wins," he says. "Because you can't get a win unless you are willing to lose." Gordon says his time at Sony matured him and allowed him to learn the business. He worked on many projects in the four years he was there. This included projects with Mariah Carey, Will Smith, Wyclef Jean,

50 Cent, Alicia Keys, and TrackMasterz. He also worked on Destiny's Child's first album, the *Love Jones* soundtrack, and the *Men in Black* soundtrack.

While he was at Sony Music, Lauryn Hill asked Gordon to work on her solo project. Gordon was the engineer and production supervisor for the album. Because he was working so hard on getting the album completed, he didn't think too much of how the public would react to the record. But it was when he began mastering the record, he knew he had something special. However, he did not know it would reach the heights that it did. "I couldn't have seen this for what it became in terms of people referring to it as a classic," he says. Gordon praises the talent for the quality of the music and its staying power. The album has sold over 20 million copies worldwide and is considered one of the greatest albums of all time. It earned Gordon two Grammys, including Album of the Year, at the 41st Grammy Awards in 1999. *The Miseducation of Lauryn Hill* would be the first out of two hip hop albums to win Album of the Year at the Grammys.

With the increased importance of branding and image in the music industry, Commissioner Gordon Williams believes focusing on the music is important for emerging artists. "I think we have swung away

from focusing on the music part of the music business," he says. "I see a lot of young people who want to be famous more than they want to be great artists." He wants artists to get back to making art for art's sake. "Yes, we need to be compensated properly for our work, but don't lose the art," he says. "Be a student of the music and learn its language."

Gordon is currently a Goodwill Ambassador for the island of St. Lucia, his mother's home. His company, Lalabela Alliance, is a multi-faceted collective of companies focused on musical education, youth development, film and television, music production, and publishing. "We work with young people who are not just looking to be inspired in music, but are also inspired to be better people," Gordon says. He also advises new artists to find great mentors in music like Quincy Jones was for him. Finally, in addition to Lalabela, Gordon is part of the White Tiger Society, a music collective fronted by Tunisian singer-songwriter, Dajla. Gordon is continuing to look for new musical talent for Lalabela and is developing a production base on the continent of Africa.

When Gordon is relaxing, he turns the music off. "I don't even want to listen to music at times because I listen to so much music," he says. Because of his work in music supervision, he's been binge-watching films from that perspective. He has worked as a music supervisor for films like *The Banker* with Samuel Jackson and Anthony Mackie, and the film, *Last Looks,* with Mel Gibson. "I love good stories," he says. "I love to read, too." But what would be nice for Gordon is a vacation on a beach in the Caribbean. Because when you have worked on your craft as intensely for decades as Gordon has, you deserve to spend time in a place where the water is calm and the sky is as clear as the ocean itself.

Commissioner Gordon Williams Documentary. To learn more about Commissioner Gordon Williams, you can follow him on Instagram.

"You have the tools
needed to succeed."

Tatia L. Williams:
The NBA's Key Player

Tatia L. Williams remembers the larger-than-life figures who visited her home as a child. She grew up in Washington, D.C., and looked up to these figures that she could call family friends. "There were people like Vernon Jordan and Jesse Jackson and other men and women who were very successful doctors, lawyers, politicians, and business people who were very successful," she says. "I was very blessed to be in a place where I grew up with a variety of professionals and people who were thinkers and doers." Early on as a child in preschool, Tatia recalls understanding the lesson of whom much is given, much is expected. "It was always about thriving to do your best to succeed," she says. "You have the tools needed to succeed and so there is no excuse not to do your best."

Tatia currently resides in New York City and is the vice president and assistant general counsel of the NBA. She is primarily responsible for the legal and business affairs of the league's social responsibility and player programs department. Tatia never thought she'd be where she is today. "I didn't set out to be in sports. I was focused on getting into entertainment," she admits. After graduating from Harvard Law, Tatia worked in the New York City office of Simpson Thacher & Bartlett when a door to join politics opened.

"The White House was looking for smart lawyers," Tatia says. "I got in and thought, 'This is something interesting and fast-paced.'" She loved it. When her political stint was nearing its end, she yearned to be in entertainment. After attending a Janet Jackson concert, something finally clicked, and she decided to take the necessary steps to pursue that passion.

Tatia went on to work as vice president of legal and business affairs for Oxygen Media and as director in the sales planning and strategy/media distribution group at MTV Networks. Tatia sees the NBA as a nice mix between sports and entertainment. "I felt like I had achieved my dream when the NBA came calling. I never really thought about it," she says. "I always liked sports and interestingly enough, it ended up becoming the job that I've been at the longest."

"I was very blessed to be in a place where I grew up with a variety of professionals and people who were thinkers and doers."

In recent years, the NBA has doubled down on its support for Black youth and young people with the establishment of the NBA Foundation and other efforts. The NBA has continued its decades-long support of the Thurgood Marshall College Fund (TMCF), a nonprofit organization that supports and represents students at Historically Black Colleges and Universities (HBCUs). The late NBA Commissioner, David Stern, was a huge supporter of TMCF and an inaugural board member. Tatia is currently a member of TMCF's board of directors. In an extended effort to support HBCUs that goes beyond TMCF, the NBA created the HBCU Fellowship Program where 60 fellows from HBCUs are granted internships at the teams and league offices. "It is a paid internship and we also pay for students' housing and relocation. The program aims to give them real-life experiences," Tatia says. "We are elevating these students at the start of their careers."

The NBA recently completed its 3rd annual NBA Innovate the Future Competition with TMCF. Students solve one of three case studies presented by the NBA and the winning team receives a $10,000 scholarship and other prizes. "I'm a judge in this competition every year and this helps our mission to elevate and create opportunities for Black youth and HBCUs," Tatia says. "These efforts were highlighted this year with our first annual NBA HBCU Classic between Howard and Morgan State ahead of the NBA All-Star Game."

BK FULTON AND NICHOLAS POWELL

For those who are interested in studying law, Tatia acknowledges that it is a competitive environment. "I think you clearly have to be willing to work hard," she explains. "You may have to work hard for a little less pay than you'd make in other industries, but if it is something you really want to do, then you will find a way." She explains that competition will always be there, especially in major cities like New York and Los Angeles, so don't give up because things are challenging. This advice is extended to anyone who is a recent graduate in a competitive industry. The NBA received thousands of applicants for the 60 spots in its HBCU Fellowship Program. "There are a lot of people who are going to be disappointed," Tatia says. "If you are young and have the ability to move around, why not live someplace else for a summer or a couple of years in another market? Some markets may not be as appealing as one might like, but you will have a greater chance of learning the ropes and those skills are transferable. Once you are in, you can always parlay that. Getting in is the hardest part."

"I didn't set out to be in sports. I was focused on getting into entertainment."

Recently, Tatia became a mother. This has been a blessing for her. "Better late than never," she says jokingly. "My son's name is Decker Robert Julian and he's my little pandemic wonder." She takes Decker on walks every night as a way to bond. It calms and relaxes her. If she really needs to, she will catch up with a friend on these walks and have a laugh. With such a busy and demanding job as hers, she needs that time for herself. When we asked Tatia what she will do next, she didn't give us a specific answer. Years ago, she was interviewed while at MTV and the interviewer asked her a similar question. "I said something big and fun, and it turned out to be the NBA, so here I am putting that out there again," she says.

TATIA WILLIAMS WITH HER SON, DECKER ROBERT JULIAN.
PHOTO BY ALISON SHEEHY.

PHOTOS BY J. BOLIN

Deborah Joy Winans:
More to Come

When Deborah Joy Winans was growing up in the influential and legendary Winans family, she knew that acting would be one gift that she would share with the world. "I am an actor," she proclaims. "That is all that I have ever loved and ever wanted to do as a career. I got my BFA in acting, spent a month in Moscow training in the Moscow Art Theatre School, and received my MFA in acting from the California Institute of the Arts." While Deborah Joy trusts her singing ability, her role as Charity on the hit show *Greenleaf* was what got her to reveal her acting talent to the world. Singing (she will be releasing new music in April) is secondary to her acting. "Acting is my passion and love," she says.

Looking back at her childhood, Deborah Joy remembers the seasons and the extreme temperatures they produced: "The winters were extremely cold and the summers were extremely hot." The members of her family were hard-working individuals who loved what they did. She remembers the people of Detroit who were "resilient and loyal." As she navigated through the entertainment industry, she knew that it wouldn't be easy to land work. "I learned that I am in a career where you get a lot of no's," she says, "but you have to keep moving forward if this is something that you love and have been called to do."

From playing her aunt, CeCe Winans, in the Lifetime biopic, *Whitney,* to her role as Charity on *Greenleaf,* Deborah Joy has shown range as an actress. "When you think you are done growing, I think that means you should look at doing something else," she says. "There is always room to grow." As she continues her acting journey, she says she is grateful for the opportunities she has had. She continues to learn from her mistakes and she is aware of the importance of being present in the moment.

When deciding on a role, Deborah Joy considers if the character has enough meaning and substance. The character cannot be one-dimensional. "At the end of the day, you want to make sure that you are doing something that touches people," she says, "that changes people, that makes them feel good, that makes them start a conversation. You want your art to mean something." Her fans appreciate this. They have sent Deborah Joy inspirational messages, telling her how her work has given them a new perspective on life. "It has been beautiful," she says.

Faith, of course, is a big part of Deborah Joy's makeup and because of this, faith has influenced her career.

"I am meant to bring light and life to somebody," she says. When Deborah Joy walks into an audition, she goes in with the attitude that what is meant for her will find its way to her. She does not need to be anyone else to achieve success. "You cannot steal what God has for me," she says. "My faith has allowed me to rest a bit easier and understand that no matter where I go, I can always be kind and I always know my love for God will come through regardless."

In her new Lifetime film, *The Color of Love*, Deborah Joy plays Monica Henderson, a widow with two kids who takes in foster children from time to time. After two of the children, Peter and Rachel, flee their current foster home, she takes them in. There is one conflict: Monica and her family are black, and Peter and Rachel are white. Monica's boyfriend, Theo, thinks they would be better with a family who is of the same race. But this goes against Monica's belief that love can conquer all.

Deborah Joy was given the script by her dear friend, Tamara LaSeon Bass, the director of the recent TV One film, *Don't Waste Your Pretty,* in which Deborah Joy starred as a lead opposite of Keri Hilson. After reading the script for *The Color of Love*, Deborah Joy fell in love with the character and message. "It is about how love, unconditional love, can show through regardless of how people feel or what people say," Deborah Joy says. "Monica has a really big heart and suffered a lot of loss. She is at a point where she does everything that she can to make not just her home a better place, but the world a better place." Deborah Joy hopes that

BK FULTON AND NICHOLAS POWELL

viewers can be more tolerant and open towards each other in a time where many of us are having uncomfortable but necessary conversations about race. "This is something that is not often told and is something that people need to hear and see right now," she says.

Reflecting on COVID and her 2020, she says that, like many of us, she took the time to reflect on what was working and what wasn't. "I've been reflecting and making sure I am where I am supposed to be," she says. "Not just workwise, but spiritually and physically. There is always something to work on for yourself."

When asked if she had any advice for young people who want to break into the industry, Deborah Joy advises that beyond hard work, having thick skin is a must. "You can never have enough training. They should be willing to work hard and understand that you will get a lot of no's before you get a yes," she explains. "All that does is help you continue to build who you are and who you are meant to be."

Deborah Joy Winans hasn't been in the industry for long but she is having a good time following her passion. "I just love what I do and I am always looking for ways to grow," she says. This is just the beginning for Deborah Joy. "I don't think I will ever say that I've made it," she says. "I will always say that I am very grateful for whatever job I've done and hope to continue to go further."

To learn more about Deborah Joy Winans, follow her on Instagram and X.

The way an actor learns

Jeffrey Wright:
Next Level Cinema

Jeffrey Wright is a thoughtful and immensely talented actor who makes it a point to find roles that are meaningful. His roles often speak to social and political issues. Jeffrey's career began in the theater. Finding a passion for acting in college, Wright's dedication to his craft paid off in the form of a Tony award for his breakout role as Belize in *Angels in America.* He would later reprise this role for the HBO miniseries adaptation of the play that earned him an Emmy and a Golden Globe. On screen, one of his earliest roles was his portrayal of Jean-Michel Basquiat in *Basquiat*. He exposed audiences to the complicated, brilliant, and tragic life of the highly esteemed artist.

Beyond the screen, Wright is deliberate in his political and social activism. He has used his voice to speak out against injustice and to help others. He most recently created Brooklyn For Life! that helps feed frontline pandemic workers in Brooklyn, NY. In our conversation with the actor, he eloquently lays out the current condition of our political state and muses over the difficulties of finding adequate solutions to many of today's challenges.

Over the years, Wright has garnered respect from directors and producers alike. Once viewed as one of the more underappreciated actors of his generation, that moniker is no longer applicable. As he plays Bernard Lowe in *Westworld*, Commissioner Gordon in *The Batman*, Roebuck Wright in Wes Anderson's *The French Dispatch*, and returns as Felix Leiter in the new James Bond film, *No Time to Die*, Wright has worked smart and hard to earn his success as an actor. In the very honest and open interview below, Jeffrey Wright tells us exactly how he arrived at the next level of cinema.

Where are you from and what was it like growing up there?

I grew up in Southeast Washington, D.C., for the most part, but I spent a good deal of my childhood in the Tidewater area of Virginia, where my mother grew up and my grandparents lived. I would go down there after the last week of school. My mom would drive me down, drop me off, hang out for a couple of days, and then go back to D.C.. The next time I would see her was at the end of the summer when she would come back to pick me up.

My childhood was pretty much spread between those two places. I'm a city boy but I got a little bit of "country" in me too. My grandfather was a waterman and farmer. He was the main father figure in my life. I got a little bit of that watery ground, salt air and seawater in my veins.

Who was your biggest inspiration growing up?

My mother was a lawyer. She was my biggest inspiration. My mother was the person who gave me all of the tools and the opportunities that shaped my life and journey.

She was a woman who came to D.C. in 1957 after graduating from the Hampton Institute, as it was called then, and she made her way to Howard University Law School. She was the first in our family to go to law school and become a lawyer. Her older sister had gone to nursing school at North Carolina A&T after graduating from the Hampton Institute. She was the first to go to graduate school and the first to go to college. She was a nurse at D.C. General Hospital for 30 odd years. I was raised by both of them in D.C..

They were a part of that generation of black folks who came up from the South who represented and embodied the values of the Civil Rights Movement. They were people who had faith in hard work, faith in their abilities, and an insistence that society provides a means for them to express all that they can be.

I was born in the middle of all of that. I was born in 1965. I was born at the height of the Civil Rights Movement. I was born as the black power

BK FULTON AND NICHOLAS POWELL

movement emerged. I was born as the women's rights movement emerged. So, growing up in Washington, D.C. was really inspirational to me. It shaped the way I viewed the world and the way I do my work.

The roles that strike me and compel me are roles that have some kind of relevance beyond entertainment. They often have social relevance and at times, political relevance. These themes can be implicit or overt, but they draw me in. I want my work to mean something. It really is a function of having come of age in the household, city, and time I grew up.

I'm more inspired and starstruck by people like Angela Davis and Shirley Chisholm and all of these people who represented an insistence that our country, as Dr. King said, "Be true to what it said on paper."

What was the most important lesson you learned in the early phases of your career?

Our family was really defined by the character of my grandfather and grandmother. Aside from the fact that my grandfather was a showman in his own right, he was a master storyteller, or as they say down there, "He could tell those lies," as guys who lived on the water often do. He also sold a bit of liquor in his day. He had a lot of folks come by the house looking for fish, for vegetables, looking for a "taste" [a drink] and so he had a stage on which he performed. But beyond that, what they really taught me and what I don't think I truly appreciated then but I certainly do now because I recognized its influence on me, was the lesson of hard work.

My grandfather woke up at 5:00 AM. I was asleep, and he was off to work. He was an older man at the time. He was off on the water gathering his crab pots, oysters, whatever the season brought, and he came back home after selling what he caught, grabbed a bite to eat, and headed out into his field. He had a couple of acres that he farmed. After he finished, he came back home and went out there again to sell his goods in the yard. He worked from sun up 'till sundown every day and loved it. It strengthened him and his family and our community.

> "The roles that strike me and compel me are roles that have some kind of relevance beyond entertainment.... I want my work to mean something."

Right, your grandfather's example influenced you to be dedicated to what you do?

A lot of people look at acting and see the glitz and the glamour of it. They see the award shows and all. What they don't appreciate is that underneath all of that is a lot of hard work and a lot of persistence to be able to sustain yourself in the business. For example, on *Westworld*, at times, we pull 20-hour days. We average about 16-hour days and it's not a lot of hanging out and sitting in your trailer. We get there on set and hustle because we have a lot of work to do. We have a lot of film to put in the can.

It is a 10-episode (season 3 was 8) TV series. That is really four or five movies we are shooting in the course of maybe 6 months. Sometimes I get called to set like, "Hey you got to be on set at 2:00 in the morning." I'm like, "What? The bar just closed. What are you talking about?"

We have to use all of the sunlight we can on the first day of the week, Monday. You got to get out there early so you can get a start on the week. So by the time you hit Friday, because of the union rules and turnaround and things like that, you might end up on Friday with like an 8 am call that will have you working until Saturday morning.

I say that all to say, I love what I do. I love my work. I love the people that I find myself working with now. I've chosen great collaborators. I've chosen great parts. I make a good living. This is all true. But it takes a lot of work and it takes a lot of time away from my family. It takes a lot of flights here and there and I guess I owe the ability to handle that from the lessons I was taught by the country folks that raised me.

At what point in your career did you begin to feel you had made it?

"Made it" can mean many things. The thing about our profession is that there are very few guarantees in our business. There is a lot of uncertainty. In the last five years, I have only reached the place where I can project out what I will be doing for a couple of years or a year even. That's really because of *Westworld*. It has given me some kind

BK FULTON AND NICHOLAS POWELL

of security that if we do well, and there is still that if, we will return the next year or shortly thereafter. I've put myself in a position now where there are directors seeking me out to work on their projects.

I thought I had made it after the first play I had ever done in college. The play was called *Bloods.* It was the reworking of a novel about black Vietnam veterans and their experiences. It was a novel written by Wallace Terry. There was a student named Kevin Frasier who passed away from AIDS a couple of years from graduating. This was at Amherst College during my junior year of college. Kevin had put together this evening of monologues based on that novel. I think it was the winter of 1986 when I started acting. This was my first performance and we did it in a small black box theater. People saw that production and were moved by it. They were compelled by what I was doing. In some ways, you ask me when I had made it or what was my big break; it was that night when I went out there, did what was being asked of me, and people responded. Once you've proven the case, the momentum builds from there.

Where did you go from there?

At the end of the day, you are not reliant on what someone is offering you, but you are reliant on your own abilities to work in this space. From there it was about developing my skills and training and working in the theater. I had worked in the theater professionally for seven years before I got to Broadway.

While my beginning helped me to appreciate that I had something, it wasn't until I did *Angels in America* on Broadway, and it was about halfway through that run—which was a year and a half run, where I had finally said to myself, "You know, I'm an actor now." It is not so much that you achieve a particular point or receive awards and jobs pay well. I think success is more about a kind of quiet understanding of your value. Once you have acquired that understanding and sense of clarity about what you are doing, then you might be able to say that you've made it.

What would you consider to be your greatest achievement?

My current greatest achievement? Well, that's a work in progress too. That's called parenting. That is the hardest work that I have undertaken and the most rewarding but also the most demanding. I have an 18-year-old son who just graduated high school and a 15-year-old daughter. No character that I can create can surpass them as my reward.

"I think success is more about a kind of quiet understanding of your value."

We are living in a time of a lot of turmoil and pain. What are your thoughts on the state of our country and do you believe this is a watershed moment for racial justice?

I'm deeply concerned about what is happening in our country right now. I'm really awestruck by the ways in which our national dialogue has deteriorated. It is a result of a couple of things. It is a result of the tragic lack of competent leadership at the top and the malevolence and divisiveness that emanates from the White House every day, practically every hour. It is also the result of the technology that allows these kinds of destructive messages to be disseminated by the hour and the technology that allows this messaging and divisiveness to be amplified in real-time.

We have the person in the highest seat in the land who speaks only to a narrow base of concerns relative to the larger population of the country, who refuses to work in any way to define and cultivate a common sense of Americanness, who works solely for what he perceives is his own personal, political and financial benefit, all while using the tools of misinformation, disinformation, deception, deception of the country, and self-deception. I am very concerned.

You have all of these political tools with technology like social media that we carry around in our pockets every day that facilitate the agenda of not only him but other bad actors who are averse to the truth and facts and are working towards their own selfish ends. So, you have a combination of things creating more tension in this country than we have seen in many, many decades.

Including the 60s?

Yes. No doubt during the 60s, we had an incredibly tumultuous period. We think of the period between 1963 and 1968 when JFK, Malcolm X, Martin Luther King, and Bobby Kennedy were assassinated. It was a decade of incredible turmoil and upheaval.

But we didn't have this technology, right? That pours gasoline on those fires. We all could somehow manage to find something that looked like common ground: that provided a place where we could stand and take in what was happening to us as a collective. We are so disjointed right now. We have such chaotic relationships with one another and it

BK FULTON AND NICHOLAS POWELL

is incredibly dangerous. Even when we vote this guy out of the White House, the genies that the technology has allowed out of the bottle—disinformation and misinformation—will be extremely difficult to jam back into that bottle.

It makes it difficult to find a solution.

It makes it much more difficult to craft a way forward that leads to the type of progress and expansion of equal rights and justice in our country. Even while there are these cataclysmic things happening in the country around race relations, and the need for police and criminal justice reform. The way forward is still very cloudy because we lack clarity, the clarity of leadership. I think it is well on the side of those who are protesting for change. I still think we lack a clarity of leadership and it concerns me.

It is wonderful that we have multigenerational energy but how do we achieve the political and legislative outcomes that are going to speak to and facilitate the kind of systemic change we need in this country? I think too many of us—because year after year, decade after decade of corroding trust in government—have given up hope that there can be real seismic movement in the right direction.

Please elaborate.

When the violence erupts, the frustration erupts, the anger erupts, and it is understandable. So how do we regain the trust that we can afford in a way that is going to push this country to a more perfect union? How can we regain control over the facts so that we all can agree that the sun came up in the morning as opposed to the sun setting in the morning? We can't even agree on basic truths now. So, I'm really concerned. I'm trying to do what I can to help provide an understanding and clear messaging around these things.

I've been involved in some projects around voter suppression, such as the film called *Rigged,* that I narrate and kind of walk the audience through. I just finished narrating a film called *American Pathogen*, a documentary that chronicles the Trump administration's failure to respond to this pandemic in an effective way. *American Pathogen* outlines all of the steps that it took to dismantle the work that has been done by the Obama administration to prepare the country for something like COVID-19, and it chronicles all of the missteps and malfeasance associated with the Trump administration's response from the beginning of COVID in January and February.

These are projects that I've been involved in with the hopes to shine some light on the basic facts that we are all living under, whether or not we admit to it.

Can you give us insight into how you prepare for a new role?

The only constant for me in preparing for roles is to remain open to whatever the particular project calls for. I don't have any one way of preparing, but I try to remain fluid, flexible, and adaptable to whatever the situation may be. I have to be like water in many respects.

Preparing for a role like *Basquiat* is different than preparing for the role of Commissioner Gordon in *The Batman*, so I have to just be aware of

BK FULTON AND NICHOLAS POWELL

the different needs and respond to them. For *Basquiat*, I spent about six months prior to working on that film painting, trying to absorb and study as much of his work from books and actual paintings that I had access to and trying to recreate his language, his poetry, his imagery so I could facilitate it on camera. I studied footage of him and spoke to a few people who knew him but not many because I wanted to form my own opinions of him. I tried using every tool I could to try to conjure his memory and recreate him and walk through the space in the way that he walked to do justice to his story.

It was particularly important because at the time that we made the film, very few people knew about Jean-Michel Basquiat and now he is practically a household name. So, I think it is a responsibility when you introduce someone's story to your audience for the first time that you be as beholden to the truths of his life as possible.

And that was a different process for *The Batman.*

Yes. What I've done with *The Batman* is to go back and read some of the material before our film. It is an 80-year-old set of stories. The first comic was released in 1939 by DC Comics (Detective Comics). I went back and read some of the original versions to understand how this began and then read the more modern versions to see how it has evolved.

James Gordon is a black man now, so there has been pushback from a small group of folks. For me, it was important to go back and dig deeper into what these stories represented so I could understand how I could work my way into it. What I have discovered is that there has always been an evolution of the story, an evolution of the characters, and an evolution of their narratives. For example, what is wonderful about *The Batman* series is that it is one of the very few superheroes series that is grounded in an American city (Gotham—New York City). So you have the opportunity to explore more grounded ideas and issues than you might explore in other stories. These issues are experienced through the lens of a detective genre, which I find very interesting.

You look at New York in 1939, I think New York was 90-95 percent white. So obviously, the characters that were written then reflected a Gotham that was born of those facts. Gotham today is a very different city. All you need to do is take the 7 train out through Queens to a Mets game and you will understand this city is a confluence of colors. The characters in this Batman, particularly James Gordon, have evolved from 1939 to reflect a contemporary Gotham. So, there is a different set of requirements than what would be required for *Angels In America, Westworld*, or the other projects I've done.

In Wes Anderson's movie, *The French Dispatch*, you play the character Roebuck Wright who has been described as a "mashup of James Baldwin and A.J. Liebling" by *The New Yorker.* Tell us a little bit more about this character and how you approached this role?

We met for lunch and he told me about what he had written. Before he sent me the script, he described it to me as you suggest. A couple of weeks later, he sent me the script. From the moment I read the script, the character just seared into me. The music that was expressed through his language stayed in my head like a song you hear on the radio that you instantly love. The language Wes had written was so beautiful and moving that I was hooked from the start.

Roebuck Wright is a fictional character and draws from a bit of Baldwin, a bit of AJ Liebling, and a bit of Tennessee Williams. He's kind of an amalgam but he exists in the middle. It's a film that in many ways is a love letter to writers and also in some ways, certainly my character, is an exploration of solitude—the case of the stranger in a strange land. But also, someone who is running away from home. And at the same time, trying to redefine and understand what home is for him as he finds the celebration of life through the creation and experiencing of great food.

It really is a fascinating story that he has drawn. I can't wait for people to take it in. I think it is a beautiful film with an incredible group of actors— Benicio del Toro, William Dafoe, Frances McDormand, Bill Murray, Léa Seydoux—were a part of it. Wes is just a masterful filmmaker. He has his own language, his own way of working. He is a wonderful collaborator. He is demanding, he is exacting, but he's fully committed and a wonderful on set general and brilliant writer.

When you aren't acting, how do you relax?

I've been going to California for many years since the early 90s as an actor, but it was only about five years ago when I started working out there and commuting back and forth between LA and New York, for *Westworld* that I understood Los Angeles' competitive advantage over New York and that is the Pacific Ocean.

When I'm not working over there, you can find me out in the ocean surfing. That's where I go to make myself whole. That's where I go to

BK FULTON AND NICHOLAS POWELL

clean my mind, body, spirit, and to avoid all of the nonsense on the land to the extent that I can. The ocean is where the dolphins and the whales return. They were mammals on the land. They returned to the ocean to evolve into something greater, so it has become that type of refuge for me.

I used to skateboard as a kid, almost religiously, until I broke my leg riding in a pool. It was only about seven years ago when I made a trip to Hawaii with my kids and my daughter wanted to take surf lessons that I discovered surfing and I've been hooked ever since. It has been a great gift to my life.

Before we go, what advice do you have for young people who want to not only get into acting but are seeking out roles that are meaningful and impactful?

The business is very different than when I started but my advice is probably still the same and that is to find a part. It doesn't have to be in a big movie. It doesn't have to be in a movie at all. For me, it started with a play and one thing led to another. I encourage people to still do work in the theater if you want to be an actor.

"It is wonderful that we have multigenerational energy but how do we achieve the political and legislative outcomes that are going to speak to and facilitate the kind of systemic change we need in this country?"

We've gotten so caught up in the trappings of the work, you know, the instant gratification, the fame, the money, and I think we've lost sight of how it all begins. It begins with an understanding of what you are doing. The way an actor learns the craft is on the stage so by the time you get to the film set, you can shape your role into something that is sustainable. With practice, you will develop a sense of time and a sense of proportion and a sense of control over your instrument that gives you the presence and power for acting. Always start in the theater.

PHOTOGRAPHY BY
RAYON RICHARDS

"Be the change
you wish to see in
the world."

Malik Yoba: A Creator of Opportunity

The moment four-year-old Malik Yoba laid his eyes on the eccentric costumes of the cast in the Off-Broadway production of *Alice in Wonderland,* he knew he wanted to be an actor. At 13, he joined the Metropolitan Opera's Children's Theater Guild. Feeling inspired, he gave his autograph to his teacher and said, "I'm going to be famous, you should keep this." This confidence and swagger has followed him into adulthood. He is not arrogant. His acting and his art are inspired.

Growing up, his Dad instilled in him the value of hard work. His father would tell Malik, "Build your own generator so when they turn off the power, you still have lights." His words became the philosophy Malik would live by for the rest of his life.

Malik's humble beginnings started in the Bronx, but he mostly grew up in Harlem, New York. While his neighborhood was rough, he was lucky to have parents who exposed him to the "whole city and the world through travel." In his household, his parents emphasized the importance of being a "global citizen." Lying around the living room table were publications like *Vogue, Essence, National Geographic,* and *Architectural Digest.* Through these publications, Malik could transport himself into a different world. In his childhood home, there was no television. His dad was convinced it was an "idiot box." He wanted his children to be independent thinkers. Instead of TV, Malik's childhood home was filled with books about Black culture and history.

Through his schooling, he was exposed to kids who had a lot, kids who did not have much, and those who were in-between. "I remember in middle school going to my friend's grandfather's house on Fifth Avenue, overlooking Central Park. He was an executive at General Motors," Malik says. "He lived in a building called the Park Five, which was on 61st street at Central Park. I had never seen a grand piano in anyone's house before or all white carpet. You walked to the window and you saw Central Park. I couldn't believe it."

"Build your own generator so when they turn off the power, you still have lights."

When Malik arrived in Hollywood in the 90s, he was not mystified by the glitz and glamour so many young stars get wrapped up in. He worked on his craft and created a place for himself among the distractions.

"There is a moment where you arrive in Hollywood and you are literally standing on a studio stage and you look down and say, 'I'm here,'" Malik says. "But I knew, you are only as good as your last five minutes. Fame and even the opportunity to do the work is fleeting. For me, I've never felt like I made it, no matter how much I've done. I always strive to continue to create my own way."

When speaking to Malik, you get the impression of a determined artist who knew all his life where he was going, but he also looks back in amazement that it really panned out. "When you get to grow up and do the things you dreamed about as a kid, you realize that for one, you're very blessed. There is also something very satisfying about it. I wrote plays as a kid and performed them in front of my parents and charged them money. I still do that as an adult," he explains.

"There is a moment where you arrive in Hollywood and you are literally standing on a studio stage and you look down and say 'I'm here.'"

Malik was taught to not let his environment limit his possibilities. He believes in the law of attraction that says, 'What you think about is what you become.' "Many people don't believe it's possible to invent your future, and they prove themselves correct. The Bible says, 'You ask it and you are given.' If you aren't religious, you can refer to so many other teachers like Wattles, Napoleon Hill, or Abraham-Hicks that also convey this principle," he explains.

"That truth is absolute—you dream about things, think about them, speak them into existence, and step into the vision from them. Even

BK FULTON AND NICHOLAS POWELL

when proper circumstances do not show you that it is possible with the naked eye, you still have the ability to manifest ideas based on the power of thinking and then doing," he says. In Malik's life, there are specific moments that serve as testament to these beliefs. He remembers the time he wanted to be an Olympic bobsledder and ended up playing the fictional Olympic bobsledder, Yul Brenner, in *Cool Runnings*. Consequently, he wanted to know how it felt to get shot, and at 15, he was shot and left for dead. The power of the mind is no joke.

The law of attraction came to him recently when he received the news that ABC was rebooting *New York Undercover*. Malik recalls meeting with TV producer, Dick Wolf, many years ago to reboot the 90's police drama. It wasn't until this year when that wish began to fully materialize. The show began shooting last month. "I remember in 2018 telling my former co-stars that I'm no longer going to push for the reboot, and for it to manifest anyway is very powerful. It's something that speaks to a collective consciousness. I can tell you, after 30 years in this business, out of all of the things I've ever done, I've never had something with such strong and focused support from so many people."

He explains that Dick Wolf wasn't necessarily looking to reboot the series, but ABC came to him with the idea because they needed more diverse content. "We were looked at as the little ghetto show that could," he says. "Something that they would say mainstream audiences were not ready for, and now it's as if the world has caught up and understands the need for more diverse content."

Malik is excited for new talent to have their chance on the show. He always tells young people to "build their own generator," but he also wants them to realize the power of doing and believing they are capable of greatness. "Create, ask a lot of questions, surround yourself with people who are smarter than you," he advises. "Believe in the magic because the magic is real. It is as simple as that. One ounce of doubt and you're out.".

"If you believe you can't do it, then you're correct. If you believe you can, then you can. Just know it's not easy. It takes tenacity."

"We are all capable of greatness as part of this abundant universe and too often the politics of distraction tell us we are not worthy."

BK FULTON AND NICHOLAS POWELL

He believes we are more alike than different and negative forces try to divide us and allow people to feel lesser than. "The biggest challenges in the world— from immigration to racism—are often about fear and lack of opportunity," Malik explains. "We are all capable of greatness as part of this abundant universe and too often the politics of distraction tell us we are not worthy."

Malik is always making connections and working to help others, even in moments of supposed relaxation. While staying at a bed and breakfast recently, he noticed an inconsistency in the service. The owners, a couple fairly new to the resort business, had invested millions and were still learning. Malik pulled the wife to the side and spoke to her about what he had observed. He shared with her his expertise in the restaurant business. After all, he owned the Soul Cafe for nine years and was trained by one of the top restaurateurs in the country, Keith McNally. She was grateful for his advice. The next day, he ends up talking to her husband who does business in Boston. Malik is on the board of the Boston Arts Academy (BAA). They make that connection and Malik ends up getting support for BAA's fundraising gala. "Even when I'm on vacation, there is always an opportunity to push my dreams forward or create new opportunities for myself and others," says Malik.

> "Even when proper circumstances do not show you that it is possible with the naked eye, you still have the ability to manifest ideas based on the power of thinking and then doing."

If there was one man that could lift the whole world with his hands, Malik Yoba would be the first to try. Be the change you wish to see in the world and "build a generator!"

BK Fulton is a modern renaissance man. He believes in authentic expression, high integrity, and moral leadership. While many know him as the former President of Verizon, since his retirement in 2015, BK has turned full media mogul producing more than 20 films, 19 books, and four number one Broadway shows including *The Piano Lesson* with Samuel L. Jackson, John David Washington and Danielle Brooks. The play was nominated for two Tonys and remains the highest grossing Broadway revival of all time.

He is currently a team member for the 2024 Broadway revivals of *The Wiz* and *The Outsiders* (nominated for 12 Tonys, winning 4, including Best Musical). His *Mr. Business* children's books are being considered for a movie and HBO Max and Warner Brothers have released a documentary about his MoviePass business venture, entitled MoviePass, MovieCrash.

BK and his wife - Jackie Stone - are also philanthropists giving to causes that develop and expose young entrepreneurs to leaders from around the globe. A native of Hampton, VA, BK is a proud graduate of Virginia Tech, Harvard and the New School as a Sloan Fellow, and New York Law School. He is also a Smithsonian Laureate Medal winner, a Business Leaders History Maker, winner of a Nonfiction National Book Award, the Renaissance Award in media and winner of the Oscar Micheaux Award for Excellence in Film Making.

BK sits on several boards including, TowneBank, the Library of Virginia, Advantage Testing Foundation, Lewis Latimer House Museum, The National Center of Women's Innovations, and the Richard Hunt Legacy Foundation. His professional memberships include the Producers Guild of America (p.g.a.), the Writers Guild of America, Omega Psi Phi Fraternity, the Alpha Beta Boule, the Executive Leadership Council, and the Business Leaders Hall of Fame.

NICHOLAS POWELL, CO-FOUNDING
EDITOR, SOULVISION MAGAZINE

Nicholas Powell has a passion for storytelling and a deep curiosity about the world. Nicholas is currently a policy analyst for the largest electric utility in Virginia. Nicholas worked with BK Fulton as the co-founding editor of SoulVision Magazine, a digital publication focused on telling positive human stories. He is a graduate of Virginia Commonwealth University (VCU), where he double majored in political science and English. While attending VCU, he was inducted into VCU's chapter of the National English Honor Society.

BK FULTON AND NICHOLAS POWELL